On the Cultural Achievements of Negroes

W9-DGJ-935

On the Cultural Achievements of Negroes

HENRI GRÉGOIRE

Whatever their tints may be,
their souls are still the same.
—Mrs. Robinson

Translated with notes
and introduction by

Thomas Cassirer &
Jean-François Brière

University of Massachusetts Press
AMHERST

This book is a translation of *De la littérature des nègres, ou Recherches sur leurs facultés intellectuelles, leurs qualités morales et leur littérature; suivies de Notices sur la vie et les ouvrages des Nègres qui se sont distingués dans les Sciences, les Lettres et les Arts* [Concerning the literature of Negroes, or research on their intellectual faculties, their moral qualities, and their writings; followed by accounts of the life and works of Negroes who have distinguished themselves in the sciences, letters, and arts]; par H. Grégoire, Ancien évêque de Blois, membre du Sénat conservateur, de l'Institut national, de la Société royale des Sciences de Gottingue, etc., etc., etc. (Paris: Chez Maradan, Libraire, 1808)

Printed in the United States of America
LC 95-47293
ISBN 1-55849-031-0 (cloth); 032-9 (pbk.)
Designed by Jack Harrison
Set in Adobe Caslon by Keystone Typesetting, Inc.
Printed and bound by Braun-Brumfield, Inc.

Library of Congress Cataloging-in-Publication Data
Grégoire, Henri, 1750–1831.
[De la littérature des Nègres, ou, Recherches sur leurs facultés intellectuelles. English]
On the cultural achievements of Negroes / Henri Grégoire ; translated with notes and introduction by Thomas Cassirer and Jean-François Brière.
p. cm.
ISBN 1-55849-031-0 (cloth : alk. paper). — ISBN 1-55849-032-9 (pbk. : alk. paper)
1. Blacks. I. Cassirer, Thomas, 1923– . II. Brière, Jean-François, 1945– III. Title.
HT1581.G7213 1996
909'.0496—dc20 95-47293
CIP

British Library Cataloguing in Publication data are available.

This book is published with the support and cooperation of the University of Massachusetts Boston.

Dedicated to the memory of Sidney Kaplan

CONTENTS

EDITORIAL PREFACE

It was Grégoire's intention to give an international launching to *De la littérature des nègres*, on which he had been working for many years; he turned to two friends, the Swiss Paulus Usteri and the American David Bailie Warden, to have the book translated and published in German and English as well as in French.[1] He may have thought of this as a form of insurance, in case the strict censorship under Napoleon prevented publication in France, but it also expressed his awareness that the fight against racism and slavery was international, and that he was working in concert with the international intellectual community to whom he dedicated his book.

Usteri and Warden shared Grégoire's ardent republicanism and faith in democracy, as well as his intellectual curiosity and enthusiasm for the dissemination of knowledge. Grégoire made their acquaintance when they came to Paris during the reign of Napoleon as emissaries of the only two republics recognized by the emperor, Switzerland and the United States. They became personal friends and intellectual companions, and he valued them as representatives of the two countries in which he

---

1. *De la littérature des nègres* was published in Paris in 1808. Usteri's translation appeared the following year: *Über die Literatur der Neger, oder Untersuchungen über ihre Geistesfähigkeiten* (Tübingen: Cotta, 1809). Cotta was then the leading German publishing house, known particularly for its edition of Goethe's works. A second translation into German appeared in that same year: *Die Neger, ein Beitrag zur Menschen- und Staatskunde, aus dem Französischen von Saul Ascher* (Berlin, 1809). In a letter to Usteri (January 18, 1810), Grégoire expressed his surprise at this translation by a man completely unknown to him. We too were unable to find any information on Ascher.

Warden's translation, *An Enquiry Concerning the Intellectual and Moral Faculties, and Literature of Negroes* was published in Brooklyn, New York, in 1810.

placed his hopes for the survival of political and intellectual freedom in a time of tyranny and repression.[2]

Both translators also played prominent roles as cultural intermediaries between postrevolutionary France and their own countries. Usteri was first sent to Paris by his native Zurich as observer during the French Revolution; he returned in 1803 as a delegate to the convention called by Napoleon to draw up a constitution for the newly formed Helvetic Republic. He served a term as president of this republic before returning to Zurich, where he eventually became editor of *Die neue Zürcher Zeitung*, at that time the most prominent liberal newspaper in German. He and Grégoire corresponded for many years, exchanging information on new publications and on current events.[3]

David Bailie Warden was born in Ireland.[4] He participated in the unsuccessful 1798 rebellion against the British, who gave him the choice of either standing trial or removing himself forever from British territory. Warden decided to move to the United States, where he became a tutor in various schools. In 1804 General Armstrong, the newly appointed United States ambassador to France, chose Warden as secretary of the Paris legation. Although he had by now become an American citizen, Warden spent the rest of his life in Paris, first as secretary of the legation, then as United States consul, and from 1814 to 1845 as an independent cultural middleman between the American and French scientific and literary establishment. He translated into English, for publication in the United States, several books by French scientists and scholars; he also published, in French, a five-volume historical and political description of the United States, *Description statistique, historique et politique des Etats-Unis de l'Amérique septentrionale, depuis l'époque des premiers établissements jusqu'à nos jours.*

---

2. *De la littérature des nègres* contains repeated expressions of Grégoire's faith in the United States; concerning Switzerland he wrote to Usteri in 1814: "Fasse le ciel que votre pays serve d'asile à la liberté, je doute si elle pourra en trouver un autre sur le continent européen." (May Heaven grant that your country will be a refuge for liberty. I doubt that liberty can find any other on the European continent.) Quoted from the collection of letters by Grégoire to Usteri in the manuscript collection of the Zentralbibliothek in Zürich.

3. The Usteri papers in the Zürich Zentralbibliothek contain letters by Grégoire from 1808 to 1825.

4. Information on Warden is taken from the only monograph that has been published on him: Francis C. Haber, *David Bailie Warden, A Bibliographical Sketch of America's Cultural Ambassador in France, 1804–1845* (Washington, D.C.: Institut Français de Washington, 1954).

We decided on a new translation of *De la littérature des nègres* because we found the Warden text quite inadequate. In part this was due to Warden's own shortcomings, which he himself acknowledged in the preface to his translation: "I beg leave to inform the reader that this translation was made . . . with such haste, that an apology for its imperfections is necessary." This haste no doubt accounts for the many mistranslations, and perhaps also for Warden's having omitted sentences, paragraphs, and even an entire chapter. But the inadequacy of the text is also due to the passage of time and the differences between American English of 1810 and that of the 1990s. Moreover, many allusions that were familiar to a reader in the early nineteenth century now need to be explained, either in the text or in the notes. We did not want to lose the historical context and flavor of the earlier translation, however, and thus we preserved Warden's style wherever this could be done while still making the text accessible to the modern reader. We have also added notes, especially on historical references, as well as an Introduction designed to acquaint the reader with the historical and biographical context of Grégoire's work.

The edition started out as a collaborative venture by the two of us and Sidney Kaplan, a distinguished former member of the English department at the University of Massachusetts, to whose memory we dedicate this book. It was Sidney Kaplan, well known for his pioneering scholarship on the contribution of African Americans to American culture, who originally saw the need for a new American edition. He gave us advice and encouragement, and planned to contribute an essay on David Bailie Warden and the importance of the Warden translation for the abolitionist movement in America. Unfortunately his health prevented him from carrying out his intention. As we put the book together, we missed his presence and his expertise, and we are saddened that he did not live to see the completed manuscript.

While we take joint responsibility for the book in its final form and consider ourselves co-authors of the entire text, we practised a division of labor in putting together the original draft. Thomas Cassirer was primarily responsible for the translation, the editorial notes, and the Editorial Preface, while Jean-François Brière wrote the Introduction. We then jointly worked through and revised the entire manuscript into its final form.

The Formatting of the Text

In order to facilitate the reading of a text that carries a great deal of documentation, we have kept the notes to the Editorial Preface and the Introduction as footnotes for quick reference; the voluminous notes to the book itself are endnotes. These are marked (G) if they are notes by Grégoire, (W) if they are notes by Warden, and (E) if they are editors' notes. Occasionally we have also inserted very brief explanations into the text, in parentheses followed by *Ed.* Passages that were omitted by Warden are enclosed in square brackets.

The Vocabulary

Grégoire's style was largely shaped by the discourse of the Enlightenment and the rhetoric of the Revolution. We have retained eighteenth-century usage and only modernized expressions that were likely to be misunderstood by modern readers. But at the risk of misunderstanding, we retained Grégoire's use of *Negro, black, mulatto, men* (*or people*) *of color*, even though these expressions have quite different connotations today than they had in his time, because any attempt at modernizing would have distorted the text. Grégoire used *nègre* (Negro) and *noir* (black) interchangeably to designate individuals of African origin, while *gens* (*hommes*) *de couleur* (people or men of color) refers to those who were of mixed African and European descent (i.e., mulattoes). This was an important social and legal distinction in Grégoire's time; in the French colonies most mulattoes were free, though not considered the equals of the whites, and often were French-educated.

We have used the endnotes to comment on other expressions whose connotation has changed in the last two hundred years. There is only one, "philanthropists," that is so pervasive and so characteristic of Grégoire that it needs to be commented on here. To quote the *Oxford English Dictionary*, philanthropy meant "the disposition or active effort to promote the happiness and well-being of one's fellow men" or, in the words of an eighteenth-century quotation given by the dictionary, "a generous love for Mankind in General, or an inclination to promote Publick Good." For Grégoire, the term "philanthropists" encompassed all the men and women, of whatever nationality, race, or religious faith, whose actions were motivated by this "generous love for Mankind in General."

We give special thanks to Emma Kaplan for her interest in our project and for allowing us access to her husband's notes; to Paul Wright, our editor at the University of Massachusetts Press; to Mlle Barenne, librarian of the Société de Port-Royal library in Paris, who kindly allowed us to consult the Grégoire collection of the Société; also to the manuscript collection of the Zentralbibliothek in Zurich for giving us access to the correspondence between Grégoire and Usteri, and to François Manchuelle of New York University for information on Armistead.

INTRODUCTION

During the French Revolution and up to his death, the French Catholic priest Henri Grégoire (1750–1831) was equally admired by some and hated by others for his relentless activism in support of human rights and the abolition of slavery. His memory has often been recalled by individuals and organizations fighting racial and religious intolerance. Such was the case in the 1930s when Ferdinand Brunot founded the Société des Amis de l'abbé Grégoire as a gesture to stem the rising tide of anti-Semitism. Such was the case again in 1989, when the French socialist government decided to move Grégoire's remains to the Panthéon mausoleum, where great figures of the French Republic are buried.[1] Today, the revival of racial and ethnic intolerance throughout the world as well as the bicentennial of the first abolition of slavery by the French (1794) call us to listen to the voice of a man who spent his life fighting prejudice and oppression under all its forms. Nowhere is Grégoire's unswerving struggle for equality and justice more forcefully exhibited than in *De la littérature des nègres*, which is translated into English here.

Who Was Grégoire?

Henri Grégoire was born in 1750 in Vého, a village in the duchy of Lorraine, a region that for many centuries served as a cultural bridge

---

1. The French president and most members of the French socialist government were present at the grandiose ceremony on December 12, 1989. Yet, although the archbishop of Paris and other dignitaries of the French Catholic Church were invited, they declined to attend the event. The church refused to honor Grégoire's memory because of his prominent place in a self-governing French church that the pope rejected, and also because he was a member of parliamentary assemblies that carried out anticlerical policies during the French Revolution.

between Latin and Germanic Europe.[2] The young Henri, whose father was an artisan, became a French subject at age sixteen in 1766, when France annexed Lorraine. He grew up in the part of what became France that harbored the largest and least assimilated Jewish population.[3] Anti-Semitism was more rampant there and in neighboring Alsace than anywhere else in the country. This is likely to have made Henri aware of racial and religious discrimination at a young age. Lorraine was also a region that was particularly open to the ideas of the Enlightenment. Voltaire spent some time at the court of Nancy during the reign of Stanislas (1736–66), a monarch who prided himself on being open-minded and receptive to new ideas. Thus the young Grégoire grew up in an environment somewhat more conducive than others to questioning the way in which society ostracized some of its members. He received a clerical education and studied at a Jesuit school in Nancy before being ordained a Catholic priest in 1776. Six years later, Grégoire became vicar of Emberménil, a village in Lorraine. There, he showed an unusual interest in the education of the peasantry and the improvement of their living conditions. He created a public library where his parishioners could learn about new agricultural techniques. In 1786–87, he traveled to Alsace and Switzerland, establishing the first ties of what would later become an international network of scholarly connections.

Grégoire was still unknown outside the boundaries of his parish when he wrote his first book, a short treatise on the Jewish question, *Essai sur la regénération physique, morale et politique des Juifs*. This book won a prize in 1788.[4] In this famous work—the first demonstration of his keen interest in what we would call today "minorities"—Grégoire suggested

2. The linguistic boundary between the French and German languages cut across Lorraine: northern Lorraine was German-speaking while southern Lorraine (where Grégoire was born) was French-speaking.

3. There were fewer than 50,000 Jews in France at the end of the eighteenth century (out of a total population of 26 million). The Jews of Alsace and Lorraine were Ashkenazim Jews originating from Central Europe. The other sizable Jewish population in France lived in cities of southwestern France, especially in Bordeaux. They were Sephardim Jews originating from Spain and Portugal. They had become somewhat more assimilated to French society than Ashkenazim Jews. Before the French Revolution, Jews living in France were legally treated like foreigners and faced many restrictions in professional and public life.

4. See H. Grégoire, *Essai sur la regénération physique, morale et politique des Juifs*, with a preface by Rita Hermon-Belot. (Paris: Flammarion, 1988). The prize was awarded by the Société Royale des Sciences et des Arts de Metz.

radical changes in civil law that would allow for a full integration of French Jews into the French nation.

Propelled to some notoriety by this literary success, he was elected a representative of the lower clergy in the Estates General, a consultative assembly summoned by the king in 1789.[5] There, he became one of the first delegates of the clergy to join the delegates of the commoners after they started the Revolution. Grégoire embraced with enthusiasm the profound changes put forward by the National Assembly's radical wing to create a new civil order based on freedom and equality. He quickly became known as a sharp-tongued and pugnacious advocate for people oppressed because of their religion or their race in metropolitan France and in the colonies. He joined the Jacobin Club, a group of avant-garde reformists with much influence within the Assembly. Gifted with an eclectic mind, he showed a special interest in the writing of the Declaration of the Rights of Man (issued August 26, 1789), the drafting of the Constitution (issued September 3, 1791), the status of blacks in French colonies and of Jews in France, education, new agricultural methods, and the reform of the French church.

For two centuries, a fierce debate had raged in France between *Gallicans*, who longed for a self-governing French church autonomous from Rome, and *Ultramontains* for whom the pope was an absolute monarch with full authority over all church matters anywhere in the world. The Revolution, with its nationalistic overtones and antiabsolutist calls, gave the Gallican side an edge in this conflict. The French church was completely reorganized as a religious branch of the state. Grégoire embraced this new "Constitutional" church. He saw it as a regenerated institution,

---

5. The Estates General were an assembly elected by the French people, summoned by the king on an occasional basis to discuss matters of great importance for the kingdom. Each of the three "orders" of society (clergy, nobility, commoners or Third Estate) elected its representatives. In May 1789, King Louis XVI summoned the Estates General to find a solution to the catastrophic financial situation of the French Crown. The French Revolution started in mid-June, when delegates of the commoners made the decision to become a National Assembly representing the sovereignty of the French people. Later on, some delegates of the other two orders joined (as individuals) the National Assembly. On June 20, members of the Assembly took an oath pledging to remain in session until they had drawn a constitution (Serment du Jeu de Paume). With great reluctance, Louix XVI formally accepted the new regime, making France a constitutional monarchy. Grégoire is one of the central figures in David's famous painting depicting the oath taken by members of the National Assembly on June 20.

"L'Abbé Grégoire," 1791, oil sketch by Jacques-Louis David. (From Musée des Beaux-Arts et d'Archéologie, Besançon, courtesy Lauros-Giraudon)

reorganized, like the state itself, along democratic principles. Yet, although he fiercely opposed the pope as an absolute monarch in worldly matters, he fully recognized his authority in spiritual matters and did not advocate a split between Rome and the French church.[6]

Grégoire's interest in "men of all colors" and colonial matters began in September 1789, after he had been appointed to the Credentials Committee of the National Assembly.[7] Among other issues, this committee had to examine a most volatile question: Do free mulattoes of the French West Indies—and especially those of Saint Domingue (today Haiti)— have a right to be represented along with the white colonists in the colonial deputation to the Assembly?[8] In August 1789, a delegation of mulattoes had petitioned the National Assembly to ask for mulatto representation. But the white planters, who were opposed to such request, had powerful connections in Paris through the Massiac Club, a new organization of wealthy planters who lived in France.[9] The mulattoes then turned for support to the Société des Amis des Noirs, an organization created in 1787 to promote the abolition of the slave trade.[10]

6. The Constitution Civile du Clergé of July 12, 1790, reorganized the French Catholic Church. Church property (10% of the land) became property of the state. Bishops were no longer appointed by the king nor vicars chosen by the episcopate; they were elected by the civil electoral assemblies and paid by the state. The Catholic clergy had to adhere to this new system formally by taking an oath. This reorganization was designed to integrate the French church into the new civil order of the country. The quick condemnation of this new system by Pope Pius VI caused a split in the church within France. Many members of the French clergy (most bishops) followed the pope and refused to take the oath; they were the *clergé réfractaire*. Others, like Grégoire, embraced the new church (sometimes called the Gallican Church); they were the *clergé constitutionnel* or *clergé jureur*.

7. For a history of Grégoire's action in favor of black people, see P. Grunebaum-Ballin, *Henri Grégoire, l'ami des hommes de toutes les couleurs. La lutte pour la suppression de la traite et l'abolition de l'esclavage, 1789–1831* (Paris: Société des Amis de l'Abbé Grégoire, 1948.) See also parts 1, 2, and 3 in Ruth Necheles, *The Abbé Grégoire, 1787–1831: The Odyssey of an Egalitarian* (Westport, Conn.: Greenwood, 1971.)

8. In late eighteenth-century France, mulattoes were also called *gens de couleur* (colored people) or *sang-mêlés* (mixed blood). Blacks were called *nègres* (Negroes). In the colonies—particularly in Saint-Domingue—mulattoes represented a rapidly growing share of the total population. They were the only segment of the population that was not composed mostly of immigrants. They formed a distinct racial caste socially subordinate to whites and superior to both free blacks and slaves. Some of them were educated in France. Mulattoes and free blacks in general were not opposed to slavery; many of them owned land and slaves.

9. The Société de correspondance des colons français was created in April 1789. Its members were wealthy aristocrats who owned large estates in Saint-Domingue (among them was Louis XVI's minister of war, the maréchal de Ségur.) They met at the marquis de Massiac's mansion in Paris and became known as the Massiac Club.

10. The Société des Amis des Noirs was founded by Brissot, Condorcet, Pétion, Clavière, and Lafayette, all leading political figures in 1789. They were inspired by the American and British

The Société introduced the mulattoes' petition in the National Assembly where it was referred to the Credential Committee. Grégoire and a majority of committee members voted to recommend mulatto representation. It was as a partisan in this struggle that Grégoire began to publish on the rights of people of African descent. At the same time (September 1789), Grégoire became interested in the anti-slave-trade cause and in the slavery problem; he was influenced in these matters by Thomas Clarkson, an English abolitionist whose visit to Paris was sponsored by the Amis des Noirs.

Alarmed by the threat to white supremacy presented by mulatto representation, the white planters tried to establish a special committee in the Assembly where decisions about colonies could be indefinitely delayed. Grégoire and the Amis des Noirs were fiercely opposed to the potential "confiscation" of colonial matters by the planters' lobby. In a speech before the Assembly on December 3, 1789, Grégoire, for the first time, publicly sided with the abolitionists. Soon thereafter, he was elected a member of the Société des Amis des Noirs, quickly becoming their main spokesman in the Assembly. The stage was set for a long and bitter struggle. On one side, the white planters wanted to prevent the ideas of liberty and equality from spreading to the colonies. On the other side, Grégoire and the abolitionists attempted to use the political momentum of the Revolution to improve the situation of mulattoes and blacks. The majority of deputies in the National Assembly did not have a clear idea about what should be done, but they feared that hurting the planters' interests might lead to the colonies' secession from France.

In order to present more forcefully his arguments in support of mulatto representation, Grégoire published a pamphlet entitled *Mémoire en faveur des gens de couleur ou sang-mêlés de Saint-Domingue et des autres îles françaises de l'Amérique.* He fiercely attacked the racial discrimination on which colonial society rested and demanded that mulattoes and free blacks enjoy the same rights as the whites in every aspect of life. "And you, white planters who are obsessed by ancestry," he wrote, "let me ask you: who were your fathers? Some were the buccaneers and pirates who

---

antislavery movements. Their goal was not the immediate abolition of slavery, which they saw as leading to potentially catastrophic consequences, but incremental progress beginning with the abolition of the slave trade. Necker, Mirabeau, and the Abbé Sieyès, among others, were briefly members and continued to sympathize with the Society's goals (see Necheles, *Abbe Grégoire,* 65).

made humanity tremble and ashamed of itself. . . . Who were your mothers? Don't you know that the scum of Paris' streets, the disgusting remains of debauchery were repeatedly collected and sent to the New World?"[11] Despite Grégoire's efforts, no decision on mulattoes was made and, in March 1790, the white planters managed to seize control of the newly formed Colonial Committee.

In the West Indies, voting rights were denied to mulattoes. Mulattoes began to revolt and white planters, wary of the National Assembly's future decisions, threatened to institute colonial self-rule. In October 1790, the Assembly defused these threats by promising that nothing would be changed in matters of civil rights in the colonies. Grégoire, seeing his hopes for mulatto rights thwarted, published his *Lettre aux philanthropes*: "The volcano of freedom which has erupted in France, will soon bring a massive explosion and will change the fate of the human race in both hemispheres. . . . Everywhere, mulattoes see the emblem of the Revolution which will spread around the world; they see the flag of revolution proudly waving; how can they hear the unceasing cries of freedom without being awakened to their rights?"[12]

Although the abolition of slavery was his ultimate aim, Grégoire was very cautious not to lead a frontal attack against such a formidable institution. He believed that the offensive had to be launched indirectly, beginning with changes affecting free blacks and mulattoes, and he pretended to favor the status quo regarding slaves. The white planters, of course, were not duped. They and their supporters in France hated Grégoire and the Amis des Noirs, mocked them as "nigger lovers" (*négrophiles*) and accused them of being traitors on Britain's payroll. The acrimonious debate about mulatto voting rights continued to rage until May 1791, when, faced with a large mulatto uprising in Saint Domingue, the Assembly finally gave political rights to both mulattoes and free blacks in future elections (decree of May 15, 1791). A triumphant Grégoire wrote his *Lettre aux citoyens de couleur et Nègres libres de Saint-Domingue et des autres isles françaises de l'Amérique.*[13] White planters vowed to block en-

---

11. Grégoire, *Mémoire en faveur des gens de couleur ou sang-mêlés de Saint-Domingue et des autres îles françaises de l'Amérique*, December 1789. Bibliothèque Nationale (Paris), Lk9.70

12. Grégoire, *Lettre aux philanthropes sur les malheurs, les droits et les réclamations des gens de couleur à Saint-Domingue*, October 1790. Bibliothèque Nationale (Paris), Lk9.119.

13. Bibliothèque Nationale (Paris), Lk9.162.

forcement of the decree and threatened to secede from France. Alarmed by such a menace, the Assembly rescinded in September 1791 its decree of May 15. Meanwhile, a slave rebellion erupted in Saint Domingue (August 1791), which the white colonists said had been induced by Grégoire's pamphlets.

In October 1791, elections were held for a new Legislative Assembly and members of the preceding National Assembly, such as Grégoire, were declared ineligible. But under the revolutionary reorganization of the church, Grégoire was now eligible for a bishopric, and the citizens of the *département* of Loir-et-Cher elected him bishop of Blois.

After the Legislative Assembly was convened, Grégoire's unrelenting struggle in favor of mulattoes and blacks continued through the Jacobin Club. He fiercely attacked the September 1791 decree and warned that it would lead to further rebellion and bloodshed.[14] Brissot, founder-president of the Amis des Noirs and leader of the Jacobin leftist faction at the Assembly, became the major voice of the antislavery movement. Thanks to his efforts, the Assembly finally decided, on April 4, 1792, to give voting rights to free blacks and mulattoes. Grégoire, from his Blois bishopric, could savor a belated victory. Four months later, on August 12, 1792, the Assembly suppressed all bounties and special privileges given to the slave trade (without making it illegal). Having achieved one of the abolitionist movement's major goals and very much preoccupied with internal affairs (France was at war), Brissot and his friends let the Société des Amis des Noirs fade out of existence.

In order to ensure that the decree of April 4, 1792, would be enforced, the Legislative Assembly sent three commissioners, Sonthonax, Polverel, and Ailhaud, with 6,000 soldiers to Saint Domingue. Both Sonthonax and Polverel were friends of Grégoire, Brissot, and the Amis des Noirs. When they arrived, the island was in total chaos. The slave rebellion had developed into a well-organized resistance under the direction of Jean-François, Biassou, and Toussaint Louverture. They were receiving help from the Spaniards (in their colony of Santo Domingo) who offered them and their followers freedom in return for fighting the French. The whites were divided between the royalists (Louis XVI had just been imprisoned) who called for a British invasion of Saint Do-

---

14. *Addresse aux députés de la seconde législature, par M. Grégoire, membre de la première*, Paris, September 26, 1791. Bibliothèque Nationale (Paris), Lc 40.637.

mingue and the pro-revolutionary faction, which favored the new regime in Paris but not its colonial policy.

Meanwhile, in Paris, a new and more radical assembly, the Convention, replaced the Legislative Assembly in September 1792. While remaining bishop of Blois, Grégoire was elected a representative of the
Loir-et-Cher *département* and immediately became a major figure in the
new Assembly. At its first meeting, it was he who moved to abolish
formally the monarchy in France.[15]

Grégoire joined several committees, becoming most active in the
Committee of Public Instruction. He was very much interested in education, which he saw as a key factor in the creation of a new France.
Convinced that absolutism and feudal oppression were rooted in ignorance, he believed that a genuine cultural revolution was necessary to
bring knowledge, progress, and freedom into the rural world. Such a
revolution was possible only through the adoption of French as the
common language of all the inhabitants of France. Latin, an idiom
incomprehensible to the vast majority of the population, was to be abandoned in churches. French had to become the language of the people,
not only of cosmopolitan courts and educated elites: "The time is coming when the words cow and manure will be recognized as much as the
words princess and courtier. French, the language of freedom, must be
written on all monuments; all walls and marble must speak to the people."[16] After a long inquiry on language usage in France, Grégoire published his famous *Rapport sur la nécessité et les moyens d'anéantir les patois
et d'universaliser l'usage de la langue française* (Report on the necessity
and the means to eradicate dialects and to make the use of the French
language universal).

Meanwhile in Saint Domingue, the situation of the two commis-

---

15. King Louis XVI was imprisoned in August 1792 and later tried for having allegedly conspired with Austria, a country at war with France. Grégoire believed that the king was guilty, but he
was opposed, as a matter of principle, to the death penalty. When the final vote was taken on the
king's sentence at the Convention, Grégoire was away on a mission in Savoy and his written opinion
was not taken into consideration. Louis XVI was beheaded on January 21, 1793.

16. H. Grégoire, *Oeuvres* (Paris: EDHIS, 1977), 2:141. About one-third of the French people
spoke other languages than French in the late eighteenth century. A large portion of the other two-
thirds spoke various French dialects more or less remote from the standard French of the educated
elite. Grégoire's dream of spreading the French language all over the country was not fulfilled until
the late nineteenth century through compulsory elementary education (Ferry law of 1882). French
replaced Latin in the Catholic liturgy in France in the 1960s.

sioners became untenable. Diseases killed half of their European troops within two months. Galbaud, the royalist pro-planter governor of Saint Domingue, tried to have them arrested. White planters were pleading with Britain, who had just declared war on France, to invade the French colony. Jean-François, Biassou, Toussaint, and their followers formally sided with Spain, a country also at war with France. In desperate need for support from blacks, Sonthonax and Polverel took it on themselves to abolish slavery on August 29, 1793.[17] Of the five representatives elected in Saint-Domingue to the Convention, three (one white, one mulatto, and one black) managed to reach France, carrying the commissioners' request that the Convention confirm their decision to abolish slavery. On February 4, 1794, they arrived in Paris and took their seats. For the first time ever, black people were members of a national parliament in Europe. The same day, with Grégoire attending, the Convention officially confirmed the abolition of slavery in all French colonies, with no indemnity for slave-owners. It was hoped that such a move would not only induce slaves to join the French government's side in Saint Domingue, but also ignite slave rebellions throughout British colonies.

Because of the growing rift among the Jacobins between the Girondins and the more radical Montagnards, the antislavery cause became entangled in the bitter fights between these two factions. The Saint Domingue planters sided with the Montagnards in their attacks against Brissot and his Girondin friends, and pushed for the removal of Sonthonax and Polverel from Saint Domingue. The Convention indicted the two men, but being unable to arrest them, was forced to continue relying on them. Grégoire remained cautiously neutral, avoiding any involvement in the power game that could have jeopardized his safety. Surprisingly, when abolition came in February 1794, Grégoire did not play any role in it. He had indeed good reasons to be extraordinarily cautious at that time. Many of his friends (Brissot among them) had been executed

---

17. Sonthonax's proclamation read: "Men are born and die equal. Citizens, this is the Gospel of France. . . . Never forget that you have fought for the French Republic; that of all white people in the universe, the only ones who are your friends are the French from Europe. The French Republic wants freedom and equality between all men without distinction of color. . . . The Republic adopts you as her children." However, in order to maintain some degree of socioeconomic order on the island, Sonthonax forbade former slaves to leave the service of their former masters during a transitional period. See Grunebaum-Ballin, *Henri Grégoire l'ami des hommes de toutes les couleurs* (Paris: Société des Amis de l'abbé Grégoire, 1948), 63–65.

a few months earlier and the very initiators of abolition (Sonthonax and Polverel) were facing arraignment. Grégoire himself was under attack from the fiercely anticlerical Montagnards for his religious beliefs as well as from the planters' lobby in France.[18] Moreover, there is little doubt that the politics of the abolition decree must have been disturbing for Grégoire. Abolition was for him a matter of principle, not of political opportunism. He cannot have failed to ask himself the obvious question: If the abolition of slavery is a tactical move designed to gain the support of slaves against the British and spark slave rebellions in British colonies, what will happen when the war ends and the help of former slaves is no longer needed?

In July 1794 (9 Thermidor), the rule of the Montagnards and the period known as the Terror came to an end. The de-Christianization policy of the Terror period officially ended. Worship in the Constitutional Church was allowed again, although the largely anticlerical government and legislature of the Directoire, the new political regime, remained hostile. Grégoire, still a bishop, became particularly interested at this time in the organization of the Constitutional Church in the French West Indies. Now that slavery was abolished, he saw the church as a privileged instrument for educating former slaves and transforming them into good citizens and good Christians. Grégoire strongly feared that the lack of priests (most had left Saint Domingue in 1792–93) would lead blacks to revert to paganism. It was therefore urgent to reestablish the colonial church: any hope of regeneration rested on that foundation. Up to that time, the all-white colonial clergy operated under the direct rule of the pope. Grégoire wanted to create a new kind of colonial clergy, one that would be part of the French Constitutional Church, with locally elected black priests and bishops.

The abolition policy of Sonthonax and the Convention worked as intended. Faced with the immediate threat of an Anglo-Spanish takeover of Saint Domingue that would restore slavery, Toussaint Louverture switched sides and allied himself with the small French army of General Laveaux, an abolitionist (May 1794). Their troops repelled the Spaniards and contained the British offensive. Toussaint, who was ap-

---

18. In 1793 and 1794, the Montagnards advocated the de-Christianization of France. The Christian religion was to be replaced by civic and patriotic cults. Those who supported such aims began destroying all religious symbols and pressed the clergy to renounce their faith.

pointed general by the French in 1795, ruled the northern part of the colony for seven years (1794–1801) without much interference from the French government.[19] Meanwhile, the planters continued to lobby for the restoration of direct French authority and of slavery on the island.

In 1795, Grégoire was elected to the Conseil des Cinq Cents, the new parliamentary body, but he was no longer a central figure in French politics and his fellow members tended to ostracize him. Indeed, the tragic events of 1793–94 had completely changed the political spectrum in France, in a way that left Grégoire painfully isolated. The royalists, who were the main defenders of the Catholic Church, condemned him as an accomplice of the "monsters" who had perpetrated the massacres of the Terror. They spread the enduring myth that he had voted for the king's death at the Convention. Their adversaries, those who wanted to perpetuate the heritage of the Revolution, were in power but they dismissed Grégoire as a cleric and a defender of the Catholic faith. From that time on up to his death (1831), Grégoire remained a sort of political outcast, unable and unwilling to fit into the polarized ideological structure of early nineteenth-century France. The deep rift that opened between the Roman Catholic Church and the French Revolution became a personal tragedy for Grégoire. It separated him from most of his contemporaries, who did not share or even understand his position: How could he support both republicanism and Catholicism and not take sides? And it sealed the fate of the Constitutional Church, which had never gained mainstream support among French Catholics and suffered deadly blows from the converging attacks of the Montagnards and the supporters of Rome.

After 1795, Grégoire's main fields of action were the Institut (the new national academy) and the second Société des Amis des Noirs, both of

19. After 1794, the French government remained preoccupied with military operations in Europe and later Egypt (1798). Communications between France and Saint Domingue were hampered by the war with Britain. In 1798, the British left their last positions in Saint Domingue. In 1800, Toussaint took control of the southern part of Saint Domingue and invaded (without the consent of the French government) the formerly Spanish side of the island, which had become French since 1795.

20. All royal academies were consolidated into an Institut national des sciences et des arts, created in 1795. It had 144 members in Paris and associated members in the rest of the country. It was divided into three *classes*: mathematical and physical sciences, moral and political sciences (we would say today, social sciences), literature and arts. Grégoire was a member of the moral and

which he helped to create.[20] Grégoire realized that, although slavery had been abolished in French colonies, such was not the case in the British and Spanish empires nor in the United States. Saint Domingue was in turmoil, its economy in shambles. In order to succeed, it was essential for the abolitionist cause to demonstrate that black societies could thrive in freedom. The French West Indies had to become a model for the rest of the world. Faced with government inaction, Grégoire, his friend Lanthénas, and the Swedish naturalist Wadstrom decided to create in the spring of 1796 a new Société des Amis des Noirs et des Colonies designed to provide assistance toward the economic and social recovery of Saint Domingue. Contrary to its famous predecessor, the new Société des Amis des Noirs kept a low profile, did not meddle in politics, and limited its work to economic projects. With no means at its disposal and no official support, the Société remained a sort of discussion group.[21] We know that by 1799 Grégoire had been working for some time on a work devoted to the capacities of black people: during the meeting held on February 4, 1799 (29 Pluviôse year 7) to celebrate the fifth anniversary of black emancipation, "Citizen Grégoire read excerpts from a piece that he has been working on for a long time concerning the moral qualities of people of color. He narrated sentimental anecdotes which greatly moved the audience."[22] Nonetheless, most members lost interest in Grégoire's moral and religious program, and the Société collapsed at the end of 1799.

Grégoire had long dreamed of an institutional framework that would help the community of enlightened scholars to exchange opinions and projects throughout France and Europe. The newly created Institut, with its network of corresponding members, was part of such a scheme. There, he also tried to advance his ideas. At the beginning of 1797, he read to his colleagues a *mémoire* on the history of black people's freedom.[23] In May 1799, he read another paper on the intellectual, spiritual,

---

political sciences *classe*. The Institut still exists today, although its structure has changed since Grégoire's time (it is called the Institut de France and includes the Académie française).

21. Among the members were Lanthénas, a founding member of the first Société des Amis des Noirs; Sonthonax, the administrator who had freed the slaves in 1794; the economist Jean-Baptiste Say; and the director of the colonial office, Granet (Necheles, *Abbé Grégoire*, 161).

22. *Chronique Universelle*, 29 Pluviôse year 7 (Bibliothèque de Port-Royal, fonds Grégoire, Colonies).

23. This *mémoire* was never published.

and moral characteristics of black people.[24] But Grégoire faced the same obstacles there as he did in the Société des Amis des Noirs et des Colonies. His colleagues at the Institut did not care about former slaves or the moral regeneration of colonial society. France was embarked on a vast continental struggle for the domination of Europe. Colonies were far away and communication with them nearly cut off by the war.

After the November 1799 coup d'état, a new system of government, the Consulat, was put into place.[25] Grégoire, still bishop of Blois, was elected to the Corps Législatif (the lower legislative chamber) but, un-compromising on democratic and republican principles, he quickly opposed the authoritarian rule of the new regime. In 1801, he was co-opted to the Senate, a move that angered Bonaparte. The leader of France respected Grégoire for his role in the early days of the Revolution; but he viewed him as politically naive and despised what he considered his bizarre pro-black ideas. It would have been difficult indeed to find someone more different from Grégoire than the future emperor Napoleon, a man notoriously insensitive to human suffering.

In 1800, Mauviel, bishop-designate of Saint Domingue and a friend of Grégoire, was finally allowed by the French government to reach his diocese. Grégoire had great hopes that Mauviel would be able to develop the influence of the Constitutional Church and create a native clergy in the colony. Unfortunately, Mauviel played politics, clashed with Toussaint Louverture, and later sided with the French military expedition sent by Bonaparte to retake control of Saint Domingue.[26]

In 1801, Bonaparte negotiated an agreement (a Concordat) with the pope to normalize relations between France and the papacy.[27] The Con-

---

24. Necheles, *Abbé Grégoire*, 164.

25. Bonaparte established this regime by the coup d'état of November 9, 1799 (Brumaire 18, year 8 in the revolutionary calendar). He then became premier consul and later (1804) emperor.

26. Bonaparte decided in 1801 to put an end to Saint Domingue's de facto autonomy from France since 1794. In January 1802, with Britain's approval, a French armada carrying 22,000 troops landed in Saint Domingue to retake control of the colony. Toussaint was captured and died in captivity in France in 1803. The French were not able to overcome black resistance and their operations were hampered by large losses due to disease. They left Saint Domingue at the end of 1803. Haitian independence was proclaimed on January 1, 1804. France recognized the independence of its former colony only in 1825 after Haiti was forced (under the threat of an armada) to pay 150 million francs in damages to former French planters. Haiti remained the first and only nonwhite colony to gain independence until the Second World War.

27. Bonaparte did not care about church reform. He needed the political support of the Catholic Church and the pope to reorganize Europe as he wished. The 1801 Concordat gave the pope full

stitutional Church was to be abolished and full papal authority restored. Grégoire and other prominent bishops of the Constitutional Church had to resign. For the rest of his life, Grégoire remained excluded from clerical functions.

In 1802, things worsened: under pressure from the planters' lobby, Bonaparte's government restored slavery in French colonies and forbade the publication of all works related to colonial affairs.[28] Blacks and mulattoes were no longer allowed to enter France.[29] By 1804, when Haitian independence was proclaimed and the French left the island, nothing had been accomplished of the educational and religious plans set forth by Grégoire.

Distressed and disgusted, Grégoire left France in June 1802 for a short visit to England (the Peace of Amiens had temporarily stopped the war). He was, of course, interested in meeting members of the influential British abolitionist movement and also in getting material for his projected study of black people's capacities. He met prominent abolitionists such as William Wilberforce and Granville Sharp, but was not particularly welcome. In a country that had just fought against the French Revolution for ten years, his republicanism was suspect and his egalitarianism too radical. The only British abolitionist with whom he maintained a close friendship was Thomas Clarkson. In London, Grégoire also bought books and other printed material on slavery and the slave trade from the abolitionist bookseller Philips. He collected nearly 150

---

authority over clerical appointments (which he did not have before 1790 when kings appointed bishops) while the clergy continued to be paid by the state. This system remained in force until the separation of church and state in 1905.

28. This is the only case of "restoration" of slavery after its abolition. Bonaparte, who had no interest in colonial affairs and the fate of blacks, later recognized that he had made serious mistakes in his policy toward Saint Domingue and put the blame on the influence of his wife Joséphine, daughter of a wealthy planter from Martinique. The slave trade was reluctantly outlawed by the French government in 1815, but lax enforcement of the ban allowed it to continue until 1831. Slavery was abolished for a second (and last) time in French colonies in 1848.

29. In the eighteenth century, planters from the West Indies often traveled to France with slave servants. This custom was not looked upon favorably by French authorities. Until 1777, slave servants were not allowed to remain in the country for more than three years. As of 1777, all black persons were prohibited from entering France. These rules were routinely ignored by planters and not enforced by authorities. The situation of slaves who escaped from their master's service raised complex legal issues, since slavery was not lawful in France. Many slaves were declared free by French courts. A 1791 law stated that any individual of any race entering France would be free. Bonaparte's decision was a return to the laws of 1777. See Pierre Pluchon, *Nègres et Juifs au XVIIIe siècle* (Paris: Tallandier, 1984), part 3, II.

books and brochures in English, which he would later use extensively to write *De la littérature des nègres*. The following year, he traveled to Belgium and the Netherlands. In 1805 and 1806, he went twice to Germany, visiting learned societies in Mainz, Frankfurt, and Berlin. From that time on, Grégoire became increasingly interested in the creation of an international network of scientists, scholars, writers, and artists who would exchange their knowledge and talent through publications, correspondence, and regular meetings across Europe.[30] He saw the creation of such a network as a way to compensate for the failures he had experienced on the domestic front. Relying on the outside world now appeared to be his last chance at achieving at least some of his major goals.

Grégoire's vocal opposition to Bonaparte in the Senate increased after the general proclaimed himself emperor (1804), but it remained politically ineffective. The small cohort of republicans who, like Grégoire, opposed both Napoleon and the monarchy were powerless. Posing no threat to the government, which enjoyed widespread support, Grégoire was left alone. He even kept his long-standing personal friendship with the minister of police and former priest Joseph Fouché, who saw him as a harmless idealist.[31] With little support for his ideas in the pro-Napoleon Senate and new restrictions on the freedom to print, few options were left to Grégoire for attacking the colonial status quo. In order to be read, he had to avoid a frontal assault against Napoleon's policies and could only strike cautiously and indirectly. Thus in 1804, he gave a lecture at the Institut in which he defended Las Casas, the sixteenth-century supporter of Amerindians, against those who tried to tarnish his reputation (*Apologie de Don Barthélémy de Las Casas, évêque de Chiappa*).

It was during the years that followed that Grégoire decided to write *De la littérature des nègres*, a book summing up the research he had done since 1797 on the history of black people. Published in 1808 and translated into English and German, this work refuted the arguments in support of slavery and the inferiority of black people. That same year, feeling that he had reached a turning point in his life (he was fifty-eight), Grégoire published his *Memoirs*, an account of his religious and political

---

30. Grégoire published in 1817 a *Plan d'association générale entre les savants, gens de lettres et artistes pour accélérer les progrès des bonnes moeurs et des lumières* (Project for a universal organization of scholars, writers, and artists to promote the progress of morality and knowledge).

31. Fouché was a former Montagnard at the Convention.

careers. Napoleon, who was adept at neutralizing his opponents with honors, had granted him the Legion of Honor in 1804 and a title of nobility in 1808, all of which Grégoire openly despised.

Grégoire's situation significantly worsened after the monarchy was restored in France in 1815 with Louis XVIII as king. Royalist "ultras" did not merely dislike Grégoire, they hated him, and they were back in power. Although (inaccurately) accused of being a former regicide at the Convention, Grégoire was allowed to remain in France. He nonetheless became an exile within his own country. He was expelled from the Institut and his pension taken away, leaving him penniless. He had to sell part of his library to support himself until he was granted a small pension as retired senator. In 1819, when Grégoire, with the support of liberals and republicans (among them Lafayette), was elected as representative of the Isère *département* to the Chambre des Députés, royalist "ultras" managed to have his election invalidated. Despite these persecutions and the increasing isolation to which he was submitted in his old age, Grégoire continued to fight relentlessly against his opponents, publishing until the age of eighty.[32] He continued to keep up a huge international correspondence with scholars throughout Europe and America, sending them books and documents that could serve the cause of freedom. He lived very thriftily, helping people in greater need than he. He was interested in the struggle for independence of small nations such as Ireland and Greece. Above all, he remained especially sensitive to the fate of Haiti, whose government repeatedly invited him to visit the island (and even offered him a bishopric). Grégoire saw independent Haiti as a regenerated society in which blacks and mulattoes, at last free from oppression, would be able to develop a new brotherly Christian civilization. He devoted several of his writings specifically to the Haitians.[33]

---

32. *De la constitution française*, 1814; *De la domesticité chez les peuples anciens et modernes*, 1814; *De la traite, de l'esclavage des noirs et des blancs; par un ami des hommes des toutes les couleurs*, 1815; *Plan d'association générale entre les savants, gens de lettres et artistes, pour accélérer les progrès des bonnes moeurs et des lumières*, 1817; *Histoire des confesseurs des empereurs, des rois et d'autres princes*, 1824; *De l'influence du christianisme sur la condition des femmes*, 1821; *De la noblesse de la peau ou du préjugé des blancs contre la couleur des Africains et celle de leurs descendants noirs et sang-mêlés*, 1826; *Des peines infâmantes à infliger aux négriers*, 1822; *Appel à la raison, par un proscrit*, 1830; *Considérations sur la liste civile. Se vend au profit des blessés dans les journées des 27, 28 et 29 juillet*, 1830.

33. *Manuel de piété, à l'usage des hommes de couleur et des noirs* (Paris: Baudouin Frères, 1818); *De la liberté de conscience et de culte à Haiti* (Paris: Baudouin Frères, 1824); *Epître aux Haitiens* (Port-au-Prince: Imprimerie du Gouvernement, 1827)

Grégoire was struck by cancer in the spring of 1831 and his health deteriorated rapidly. The archbishop of Paris forbade all clerics to give him the last rites unless he retracted in writing his oath to the Constitutional Church. Grégoire steadfastly refused to do so. This quickly burst into a major *affaire* that worried the government. Finally, the queen's confessor, Guillon, assisted Grégoire, a move that infuriated the archbishop. The "friend of men of all colors," as Grégoire called himself, died in May 1831. About 20,000 persons accompanied him to the Montparnasse cemetery. The Haitian government ordered three days of national mourning.

In his will, Grégoire set aside a sum of money to create a prize for the best essay on the topic "How can we annihilate the unjust and barbaric prejudices of whites against blacks and mulattoes?" In 1839, the prize was awarded to a young man named Victor Schoelcher who, nine years later, was responsible for the passage of the bill that abolished slavery forever in the French colonies.

Grégoire's Beliefs

Throughout his life, Grégoire's basic assumptions on humanity and society remained deeply rooted in the universalist and philanthropic principles of the eighteenth-century Enlightenment. At the very core of Grégoire's thought was a strong belief in the essential unity of the human race and its perfectibility. He saw such unity as being not only physical and spiritual (we are all children of God), but also moral and cultural. For him, civilization is progress under all its forms. Therefore, there is really only one civilization in the world, just as there is only one God and one type of human being. Civilization is unity in the making, not diversity; it makes people the same, not different.[34] Civilization is the process through which all branches of humanity become one, physically (through mixed marriages) as well as culturally. Civilization is humanity achieving its unity of essence.

Thus—and this point is crucial—civilization is not French or European culture. It is universal, it belongs to all human beings; every people on earth can bring its share to it, although this was not done equally by

---

34. Similar concepts have strongly influenced traditional French attitudes toward cultural diversity and remain part of the core assumptions of French national culture.

all throughout the course of history. In ancient times, an African country, Egypt as well as Middle Eastern countries were at the forefront of civilization. Then, it was Mediterranean Europe's turn. Since the Middle Ages, Western Europe (and France particularly in the late eighteenth century) emerged as the bearers of civilization, not because of any innate superiority of their inhabitants, but as a result of historical contingency, of chance. "Talent, writes Grégoire, is not linked exclusively to any country or variety of mankind."[35] That early nineteenth-century Europeans were more "advanced" than peoples from other regions of the world seemed indisputable to him. But, contrary to theoreticians of racism, he argued that the reason why civilization lacked the full participation of these people was not their inability to be so "advanced" as Europeans, but the conditions under which they lived, which often were imposed upon them by Europeans. To a large extent, he believed, slavery and other forms of oppression by Europeans accounted for the marginalization of entire races from civilization: "your virtues and talents are your own; your vices are the work of nations who call themselves Christian. The more you are vilified, the more they are indicted."[36] Grégoire, therefore, turned the arguments in favor of slavery upside-down: it is not because blacks are less "advanced" than whites that they can be enslaved, he says; it is because they have been enslaved that they remain less "advanced." Slaves are lazy because they are slaves, not because they are black. The violence of slave rebellions simply replicates the violence of the masters. Thus, slavery is based upon a sinister hoax: it takes its consequence as its justification. For Grégoire, slavery is, like torture, superstition, or the absolute monarchy, an intolerable legacy of Europe's barbaric past. Free black people from slavery, he says; let them be full human beings with the same rights and duties as Europeans, and they will equal white people in their contribution to civilization: "The natives of Africa and America would long ago have risen to the highest level of civilization if this good purpose would have been supported by a hundredth part of the efforts, the money and the time that have been given over to tormenting and butchering many millions of these unfortunate people, whose blood calls for vengeance against Europe."[37]

35. *De la littérature des nègres*, chap. 7, 195 (1808 French ed.).
36. *De la littérature des nègres*, chap. 2, 87.
37. *De la littérature des nègres*, chap. 6, 174–75.

Grégoire's ideals always remained very much tuned to the emerging values of the time of his youth in the 1770s and 1780s: sensitivity, emotion, moral virtue, civic equality, patriotism, family spirit. The influence of Rousseauism on him is obvious. Like Rousseau, Grégoire came from a French-speaking region near the eastern border of France that had close connections with the Germanic Protestant culture. Grégoire clearly shared with Rousseau a nostalgia for an agrarian and egalitarian society governed by principles of civic virtue. Like him, Grégoire abhorred the world of courtiers and other high-society sophisticates, which he saw as ruthless, corrupt, and decadent. He put the upper hierarchy of the Roman Catholic Church into a similar category, believing that most of its members had betrayed the Christian message. He was convinced that a regeneration was finally coming, which would make society and the church more fraternal, more equal, and therefore more Christian.

Grégoire's beliefs and activism cannot be understood without reference to the fundamental role he ascribes to the Christian religion. His vision of Christianity is both messianic and evangelic. Like other thinkers influenced by the Enlightenment philosophy, Grégoire believed that civilization meant not only progress in the arts and sciences, but also social and moral progress. What made him unique was his strong belief that the Christian evangelic message (sanctity of human life, fraternal love for others, dignity and equality of all human beings) was the essence of such social and moral progress:

> The Christian religion is an infallible means of expanding and securing civilization; such has been and will always be its effect. It was by its influence that our ancestors, the Gauls and the Franks ceased to be barbarians, and that the sacred woods were no longer stained with the blood of human sacrifices. . . . It is the glory of the Christian religion alone to have sheltered the weak from the strong. It is this religion that, in the fourth century, established the first hospital in the West. It has constantly labored to console the unfortunate, whatever be their country, their color or religion. The parable of the Samaritan marks persecutors with the seal of censure. It is a curse laid for all times on anyone who would exclude a single member of the human race from the circle of society.[38]

From his childhood in Lorraine, Grégoire remained strongly influenced by a specific brand of Catholicism called Jansenism. Jansenism

---

38. *De la littérature des nègres*, chap. 2, 75–76.

developed into a major movement with the French church during the second half of the seventeenth century. Although Grégoire was not so pessimistic about human nature as the Jansenists, he always remained impregnated with Jansenism's moral rigor, its longing for moral purity, and its deep-seated hatred for all forms of absolutist power.

Grégoire believed that Christianity inspired the protests of Las Casas in favor of Indian slaves; it inspired the Enlightenment; it would soon change the whole world. For him, the message of the French Revolution (liberty, equality, fraternity of all human beings) was in essence a Christian message. He saw democracy and civic egalitarianism as the extension of Christian principles to the political organization of society. Therefore, the French Revolution had to spread to the whole world. He adamantly opposed any separation between church and state or between religion and civil society: "if all citizens behaved as true Christians, society would resemble paradise on earth."[39] Unfortunately for Grégoire, such a vision was not shared by mainstream supporters of the French Revolution, for whom religion usually meant oppression and superstition. Bourdon, a fellow *conventionnel*, accused Grégoire of trying to "Christianize the Revolution." Above all, these views were absolute anathema to the fiercely antirevolutionary Roman Catholic Church of the early nineteenth century. As a result, Grégoire quickly found himself rejected as an outsider by both sides on the ideological battlefield. Yet, despite his deep repulsion for Rome's reactionary dispositions and his close contacts with Protestant scholars (something extremely unusual for a Catholic priest at that time), he never broke with the church. He knew that he had better chances of maintaining his influence by fighting from inside, and his struggle was strictly a matter of political ideology. Thus the Catholic hierarchy was unable to expel formally Grégoire from the clergy for heresy or misconduct; all they could do was treat him like a pariah.

The degree to which Grégoire's ideas can today be described as "Eurocentric" calls for some clarification. Grégoire saw the world with the eyes of a late eighteenth-century European imbued with the messianic vision of universal regeneration brought by the modern revolutionary paradigm. This did not prevent him from rejecting the idea that Euro-

---

39. *Manuel de piété à l'usage des hommes de couleur et des noirs* (Paris: Baudoin, 1822), 6.

"Bénédiction Nuptiale," from *Manuel de piété
à l'usage des hommes de couleur et des noirs,* by
Henri Grégoire (1822). (Courtesy
Bibliothèque Nationale de France)

pean culture as a whole was inherently superior to other cultures and that non-European peoples should take Europeans as models; in his opinion, European culture was corrupt, not yet fully freed from its old barbaric ways. But he firmly believed that the concepts of the rights of man, freedom, equality, and democracy as they were developed in Europe by Europeans were valid for the whole of humanity. Their expansion was justified by their universal value, not by the fact that they came from Europe. He thought that it would be easier to implement radical changes in the colonial societies of America than in European societies, therefore raising the possibility that such societies would become models for Europe in the future.

Although he showed much support for independent Haiti, Grégoire never advocated the independence of colonies. He knew that "independence" was just a shell that could entail the best or the worst. His inclination was to go for the complete integration between colonies and Continental France with the same rights and opportunities for everyone, whatever their race. French colonies would cease to exist as such when all of their inhabitants became fully equal with their fellow citizens in Europe in a worldwide French democratic community. Grégoire's dream was one of fusion, not separation, between France and its colonies. In this respect, he remained a hard-core Jacobin.

De la littérature des nègres

While he had numerous contacts with a supportive network of scholars and friends scattered throughout Europe and America, Grégoire became, in the early 1800s, increasingly isolated from the intellectual and political mainstream of metropolitan France. The horrors (true or invented) of the Terror and of the Saint Domingue rebellion had cast in many minds a dark shadow on the legacy of the French Revolution. The Enlightenment philosophy was attacked for being at the root of all these violent upheavals. The new "regenerated" world that in the 1790s Grégoire believed was coming into existence was now collapsing in front of him: in politics, as in colonial and religious affairs, the hard-won gains of the Revolution were being dismantled by Bonaparte's government. The intense fear of social disorder that was gripping members of the French bourgeois class fueled a spirit of regression directed at the most radical changes accomplished since 1789: the Revolution, they thought, had gone too far; restoring order and stability in the colonies as well as France became paramount.

This new atmosphere, coupled with the immediate prospect of the reconquest of Saint Domingue, seemed to offer unique opportunities for the planters' lobby and their supporters. During the Consulate, and especially in the years 1801–3, the advocates of slavery launched an all-out offensive for a return to the old colonial system. One book after another was published in defense of slavery and the slave trade; essays by Barré de Saint-Venant, Descroizilles, Cossigny, Bory de Saint-Vincent (all former planters), and Malouet, future minister of the navy, were the most noticeable among them. They all tried to prove that the very existence of French colonies and French overseas trade rested on slavery: there was simply no other option than to force black people to work to sustain a colonial economy; what had just happened in Saint Domingue proved that freedom for blacks meant the destruction of colonies; more-over, blacks were already slaves in Africa, where their fate was far worse than in the West Indies. About 6,000 white colonists had taken refuge in metropolitan France where they spread their own views about black people and the events they had witnessed in the colonies. New novels, poems, and plays narrated in full detail the "horrors" perpetrated by black insurgents against whites during the Saint Domingue rebellion. The pro-slavery newspaper *Mercure de France* was a major vehicle of this offensive. Chateaubriand, its editor, added his own part to the campaign when he wrote in *Le Génie du christianisme* (1802): "who would still dare to defend the cause of Negroes after the crimes that they have committed?"[40]

Moreover, during the same period, racialist theories and a racist men-tality were beginning to take hold in France.[41] Until the end of the eighteenth century, the concept of unity of the human race remained dominant. European scholars and travelers viewed human races as mere "varieties" of a common breed that were all considered capable of "prog-ress." Both Christianity and the Enlightenment agreed on that funda-

---

40. See *La Génie du christianisme*, part 4, book 4, chap. 7. François-René de Chateaubriand (1768–1848) was born in the port city of Saint-Malo. His father had invested in the slave trade in the mid-eighteenth century.

41. See Yves Bénot, *La Démence coloniale sous Napoléon* (Paris: La Découverte, 1992), chap. 7.

mental principle. The physiological and cultural diversity of humanity was seen as exotic, amusing, interesting to observe, but did not lead to the establishment of a hierarchy between various peoples. All "nations" had their own mores and customs, and none appeared morally superior to others; if some were more "advanced" in knowledge or technology, this was due to environmental and historical factors, not race. Humanity was always perfectible and "savages" could be changed or converted. This is why the justification of slavery (of Amerindians and of black Africans) implied a denial of a people's very humanity. The struggle of the antislavery movement was for this reason centered on reclaiming black people's humanity: human, therefore equal. This had always been Grégoire's main line of action.

In the first decade of the 1800s, a major intellectual shift occurred. Some scholars and scientists, particularly in France, began to introduce the idea that humanity was divided into a permanent hierarchy of races, with each race having immutable physiological, intellectual, and moral characteristics of its own.[42] White Europeans were at the very top, African blacks at the very bottom. The unity of mankind was repudiated. This meant that it was no longer necessary to deny black people's humanity in order to enslave them: blacks were simply an inferior race of humans and would always be so. Their fate was to remain subordinate to white Europeans who alone had the ability to master knowledge and rule the world. Such theories, relying on pseudoscientific evidence, would inspire the European view of the world for the following century and a half and provide the ideological framework of the next wave of colonial imperialism. If these racist theories served to justify slavery, they also frequently coexisted with abolitionist sentiment, as one could very well assume the inferiority of blacks while opposing slavery. Two early prominent proponents of this ideology were Virey (*Histoire naturelle du genre humain*, 1801) and the naturalist Lacépède, senator and grand-chancellor of the Legion of Honor (*Discours d'ouverture du cours de zoologie de l'an IX*, 1803). Their ideas and those of their disciples could be

42. Such racialist ideas had already been suggested in the eighteenth century by some authors, notably the Englishman Edward Long in *The History of Jamaica* (London, 1774). See David Brion Davis, *The Problem of Slavery in Western Culture* (Ithaca: Cornell University Press, 1966), chap. 15, "The Changing Image of the Negro," 455–64. See also Yves Bénot, *La démence coloniale sous Napoléon* (Paris: Editions La Découverte, 1992), chap. 7, "La formation de l'idéologie des 'races humaines.'"

freely expressed under Bonaparte's rule and they quickly permeated the French political and intellectual establishment.

As could be expected, Grégoire and the abolitionists were very much on the defensive during those years and, being generally opposed to Bonaparte's authoritarian rule, had to be careful not to offend the government. Grégoire, editor (with Desbois) of the *Annales de la religion*, made the official journal of the Constitutional Church a quasi-lonely voice against the restoration of slavery. His defense of Las Casas (1804) was his first published reaction. After the *Annales* ceased to exist in 1803, *La Décade philosophique, littéraire et politique* remained the only publication defending antislavery positions, but it showed an increasing tolerance toward the new ideology of human races. In May 1807, *La Décade* published Grégoire's *Observations sur les Juifs*, a response to an anti-Semitic campaign suggesting that the civil emancipation of Jews had been a mistake. It contained, besides a defense of Jews and Irish Catholics, an attack on slavery. The same year, Napoleon ordered *La Décade* to merge into the pro-slavery *Mercure de France*.

On January 1, 1808, Britain and the United States abolished the slave trade. A few months later, encouraged by these foreign abolitions and stung by the silencing of antislavery voices, Grégoire decided to launch a major and much needed counteroffensive with *De la littérature des nègres*.

De la littérature des nègres ou Recherches sur leurs facultés intellectuelles, leurs qualités morales et leur littérature was published in late September 1808 by the bookseller Maradan in Paris. The title and subtitle overemphasized the literary content of the book in order to make it look politically inoffensive. Grégoire was concerned that it might be caught in the government censors' net, but Fouché let it go through.[43] The regime itself was not a target and Napoleon's policies were not openly criticized. *De la littérature des nègres* is a scholarly work dealing with the culture of black people, and it contains only one reference to Bonaparte's colonial policy. Nonpolitical in its form, the book was nonetheless political in its content, as it attacked a system that was endorsed by the current government.

De la littérature des nègres is first and foremost a response to racialist theories that had started spreading in France during the previous decade.

---

43. This tolerance was not repeated in 1810 when Grégoire's *Histoire générale des sectes* was banned from publication.

In 285 pages, Grégoire mobilizes all scholarly resources available to him and gives a passionate defense of the principle of the unity of mankind, the key point of contention in the racial debate at that time. Slavery, of course, is denounced, but racism is clearly Grégoire's main target.

As expected, abolitionists praised the book. Such was the case of Jean-Denis Lanjuinais, former member of the Revolutionary Assemblies and a friend of Grégoire, who gave it warm support in his *Notice*.[44] Grégoire is "an illustrious bishop, a fearless writer that nothing has been able to distract from religious and liberal ideals, and who has always been the protector of the oppressed." Generally speaking, however, *De la littérature des nègres* was not well received. The book clearly went against the grain of prevailing ideas. Grégoire lamented the bitter skepticism with which other French critics commented on his work, writing in April 1810:

> I am flattered . . . by the reviews and reports found in various German, American, etc. and even French newspapers, but most of the latter transform literary debate into an arena for gladiators. As a consequence of the revolutionary turmoil that harmed so many interests and offended so much empty pride, we are left with many individuals who, instead of returning to reason, have become even more spiteful; they are so jaundiced that they will always be angry. They distil their bile in our newspapers.[45]

In a review of *De la littérature des nègres* published in *Le Publiciste* on September 9, 1808, Grégoire is accused of being a prisoner of his one-track mind:

> The author concludes with the wish that "European nations should finally pay for their crimes against the Africans!" And when does this Senator and Bishop give us such a book? When Saint Domingue . . . To plead in favor of the slaves in our colonies when they were really oppressed, was the best use a sensitive man could make of his eloquence; nothing could be more just and reasonable than to fight against men so blind that they would deny that Negroes are human beings. One has to read it with one's own eyes, though, to believe that his enthusiasm for the well-being of humanity and his anger against those who slander the

---

44. J. D. Lanjuinais, *Notice de l'ouvrage de M. L'Evêque et Sénateur Grégoire, intitulé "De la littérature des nègres"* (Paris: Maradan, 1808).

45. Letter from Grégoire to an anonymous correspondent, April 9, 1810 (Bibliothèque de l'Arsenal, Paris, MS 13990, folio 10).

Negroes would lead him to proclaim that any rebellion is legitimate; and that because Negroes are human beings they are equal to whites in everything. It is hard to believe that infatuated with such ideas, he has learned nothing from experience; that in 1808 he still honors publicly the destroyers of Saint Domingue. Toussaint Louverture is still a hero for him and he does not have an ounce of pity for the unfortunate victims of the Negroes' freedom.

The *Journal de l'Empire* published a long and scathing review of Grégoire's book. The author accuses Grégoire of misleading the reader with unsubstantiated assertions and of grossly exaggerating the viciousness of slave masters. "We would suggest to him that he has not chosen the best time for his pleading; that the moment is not the best to praise the humanity and the virtues of Negroes." Grégoire wants to prove "with a tiring wordiness" that blacks are human beings; but, asks the reviewer, "do colonial masters really doubt it? Should we attribute the excessively severe treatment given to their slaves by some of these men to an erroneous metaphysical belief? Or rather to self-interest, greed or their violent temper? Are there not in all countries men ready to abuse a position of power in order to oppress their fellow citizens?" After accusing Grégoire of wasting a volume on useless demonstrations and attacking his style, the reviewer concludes that the book "is not very important" and that "just as it does not give us a very high opinion about *the literature of Negroes*, it will not be much of a landmark in the literature of white people."

At the same time, the chevalier de Boufflers, a former governor of Senegal, also published a review of *De la littérature des nègres* in the *Mercure de France*.[46] His criticism of Grégoire's work was less violent and more insidious than the attacks of negrophobic writers. Grégoire's book, argues Boufflers, is well-intentioned but largely useless because it strives in a very heavy-handed way to prove what everybody recognizes: that blacks are human beings. Indeed, even if blacks did not have great moral or intellectual qualities, what would that prove? "Would they be less human because of it? As if, in order to be a human being, there were other proofs to give than a little bit of reason and a lot of folly; as if it were not enough to know how to speak, to be unreasonable, to lie, to get

46. Bibliothèque Nationale, MS 238; *Mercure de France* (October 8, 1808): 61–72. Chateaubriand and his friend Fontanes were directors of the *Mercure de France* until 1807.

drunk, etc. If Mr. Grégoire could demonstrate to us that Negroes have no vices or defects, would not he be the first to prove that they are not human beings?" And when it comes to literature, he adds, "one certainly does not need to be a man of letters to be a man, not more than a face needs to be beautiful to be a face." By trying to prove too much, argues Boufflers, Grégoire weakened a position that reason and common sense alone could defend.

The most elaborate salvo fired against *De la littérature des nègres* came in 1810, with the publication of a 312-page book entitled *Le Cri des colons*.[47] The author, F. Renouvelat de Tussac, a former planter who had left Saint Domingue in 1803, attempts to refute Grégoire's book page by page. Grégoire, he says, does not really know what he is talking about; the cases of extreme cruelty against slaves selected by Grégoire are rare exceptions attributable to the wicked character of some men; most slave-owners are not cruel with their slaves; slaves were already slaves in Africa and are better off in the West Indies than left in the hands of bloody tyrants in their native country; slavery may not be a desirable system, but there is no other choice because blacks would never work to produce colonial crops if not forced to do so.

Reactions from Haiti, on the other hand, were enthusiastic. King Christophe's prime minister, the Count de Limonade, belatedly wrote Grégoire a formal letter praising his book: "We have received your great work *De la littérature des nègres*; His Majesty, in great admiration for the philanthropic principles you are defending, has always been an avid reader of it.... Everything makes us love it and instills in our hearts feelings of admiration and thankfulness for its venerable author."[48] Christophe ordered fifty copies of Grégoire's book in London, which he offered to Haitian magistrates and generals. He also had excerpts published in Haitian newspapers.

Grégoire put great hopes in the United States, especially after the

47. F. R. de Tussac, *Le Cri des Colons contre un ouvrage de M. l'Evêque et Sénateur Grégoire, ayant pour titre "De la Littérature des Nègres," ou "Réfutation des imputations calomnieuses faites aux Colons par l'auteur"* (Paris: Delaunay, 1810). This book may have been a collective endeavor in which Tussac was only one contributor; Y. Bénot, *La Démence coloniale sous Napoléon* (Paris: La Découverte, 1992), 203.

48. Bibliothèque de l'Arsenal, MS 6339, letter from Comte de Limonade to Grégoire, June 10, 1814. Limonade apologizes for not having written sooner, but "all means of communications (between Haiti and France) were cut off."

restoration of slavery in French colonies in 1802. The contrast between American democracy and the bonapartist regime in France, the abolition of slavery in the northern American states, the abolition of the slave trade by the United States—all this led him to believe that the new society to which he aspired was likely to emerge first in America rather than in Europe.

Grégoire sent a copy of *De la littérature des nègres* to Jefferson, who was far from enthusiastic, as is evident from a letter he wrote to the American poet Joel Barlow:

> I believe him a very good man, with imagination enough to declaim eloquently, but without judgment to decide. He wrote to me also on the doubts I had expressed five or six and twenty years ago, in the *Notes on Virginia*, as to the grade of understanding of the Negroes, and he sent me his book on the literature of the Negroes. His credulity has made him gather up every story he could find of men of color, (without distinguishing whether black, or of what degree of mixture) however slight the mention, or light the authority on which they are quoted.[49]

To Grégoire himself, Jefferson sent a polite thank you note that gave no hint of his true feelings about the book:

> Be assured that no person living wishes more sincerely than I do to see a complete refutation of the doubts I have myself entertained and expressed on the grade of understanding allotted to them [blacks] by nature and to find that in this respect they are on a par with ourselves. My doubts were the result of personal observation on the limited sphere of my own State where the opportunities for the development of their genius were not favorable and those of exercising it still less so. I expressed them therefore with great hesitation. . . . On this subject they [blacks] are gaining daily in the opinions of nations and hopeful advances are making towards their re-establishment on an equal footing with the other colors of the human family. I pray you therefore to accept my thanks for the many instances you have enabled me to observe of respectable intelligence in that race of men, which cannot fail to have effect in hastening the day of their relief.[50]

Joel Barlow, an old friend from the time of the French Revolution, was much more enthusiastic: "Your enlightening work on the intellectual

49. Jefferson to Barlow, October 8, 1809, in *The Writings of Thomas Jefferson*, ed. Paul L. Ford (New York: Putnam, 1898), 9:261.

50. Jefferson to Grégoire, February 25, 1809, in *The Writings of Thomas Jefferson*, ed. Ford (New York: Putnam, 1898), 9:246–47. A facsimile of the original is reproduced in "annexes" of reprint of *De la littérature des nègres*, published by Librarie Académique Perrin in 1991.

abilities of our black brothers, he writes, pleased me very much. I lent it to my friends who are fluent in your language and I am waiting for Mr. Warden's translation to publicize it as it should be."[51]

Both Jefferson and Barlow of course read the book in the original French. There is no comprehensive study of the reception of Warden's 1810 translation into English nor of its impact on the American abolitionist movement.[52] Grégoire is mentioned, however, in one of the most influential abolitionist books, Lydia Maria Child's *Appeal in Favor of That Class of Americans Called Africans*.[53] Child, who read widely in British and American authors such as Clarkson, Mungo Park, and Wilberforce, appears to have turned to the Warden translation for information not available in their works. Like Grégoire, she did not concern herself exclusively with slavery but focused on racism as the underlying evil, incorporating many of Grégoire's arguments against racist ideology in chapters 6 and 7 of her book, which bear titles reminiscent of *De la littérature des nègres*: "The Intellect of Negroes" and "The Moral Character of Negroes." She also included several of the biographical sketches from Grégoire's chapter 8 ("Negroes and Mulattoes distinguished by their talents and their writings"). Since Child's *Appeal* "recruited into abolitionist ranks a new cadre of leaders who would extend the antislavery movement in many directions"[54] Grégoire's research and ideas, rephrased by an American writer, may have had a wider impact in America than in France during the first half of the nineteenth century.

In 1848, Wilson Armistead, an English abolitionist, published a book whose title and content were clearly inspired by Grégoire's work: *A*

51. Barlow to Grégoire, March 18, 1809 (letter in French in "annexes" of reprint of *De la littérature des nègres* published by Librairie Académique Perrin, 1991). The two men had met in 1792 when Grégoire was overseeing the annexion of Savoy to France; Barlow was then running for election to the Convention in that province. Barlow became U.S. ambassador to France in 1810.

52. H. Grégoire, *An Enquiry concerning the Intellectual and Moral Faculties, and Literature of Negroes*, trans. David Bailie Warden (Brooklyn, N.Y., 1810). Warden was U.S. consul in Paris when he translated Grégoire's book.

53. (New York: John S. Taylor, 1836). This edition was reprinted in 1968 by the Arno Press and the New York Times. Another edition, in slightly different form appeared in 1833 (Boston: Allen and Ticknor).

54. Carolyn Karcher, *The First Woman in the Republic: A Cultural Biography of Lydia Maria Child* (Durham: Duke University Press, 1994), 193. Among these leaders Karcher mentions William Ellery Channing, Wendell Phillips, and the leader of the Radical Republicans, Charles Summer. Pages 183–94 (in chapter 8) of Karcher's book are devoted to Child's Appeal, as well as the notes on 660–61. A modern edition of the *Appeal*, edited by Carolyn Karcher, was in preparation by the University of Massachusetts Press, as this introduction was being drafted.

Tribute for the Negro: Being a Vindication of the Moral, Intellectual, and Religious Capabilities of the Coloured Portion of Mankind; with Particular Reference to the African Race. Illustrated by Numerous Biographical Sketches, Facts, Anecdotes, Etc. and Many Superior Portraits and Engravings. In the preface, Armistead wrote:

> I have also derived much information from the work of the Abbé Grégoire, entitled "De la Littérature des Nègres, ou Recherches sur leurs Facultés Intellectuelles, leurs Qualités Morales, et leur Littérature," etc. I am indebted to Thomas Thompson, of Liverpool, for this scarce volume, who kindly presented me with a copy of it, which is rendered additionally valuable from its being one presented by the Abbé in his own handwriting to the late William Phillips, of London. . . . This admirable work includes a mass of information, the accuracy of which may be thoroughly relied upon, being the production of a man of great erudition and rare virtues, well known in the learned societies of his day.[55]

Armistead took directly from *De la littérature des nègres* eleven of his biographical sketches (each time giving credit to Grégoire). Through this book also, which was distributed in the United States by the Anti-Slavery Office, Grégoire's text became part of American abolitionist literature and was a source of inspiration for James Africanus Horton (1835–82), an early pan-Africanist writer from Sierra Leone.[56] Grégoire's name surfaced again much later in W. E. B. Du Bois's classic *The Negro* (1915) with a reference to Warden's translation of *De la littérature des nègres*.[57]

Although *De la littérature des nègres* has received much less attention in recent decades than Grégoire's famous appeal for the emancipation of the Jews (*Essai sur la regénération physique, morale et politique des Juifs*), it is nonetheless a book of considerable importance in the history of racial thought and of abolitionism. *De la littérature des nègres* is one of the very first attempts to launch a comprehensive counterattack on modern pseudoscientific racism.[58] Grégoire realized that the debate on slav-

55. Wilson Armistead, *A Tribute for the Negro* (Manchester, 1848), xiii–xiv. Armistead mentions that he also used Warden's translation of Grégoire's book. On Armistead, see Irene E. Goodyear, "Wilson Armistead and the Leeds Antislavery Movement," *Publications of the Thoresby Society. Miscellany* 54 (1974): 113–29.

56. James Africanus B. Horton, *West African Countries and Peoples* (London: Johnson, 1868; repr. Edinburgh University Press, 1969).

57. W. E. B. Du Bois, *The Negro* (New York: Holt, 1915), 251.

58. The word "racism" was unknown to Grégoire and his contemporaries. It was coined in the 1930s.

ery and colonization, which had been argued on economic and moral grounds before, was shifting. Racial equality was now the issue at the center of that debate, and the arguments were based on scientific evidence. Although not himself a scientist, Grégoire used all the scientific data he could gather in order to refute the new racialist theories. His aim was to demonstrate that "the most thorough research proves that there is only one human constitution, notwithstanding the different shades of skin color, whether yellow, copper, black or white. (That) the presence of virtues and talents among Negroes offers incontrovertible proof that they have the potential for all combinations of intelligence and morality."[59]

The means used by Grégoire to convey this message were adapted to his times, not ours. Grégoire wrote *De la littérature des nègres* at a time when addressing such a book to a literate European or white American public appeared to be the most effective way to bring about peaceful change. A European like Grégoire could in 1808 expect to be a convincing spokesman for people of African origin who themselves lacked access to the scholarly materials, the international connections, and the standing with a European or white American public that he could exploit.

But this message—a passionate appeal for the unity of mankind—is still as profoundly relevant today as it was two hundred years ago, and it will remain so for as long as racism exists in the world. In *De la littérature des nègres*, Grégoire is speaking to all human beings as a man of conscience who put his faith in human fraternity above everything else.

For Further Reading

A facsimile reprint of Grégoire's *De la littérature des nègres* was published by Librairie Académique Perrin (Paris) in 1991 with an introduction by Jean Lessay. The standard study in English on Grégoire is Ruth Necheles, *The Abbé Grégoire 1787–1831: The Odyssey of an Egalitarian* (Westport, Conn.: Greenwood, 1971).

Other works of interest

Bender, Thomas, ed. *The Antislavery Debate: Capitalism and Abolitionism as a Problem in Historical Interpretation.* Berkeley and Los Angeles: University of California Press, 1992.

59. Grégoire, *De la littérature des nègres*, chap. 2, 69 (1808 French ed.).

Blackburn, Robin. *The Overthrow of Colonial Slavery, 1776–1848*. London: Verso Press, 1988.

Bolt, Christine, and Seymour Drescher. *Anti-Slavery, Religion, and Reform: Essays in Memory of Roger Anstey*. Folkestone: Dawson, 1980.

Cohen, William B. *The French Encounter with Africans: White Response to Blacks, 1530–1880*. Bloomington: Indiana University Press, 1980.

Cooper, Anna J. *Slavery and the French Revolutionists (1788–1805)*. Lewiston: Mellen, 1988. First published translation of a 1925 doctoral dissertation (University of Paris) by a sixty-seven-year-old black American expatriate woman who had been born a slave.

Davis, David Brion. *The Problem of Slavery in the Age of Revolution, 1770–1823*. Ithaca: Cornell University Press, 1975.

James, C. R. L. *The Black Jacobins*. 2d ed. London: Allison, 1980.

Karcher, Carolyn. *The First Woman in the Republic: A Cultural Biography of Lydia Maria Child*. Durham: Duke University Press, 1994.

Nwoga, Donatus I. "Humanitarianism and the Criticism of African Literature, 1770–1810." *Research in African Literatures* 3, no. 2 (1972): 171–79.

Ott, Thomas. *The Haitian Revolution, 1789–1804*. Knoxville: University of Tennessee Press, 1973.

Seeber, Edward. *Anti-Slavery Opinion in France during the Second Half of the Eighteenth Century*. Baltimore: Johns Hopkins University Press, 1937.

Stein, Robert. *The French Slave Trade in the Eighteenth Century: An Old Regime Business*. Madison: University of Wisconsin Press, 1979.

——. *Léger Félicité Sonthonax: The Lost Sentinel of the Republic*. Cranbury: Associated University Presses, 1985.

Todorov, Tzvetan. *On Human Diversity: Nationalism, Racism and Exoticism in French Thought*. Cambridge: Harvard University Press, 1993.

On the
Cultural
Achievements
of Negroes

DEDICATION

To all those men who have had the courage to plead the cause of the unhappy blacks and mulattoes, whether in their writings or by their speeches in national assemblies and in societies devoted to the abolition of the slave trade, in order to relieve the sufferings of the slaves and to free them.

French Adanson, Anthony Benezet, Bernardin St. Pierre, Biauzat,[*1] Boissy D'Anglas,[*] Brissot, Carra, the Jesuit Father Cibot,[*] Clavière, Clermont-Tonnerre,[*] Le Cointe-Marcillac, Condorcet, Cournand, Demanet,[*] Desessarts, D'Estaing, Ducis, Dupont de Nemours, Dyannière,[*] La Fayette, Fauchet, Febvé, Ferrand de Baudières, Frossard, Garat, Garran de Coulon, Gatereau,[*] Le Genty, Girey-Dupré,[*] Madame Olympe de Gouges,[*] Gramagnac, Grelet de Beauregard,[*] Hiriart,[*] Jacquemin (former Bishop of Cayenne), St. John Crevecoeur, de Joly, Kersaint,[*] Ladebat, Lanjuinais,[*] Lanthenas, Lescalier, Théophile Mandar,[*] L. P. Mercier,[*] Mirabeau, Montesquieu, Necker, Pelletan, Pétion, Doctor of the Sorbonne Nicolas Petit-Pied,[*] Poivre,[*] Pruneau-de-Pomme-Gouge,[*] Polverel,[*] General Ricard,[*] Raynal,[*] Robin, La Rochefoucault, Rochon, Roederer, Roucher, St. Lambert, Sibire, Sieyès, Sonthonax, la Société de Sorbonne,[*] Target,[*] Tracy, Turgot, Viefville-Desessarts, Volney.[*]

English William Agutter, Anderson, William Ashburnham,[*] David Barclay, Richard Baxter, Mrs. Barbauld, Barrow, Beatson,[*] Beattie, Beaufoy, Mrs. Behn, John Bicknell,[*] Johm Bidlake,[*] William Lisle Bowes,[*] Samuel Bradburn,[*] Bradshaw,[*] Brougham,[*] Th. Burgess,[*] Burling,[*] Buttler, Clement Caines,[*] Campbell, T. Clarkson, John Henry Colls,[*] Th. Cooper, Cornwallis Bishop of Litchfield,[*] Cowry,[*] Charles

Crawford, Curran,* Danett,* Thomas Day, Darwin, William Steel Dickson, William Dimond junior,* Dore,* John Dyer, Charles Ellis,* Alexander Falconbridge, Miss Falconbridge,* Robert Townsend Farquhar,* James Foster, Fothergill, Charles Fox, George Fox, Gardenston, Thomas Gisborne, James Grainger, Granville Sharp, G. Gregory, Hans-Sloane,* Jonas Hanway,* Hargrave,* Robert Hawker,* Hayter (Bishop of Norwich),* Hector Saint-John,* Rowland Hill, Holder,* Lord Holland, Melville Horne,* Hornemann, Horne Took, Horsley (Bishop of Rochester),* Griffith Hughes, Francis Hutchinson, James Jamieson, Thomas Jeffery,* Edward Jerningham,* Samuel Johnson,* Benjamin Lay, Ledyard, Lettsom, Lucas, Luffman, MacIntosh, MacNeil,* Madison, Richard Mant,* Hughes Mason, Millar,* Miss Hannah More, Morgan-Godwin,* Mungo Park,[2] John Newton, Robert Boucher Nicholls (Dean of Middleham), Richard Nisbet,* Mrs. Opie, Osborne,* Paley,* Robert Percival, Thomas Percival,* C. Peters,* Pickard, John Philmore, Pinckard, William Pitt, Beilby Porteus (Bishop of London),* Pratt, Price, Priestley, James Ramsey, Reid,* Richman, Robinson (Minister at Nevis),* Robert Robinson, Mrs. Mary Robinson,* Rogers, Roscoe, Ryan, Sewall, Shenstone, Sheridan, Smeathmam, William Smith, Snelgrave,* Robert Southey, James Field Stanfield, Stanhope, Sterne, Percival Stockdale,* Miss Stockdale,* Stone (Rector of Coldnorton), Thelwall, Thompson, Thornton, John Waker, George Wallis, Warburton (Bishop of Gloucester),* John Warren (Bishop of Bangor),* John Wesley, Whitaker,* Whitchurch, J. White,* George Whitfield, Wilberforce, Miss Helen Maria Williams, John Woolman, Miss Yearsley, Arthur Young,* the anonymous authors of *Indian Eglogues, The Crisis of the Sugar Colonies, The Sorrows of Slavery,* etc. etc.[3]

Americans Joel Barlow, James Dana, Dwight, Fernando Fairfax,* Franklin, Humphreys, Imlay, Jefferson,* Livingston, Alexander MacLeod,* Madison, Magaw,* Warner Miffin,* Mitchell,* Pearce, Pemberton,* William Pinkney, Benjamin Rush, John Vaughan, D. B. Warden, Elhanan Winchester, Vining.*

Negroes and Mulattoes Amo,* Cugoano, Othello, Milscent* (under the name of Michel Mina), Julien Raimond, Ignatius Sancho, Gustavus Vasa, Phillis Wheatley.

Germans Blumenbach, Augustus la Fontaine, Juliane Duchess of Giovane,* Kotzebue,* Less,* Oldendorp, Pezzl,* Ch. Sprengel,* Usteri.

Danes Bernstorf,* Isert, Kirsten,* Niebuhr,* Olivarius, Rahbek,* Th. Thaarup, West.*

Swedes Afzelius, Euphrasen,* August Nordenskjold, Ulric Nordenskjold, And. Sparrman,* Trotter-Lind,* Wadstrom.

Hollanders Mrs. Beaker,* Van Geuns,* Hogendorp,* Peter Paulus, Mrs. Wolf,* de Vos, Peter Wrede.

Italians Cardinal Cibo, the College of Cardinals, the Abbé Pierre Tamburini, Zacchiroli.*

Spaniards Avendano.

Let us not be surprised at not finding here the name of any Spanish or Portuguese writer, except Avendano. None but he, as far as I know, has taken the trouble of proving that the Negro belongs to the great family of the human race, and that consequently he ought to fulfil all the duties and exercise all the rights pertaining to this family. On the other side of the Pyrenees,[4] these rights and duties were never problematical, and against whom do we need to defend ourselves if there is no aggressor? Only in our time has a Portuguese, through a forced and distorting interpretation of the Bible, endeavored to prove the lawfulness of colonial slavery, which is so unlike slavery among the Hebrews, where it was merely a kind of domesticity. But this pamphlet by Azeredo[5] has passed from the shop of the bookseller to the river of oblivion. Such has also been the fate of the pamphlets by Harris, who in England invoked the authority of the Bible to legitimize colonial slavery, and of the pamphlets in Poland by the Trinitarian Grabowski, who labored to prove from the Bible the right of riveting irons on the peasants of that country. This at the same time that Joseph Paulikowski[6] and the Abbé Michel Karpowitz, in his sermons,[7] proclaimed and demanded equality of rights for all. The friends of slavery are of necessity the enemies of humanity.

In the Spanish and Portuguese settlements, Negroes are generally considered brethren of a different complexion. The Christian religion, which gives us pure happiness, wipes the tear from the eye of the sorrowful, and its hand is ever ready to bestow benefits; this religion interposes itself between the slave and the master, to soften the rigor of authority and the yoke of obedience.

Thus in two colonial powers, no one has composed superfluous discourses in favor of Negroes, for the same reason that before the English author Hartlib, no one wrote on Belgian agriculture, where the practice of agriculture was so superior that it made books unnecessary.

If I should be reproached for inserting the names of certain individuals whom virtue disowns, I would answer that without intending to attenuate the faults of individuals, I present them here only in regard to their efforts to improve the condition of the blacks. Even in this regard not all whom I mention have equal merit and talent. It is regrettable that we cannot apply to every one of them the saying of the poet Churchill that "the purity of their hearts equals the legitimacy of their cause." Everyone should feel free to relegate writers to that class of men of letters, unfortunately so numerous, who are less worthy than their books.

The list is doubtless very incomplete. It ought to contain distinguished names, which I have forgotten or which are unknown to me because their works are anonymous, or have escaped my research. I shall, therefore, receive with gratitude any information that might repair these involuntary omissions, rectify errors, and make my work more complete. Many of these writers are no more. I lay my homage on their graves and offer the same tribute to those who are still living and, unlike Oxholm,[8] have not abandoned their principles but unremittingly pursue their noble enterprise, each in the sphere in which Providence has placed him.

Philanthropists! no individual can be just and good with impunity. The war that began at the beginning of time between virtue and vice, will not cease before the end of time. Possessed by the desire to do harm, the wicked are always armed against anyone who dares to reveal their crimes and who prevents them from tormenting the human race. Let us erect a wall of iron against their evil endeavors, but let us take our revenge with good deeds. Let us not tarry. Life, which is so long for the commission of evil deeds, is all too brief for acts of virtue. The earth slips from under our steps and we are about to leave this worldly stage. Crime and slavery drift toward posterity on the corruption of our times. Nonetheless, when we repose in the tomb, there will be some good men among the living who have escaped the contagion and will in some manner speak for Providence. Let us pass on to them the honorable legacy of defending liberty and those struck by misfortune. From the bosom of eternity we shall applaud their efforts, and no doubt they shall be blest by the common Father of all, who acknowledges his work in all human beings, whatever their color, and loves them as his children.

{ 1 }

Concerning the Meaning of the Word Negro. Ought All Blacks to be Included under This Name? Difference of Opinion concerning Their Origin. Unity of the Original Type of the Human Race.

Under the name of Ethiopians, the Greeks included all black people. This opinion is founded on passages of Herodotus, Theophrastus, Pausanias, Atheneus, Heliodorus, Eusebius, Flavius Josephus, and the Septuagint.[1] They are so named by Pliny the elder and by Terence.[2] They were distinguished into two classes, Eastern or Indian or Asian Ethiopians, and Western or African Ethiopians. Rome probably came to know the latter during its wars with the Carthaginians, since African Ethiopians served in their armies. That is what Macpherson asserts, and he bases himself on a passage in Frontin.[3] Since Rome had more frequent contact with the Western shores of Africa, than did Greece, blacks were sometimes called Africans by Latin authors.[4] But in the Orient they continued to be designated by the name of Arabs for quite a long time. It is also possible that Ethiopia, in its effort to pay the tribute, drew these slaves from the interior of Africa.[5] They were employed in warfare, for in Hebron and at the siege of Jerusalem in 1099 blacks with frizzy hair were in evidence, to whom William of Malmesbury also referred as Ethiopians.[6] While the name of Ethiopia is applied exclusively to a particular region of Africa in modern times, many writers, especially Spaniards and Portuguese, have employed the word Ethiopian to designate the whole race of blacks. Less than thirty years ago, Dr. Ehrlen printed, in Strasbourg, a treatise *De servis Æthiopibus Europeorum in coloniis Americae.*[7] The name Africans is the most frequently used today, but these two names are equally improper, since on the one hand Ethiopia, where the inhabitants are not of the deepest black color,[8] is only one region of

7

Africa, while on the other hand there are Asiatic blacks. Herodotus calls them long-haired Ethiopians, to distinguish them from the ones in Africa, whose hair is frizzled, because it was formerly thought that those with frizzled hair belonged exclusively in Africa, and that the blacks with long hair were only found on the continent of Asia. There were regulations that prohibited the importation of blacks with long hair into the isles of France (today, Mauritius, *Ed.*) and Reunion. But we have learned from the narratives of travelers, that Negroes with long hair can also be found on the African continent, and in Madagascar as well: such as the inhabitants of Bornu in central Africa;[9] and also the Negro shepherds of the Isle of Cerne where the Carthaginians had factories.[10] On the other hand the natives of the Andaman Islands, in the Gulf of Bengal, are blacks with frizzled hair. In various parts of India the inhabitants of the mountains have almost the same color, face, and type of hair. These facts are stated in a learned treatise by Francis Wilford, associate of the National Institute.[11] He adds that the earliest statues of Indian divinities have negroid features. These considerations support the opinion that this race formerly inhabited a large part of the Asian continent.

Since the black color is the most marked characteristic that separates a portion of the human race from the whites, less attention has been paid to the differences in physical constitution that denote varieties among the blacks themselves. Camper alludes to this when he states that Rubens, Sebastiano Ricci, and Vandertempel, in painting the Magi, represented blacks and not Negroes. Thus Camper, along with other authors, limits the name Negroes to those who have prominent cheeks, thick lips, flat noses, and woolly hair. But this distinction between them and those who have long straight hair does not indicate a racial difference. The specific character of a people is permanent as long as they live in isolation; it weakens or disappears by mixture. Can Caesar's depiction of the Gauls be recognized in the present inhabitants of France? Since the time when the peoples of our continent were, so to speak, blended one into the other, national characteristics can hardly be distinguished in either their physical or mental makeup. We are less French, or Spanish, or German, and more European; some of the Europeans have frizzled, others have straight hair. But if we claimed that we could mark the extent and limits of their intellectual faculties on the basis of this difference, and of some other differences in stature and physical appearance, would that not be laughable? What about the objection that the comparison is invalid because European frizzy hair is not woolly? Instead of quibbling about details we should limit ourselves to the question whether such a discrepancy is enough ground to deny that we are here dealing with the same racial identity. The same is true for blacks and for whites: There are remarkable differences between individuals who exhibit in their most extreme form the characteristics of these two varieties of the human species, but as we approach the line that distinguishes one from the other, these differences become weaker and difficult to discern.

Passages in the authors I have already cited, confirm that the Greeks had Negro slaves. This practice was even quite common, according to Visconti. In the *Musée Pio-Clementin* he included a very fine figure of one of these Negroes who was employed in the baths.[12] Earlier Caylus made several engravings of other Negroes.[13]

The Mosaic law prohibited the mutilation of men, but Jahn affirms, in his *Biblical Archaeology*, that the Hebrew kings purchased eunuchs, and particularly black eunuchs, from other nations.[14] He cites no authority in support of this assertion. Yet it is possible that they had such eunuchs, either through their contacts with the Arabs, or from the time when the fleet of Solomon sailed from Eziongeber to Ophir, whence it brought, says Flavius Josephus, much ivory, apes, and Ethiopians.[15] What cannot be disputed is that Egypt traded with Ethiopia, and that the Alexandrians were engaged in the Negro slave trade. Proofs of this have been furnished by Atheneus and by Pliny the Naturalist, and Ameilhon has referred to these authors in his history of Egyptian commerce.[16]

Pinkerton believes that the Egyptians are of Assyrian or Arabian origin.[17] Heeren's opinion seems more justified, that they descended from the Ethiopians who themselves, according to Diodorus of Sicily, considered Egypt one of their colonies.[18] The more we go back into antiquity, the more resemblance we find between their respective countries: the same writing, the same manners and customs. Worship of animals, which still persists in almost all Negro groups, existed among the Egyptians; their physique was that of the Negroes, although their color was somewhat whitened by the influence of the climate. Herodotus assures us, that the Colchians were originally Egyptians because, like the Egyptians, they have a black skin and frizzled hair.[19] This testimony invalidates the reasoning of Browne, who claims that Herodotus meant only that the Egyptians had a dark complexion and frizzled hair when compared to the Greeks, but that this does not indicate they are Negroes.[20] This assertion of Browne lacks nothing except proof. The text of Herodotus is clear and precise.

Everything supports the system of Volney, who recognizes the Copts as representative of the Egyptians: they have a yellowish and smoky skin, a puffy face, protuberant eyes, a flat nose, thick lips; in a word, a mulatto face.[21] The same observations induced Ledyard to believe that the Negroes and the Copts are identical.[22] The physician Franck, who accompanied the expedition to Egypt, supports this opinion by the similarity of customs, such as circumcision and excision, which are practiced among the Copts and the Negroes.[23] According to Ludolf, these customs are still preserved among the Ethiopians.[24]

Blumenbach has observed characteristics of the Negro race in the skulls of mummies, while Cuvier does not find this to be so. These two impressive testimonies appear contradictory, but they can be reconciled if we accept Blumenbach's thesis that three Egyptian varieties exist, one of which resembles the Hindu head, another the head of a Negro, while a third is indigenous to the climate of Egypt and the product of local influences. The first two have blended with the third through the passage of time.[25] The Sphinx, according to Blumenbach, reproduces a Negro face. Once again Browne disputes the validity of this observation and maintains that the statue of the Sphinx is in such bad repair that it is impossible to know its true character,[26] and Meiners is in doubt whether the heads of the sphinxes represent heroes or evil spirits. This opinion is invalidated by an inspection of the drawings of sphinxes in the writings by Caylus and by three men who examined these statues in Egypt: Norden, Niebuhr, and Cassas. More recently Volney and Olivier have also reported on their observation of the Sphinx.[27] They find that it has an Ethiopian face, from which Volney concludes that we owe our arts, our sciences, and even the art of eloquence, to the black race that is now enslaved.[28]

Gregory, in his *Historical and Moral Essays*,[29] takes us back to antiquity to demonstrate in like manner that the Negroes were our masters in science: for in the opinion of many writers the Egyptians, to whom Pythagoras and other Greeks traveled to learn philosophy, were Negroes whose native features were changed by their successive mixing with

Greeks, Romans, and Saracens. Even if it should be proven that the sciences came from India to Egypt, it would be no less true that they had to pass through Egypt to arrive in Europe.

Meiners falls back on the assertion that we owe little to the Egyptians, and a writer in Caen has published a dissertation to develop this thesis.[30] The thesis had already been advanced by Edward Long, the anonymous author of the *History of Jamaica*. He agreed that the characteristics of the Negroes were very similar to those of the ancient Egyptians, but accused the Egyptians of bad qualities, denied them genius and taste, disputed their talent for music, painting, eloquence, and poetry, and only granted them mediocre achievement in architecture.[31] He might well have added that this mediocrity is evident in their pyramids, which a simple mason could have built if a human lifespan lasted long enough. But without placing Egypt at the apex of human knowledge, we must acknowledge that all antiquity bears witness in favor of those who look on that country as a celebrated school that taught many of the learned men of Greece whom we most revere.

Although Long refuses to admit that the Egyptians have any genius, he raises them far above the Negroes, whom he reduces to the lowest degree of intelligence. Since a bad cause is always supported by arguments of the same nature, he cites as one of his arguments for the moral inferiority of Negroes that their vermin are black. This observation, he maintains, has escaped all naturalists.[32] But even supposing that this is really so, who except Long would dare to deny on this basis that all human groups are variants on one identical type, and deny to some of these groups any aptitude for civilization?

Those who have attempted to disinherit the Negroes, have called anatomy to their aid, and their first remarks concern the difference in color. A writer named Hanneman has asserted that the color of the Negroes comes from the curse pronounced by Noah against Ham. It was a waste of time for Gumilla to refute him. This question has been discussed by Pechlin, Ruysch, Albinus, Pittre, Santorini, Winslow, Mitchil, Camper, Zimmerman, Meckel the elder, Demanet, Buffon, Soemmerring, Blumenbach, Stanhope-Smith,[33] and many others. But how can they agree with regard to the consequences, when they disagree concerning the anatomical facts that ought to serve as the basis for their arguments?

Meckel the elder thinks that the Negroes owe their color to the dark color of the brain; but Walter, Bonn, Soemmerring, Dr. Gall, and other great anatomists, have found the color of the brain of Negroes to be the same as that of whites.

Barrère and Winslow believe that the bile of Negroes is of a deeper color than the bile of Europeans; but Soemmerring finds it to be of a yellowish green.

Shall we attribute the color of Negroes to that of their reticular membrane? If in some it is black, in others it has a copper or dark color. All this only sets the difficulty back a step but does not resolve it. For if we allow the hypothesis that the medullary substance, the bile, the reticular membrane, are constantly black, that still leaves the cause to be explained. Buffon, Camper, Bonn, Zimmerman, Blumenbach, his French translator Chardel,[34] Soemmerring, and Imlay, attribute the color of Negroes, and of other species of the human race, to climate, reinforced by secondary causes, such as temperature and their way of life. The learned professor of Göttingen (Blumenbach, *Ed.*) remarks that in Guinea not only men, but dogs, birds, and particularly the gallinaceous species are black; whilst near the frozen seas, bears and other animals are white. Knight maintains that black color characterizes the original species in all animals, and he is inclined to believe that the Negro is the original type of the human species.[35] Demanet and Imlay observe that the descendants of the Portuguese who settled in the Congo, on the Coast of Sierra Leone, and in other parts of Africa have become Negroes.[36] Anyone who wishes to contradict eyewitnesses such as Demanet, must do more than just deny facts, as did the translator of the last work by Pallas.[37]

We know that those parts of the human body that are least exposed to the sun, are pale, such as the soles of the feet and the area between the fingers. Thus Stanhope-Smith—who attributes black skin color to four causes: climate, way of life, state of society, and illness—has collected facts that prove the influence of climate on the complexion and the face, and on the basis of this explains very well why the Africans on the West Coast, under the torrid zone, are blacker than those on the East. He also explains why the same latitude does not produce the same effect in America. On this continent the action of the sun is inhibited by local factors, while such factors strengthen it in Africa. In general black skin color is found between the tropics, and the shadings progress according to the latitude among those peoples who have long resided in the region and have neither been transplanted into other climates nor crossed with other races.[38] If the savages of North America, and the Patagonians who inhabit the other extremity of the continent, have a deeper hue than the people who live near the isthmus of Panama, should we not explain this phenomenon with reference to ancient transmigrations, and consult local testimony? T. Williams, author of the *History of the State of Vermont*, supports this theory by his observations, which prove the connection between color and climate. Reasoning from approximate data, he conjectures that to turn the black race into whites, through intermarriage, would require five generations, each computed at twenty-five years, for a total of 125 years, while without intermarriage and by the sole action of the climate, the blacks would turn white in four thousand years. For the Indians, whose color is red, this would take six hundred years.[39]

These effects are more noticeable among slaves in domestic service, who are accustomed to a milder treatment and a better nourishment. Not only have their features and physiognomy undergone a visible change, their mental state is also improved.[40]

Besides the uncontested fact that there are albinos, Soemmerring substantiates through repeated observations, that whites have been seen to turn black or yellow, and that Negroes have whitened or become of a pale color, especially in consequence of disease.[41] In white women with child, the recticular membrane sometimes becomes as black as that of the Negro women of Angola. This phenomenon is verified by le Cat, and confirmed by Camper as eyewitness.[42] Hunter, however, affirms that when an animal race whitens, that is proof of degeneration. But does it follow that in the human species, the white variety is degenerate? Or should we say, with Dr. Rush, that the color of the Negroes is the result of an hereditary leprosy? He supports his opinion with an experiment made by Beddoes, who almost whitened the hand of an African by immersing it in oxygenated muriatic acid.[43] A journalist turned this to ridicule by proposing that companies of bleachers should be sent to Africa.[44] This joke throws no light on the subject and is out of place when it concerns so distinguished a man as Dr. Rush.

Philosophers are not agreed concerning what part of the human body ought to be considered as the seat of thought and affections. Descartes, Hartley, Buffon—each offers his system. But since thought has been generally supposed to reside in the brain, some have concluded that the largest brains are the most richly endowed with talents, and that since the brain of Negroes is smaller than the brain of whites, the latter ought to be superior to the former. This opinion is destroyed by recent observations, for there are several kinds of birds whose brain is proportionately more voluminous than the human brain.

Cuvier is not willing to accept that the extent of intelligence should be measured by the volume of the brain. He believes it should be measured by the volume of the part of the brain called hemispheres. He maintains that these augment or diminish in proportion to the intellectual faculties of all members of the animal kingdom. But since Cuvier is modest, like all true scientists, it is very likely that this is only a conjecture. For would we not need to have a better knowledge of man's mental state and of the interrelation of his faculties, in order to arrive at an affirmative conclusion? Many centuries may elapse before we penetrate this mystery.

"All that differentiates one human group from another," states Camper, "resides in a line drawn from the openings of the ears to the base of the nose, and in another straight line that touches the eminence of the coronal bone above the nose, and continues to the most prominent part of the jaw bone, it being supposed that the head is viewed in profile. The angle formed by these two lines constitutes the difference between animals and also between nations. It may be said that nature has made use of this angle in some way to identify animal varieties and to bring them, as if by degrees, up to the perfection of the finest race of men. This angle is smallest in birds, and it augments in proportion as the features of an animal seem closer to those of a human being."

"I shall cite, as an example (these are Camper's words) the heads of apes, some of which describe an angle of 42 degrees, others of 50 degrees. The head of an African Negro, as well as that of a Calmuck, makes an angle of 70 degrees, and the head of a European, one of 80. This difference of 10 degrees forms the beauty of European heads, because it is an angle of 100 degrees that accounts for the greater perfection of the heads from antiquity. Such heads represent the greatest degree of beauty and most resemble the head of the Pythian Apollo, and of the Medusa by Sosocles, two pieces of statuary unanimously considered as superior to all others in beauty."[45]

This facial line of Camper has been adopted by various anatomists.

Bonn says that he found the angle of 70 degrees in the heads of Negro women.[46] Since, on the one hand, these differences are nearly constant, and since, on the other hand, science itself is subject to the reign of fashion, this type of comment on the volume, configuration, and protuberances of the cranium, on the expansion of the brain, on the influences to which each part of the brain may be susceptible, and its relation to human intelligence, has taken the name of Cranology, ever since the time when Dr. Gall made it the object of his physiological doctrine. Gall is opposed, among others, by Osiander.[47] He disputes that Dr. Gall was the first to formulate such a doctrine and maintains that he found its elements in the *Metoscopia* of Fuchsius, and in the *Fasciculus Medicinae* of Joannes de Ketham. Dr. Gall himself states that Osiander might have added Aristotle, Plutarch, Albert the Great, Triumphus, and Vieussens.

Gall wants to base the supposed moral inferiority of the Negroes on the structure of the cranium. When he is confronted by the fact that many Negroes are unquestionably talented, he answers that in such cases the form of their skull resembles the structure of the whites' skull, and inversely he argues that stupid whites have a skull with a shape similar to that of the Negroes. Nonetheless I am quite ready to pay my respects to the talents and upright qualities of Drs. Gall and Osiander, but the most distinguished men may be led astray by their hypotheses, or may draw exaggerated conclusions from accurate observations. For example, no one will deny that the president of the London Academy of Arts is a great painter, but how would West go about proving his opinion that the physiognomy of the Jews resembles that of the goats?[48] How can it be easy to determine national traits when we see remarkable variations in all countries, even in passing from one village to the next? I noticed this particularly in the Vosges, as did Olivier in Persia. Lopez, for his part, saw Negroes with red hair in the Congo.[49]

Nevertheless, we should admit that every people has a distinct character, which is reproduced until it is altered or effaced by mixture. Yet who can determine the lapse of time required to destroy the influence of those diverse characteristics which are hereditarily transmitted, and which result from climate, education, diet, or habit? Nature is so diversified in her details, that the most skilful eye is often tempted to class congenerous plants in different species. Nevertheless she allows for only a few original types, and in the three kingdoms (vegetable, animal and mineral, *Ed.*) the fruitful power of Eternal God brings forth from these types an infinite diversity that embellishes and enriches the globe.

Blumenbach believes that the Europeans degenerate if they reside for a long time in the two Indies or in Africa. Soemmerring is reluctant to decide whether the original race of man, in whatever corner of the earth we place its beginnings, has since improved in Europe and been corrupted in the land of the Negroes. He considers that in point of physical strength and skill the Negroes are at least as well adapted to their climate as the Europeans. The Negro surpasses the European in the exquisite keenness of his senses, particularly in the sense of smell. They share this advantage with all those who frequently need to make use of their senses, such as the native peoples of North America and the Maroons of Jamaica who, at a glance, distinguish objects in the forests that are imperceptible to all whites. Their erect bearing, their proud countenance, and their vigor proclaim their superior nature; they communicate with each other by sounding the horn, and the variations of sound are such that they summon each other at a distance by distinguishing each person by his name.[50]

Soemmerring makes the further observation that the essential perfection of many plants is injured by cultivation. The beauty and short-lived freshness that we try to produce in flowers, often destroy the purpose for which they were destined by nature. The art of producing double flowers, which we owe to the Hollanders, almost always deprives the plant of the faculty of reproduction. Something analogous to this is found among men: Their mind is often cultivated at the expense of the body, and vice versa, for the more a slave is brutalized, the more suited he is for manual labor.[51]

No one denies that Negroes have great bodily strength. As for beauty, on what do you base it? No doubt on the color and regularity of a person's features; but on what grounds can anyone claim that only the color white should enter into what constitutes beauty, while this principle is not applied to other products of nature? Everyone has his own prejudices on this question, and we know that various black tribes paint the devil white, because that is the color they consider the least attractive.

As to regularity of features, it is one of those complex ideas whose elements are perhaps still unknown, and concerning which we still have to establish basic principles, in spite of the efforts made by Crouzas,

Hutcheson, and Father André. In the Manchester memoirs George Walker maintains that those forms and features that are universally approved in all nations, constitute the essence of beauty, and that whatever is in dispute is consequently a fault and an error of judgment.[52] This means that he expects erudition to supply the solution to a physiological problem.

Bosman praises the beauty of the Negro women of Ouidah,[53] Ledyard and Lucas the beauty of the Negroes of Djolof,[54] Lobo the beauty of the Negroes of Abyssinia.[55] The Negroes of Senegal, says Adanson, are the finest men of the black continent: their shape is without defect and there are no cripples amongst them.[56] In Gorée, Cossigny saw Negro women of great beauty, of an impressive stature and with Roman features.[57] Ligon speaks of a Negro woman of the isle of Santiago, who possessed such a degree of beauty and majesty, that he has never seen her equal.[58] Robert Chasle, author of *Journal du voyage de l'Admiral du Quesne*, gives the same praise to the Negro and mulatto women of all the Cape Verde Islands.[59] Leguat,[60] Ulloa,[61] and Isert[62] give the same report concerning the Negro women they have seen, Leguat in Batavia, Ulloa in America and Isert in Guinea. After such testimonies, Jedediah Morse will no doubt find it difficult to justify the mark of superiority that he sees imprinted on the faces of the whites.[63]

The theories that assume an essential difference between Negroes and white men, have been accepted by those who by every means seek to materialize man and to rob him of the hopes dearest to his heart; second, by those who look on the original existence of a diversity of human races as an argument with which to deny the story of Moses; and, third, by those who have a material interest in colonial agriculture and wish to use the supposed absence of moral faculties in the Negro as another reason for treating him, with impunity, like a beast of burden.

One of those who was accused of proclaiming this opinion, heatedly denies it. He was criticized for having stated in his *Idées sommaires sur quelques règlements à faire à l'assemblée coloniale*, printed at Cap Haitien, that there are two species of human beings, the white and the red, that Negroes and mulattoes do not belong to the same species as the whites and therefore can no more claim natural rights than the orangutan, and that thus Saint Domingue belongs to the white species.[64] Although the author denies that this is what he believes, it is worth noting that he was then a corresponding member of the Academy of Sciences and is now a member of the Institute.[65] Moreover, precisely at the time when this was written, one of his fellow corresponding members of the same Academy was a mulatto from the Ile de France (today, Mauritius, *Ed.*), Geoffroi Lislet, who will be mentioned again later.

The colonial laws did not explicitly place slaves and animals in the same category, but it was implied in various regulations and judicial decisions. From the many facts that support this I am selecting, first, a decision by the Council of Cap Haitien, which I take from a trustworthy source, the collection of Moreau St. Méry. This judgment places Negroes and hogs on the same level.[66] Second, the police regulation in Batavia that forbids slaves to wear stockings or shoes, or to use the sidewalks near the houses. They are forced to walk with the livestock in the middle of the street.[67]

But we hasten to acknowledge that the scientists who have researched this subject have not, to their honor, committed an outrage against reason by trying to reduce blacks to a subhuman state. Even those who would measure the extent of the moral faculties by the size of the brain, disavow the fantasies of Kames[68] and all the deductions that materialism or cupidity may wish to draw from them for the purpose of denying the spirituality of the soul or in order to enslave the blacks.

I have had the opportunity of conversing about this with Bonn of Amsterdam, who has the finest collection known of human skins; with Blumenbach, who perhaps has the most extensive collection of human skulls; with Gall, Meiners, Osiander, Cuvier, and Lacépède. I take this occasion to express my gratitude to these learned men. All, with the exception of one who does not dare to decide, maintain that there exists one original type of the human race, as did Buffon, Camper, Stanhope-Smith, Zimmerman and Soemmerring.

Thus physiology is here in agreement with the ideas to which we are constantly led by the study of languages and of history, and which are revealed in the sacred books of Jews and Christians. These same authors reject all assimilation of man with the apes, and Blumenbach denies, on the basis of repeated observations, that the female ape has periodic discharges which others have adduced as an indication of its similarity to the human species.[69]

There is greater difference between the head of a wild boar and that of the domestic pig, which everyone agrees are of the same race, than there is between the head of a Negro and that of a white man. But, according to Blumenbach, there is an immense distance between the head of a Negro and of an orangutan. Since Negroes are of the same nature as whites, they have the same rights and the same duties. These rights and duties precede moral development. They are doubtless put into practice better or less well according to the qualities of individuals. But should we calibrate the enjoyment of social advantages on a comparative scale of virtues and talents that would not allow a place for many of the whites themselves?

{ 2 }

Opinions Concerning the Moral Inferiority of Negroes. Discussion of This Topic. Of the Obstacles which Slavery Places in the Way of the Development of Their Faculties. These Obstacles Combated by the Christian Religion. Of Negro Bishops and Priests.

The opinion that the Negroes are inferior is not new. The claims of white superiority are defended only by whites speaking in their own interest. Before attacking their opinion we should question whether they are qualified to make such a judgment. This reminds us of the fable of the lion who sees a picture representing one of his species brought down by a man, and merely comments that lions have no painters.

In his essay on national character Hume distinguishes four or five races but maintains that only the white race possesses culture and that no black has ever distinguished himself by his actions or by his knowledge.[1] This assertion was repeated by his translator, and then by Estwick[2] and Chatelux.

Barré-Saint-Venant thinks that while nature has endowed Negroes with a certain ability to combine ideas, which raises them above other animals, nature has also made them incapable of deep feelings and sustained activity of the intellect, creative genius, and reason.[3]

To our regret we find the same prejudice in a man whose name is always mentioned amongst us with the most profound esteem and with a respect he deserves: Jefferson, in his *Notes on Virginia*.[4] To support his opinion he did not merely disparage the talent of two Negro writers; he also found it necessary to establish by argument and by a multitude of facts, that even if blacks and whites lived under the same circumstances, the blacks could never compete with the whites.

He himself raises the objection that Epictetus, Terence, and Phaedrus seem to prove the opposite, since they were slaves (he might have added the names of Lokman, Aesop, and Servius Tullius). He answers this objection by begging the question; that is, by saying that they are white.

Jefferson was attacked by Beattie, and since then with considerable heat by Imlay, his compatriot, especially concerning Phillis Wheatley. Imlay transcribes moving passages from her work. But he is also in error when he says to Jefferson that to cite Terence is awkward, since Terence was an African and in fact a Numidian, and thus a Negro.[5] It appears that Terence was a Carthaginian. Numidia corresponds to what is now named Mauritania,[6] whose inhabitants, of Arabian descent, invaded Spain and became the most enlightened people of the Middle Ages.

Moreover, Jefferson furnishes arms against himself in his answer to Raynal, who reproached America for not having produced, so far, any famous men. Once we have been in existence as a nation, says this learned American, as long as the Greeks before they had a Homer, the Romans a Virgil, or the French a Racine, observers will have a right to be astonished. In like manner we can say that once Negroes have lived in a state of civilization as long as the inhabitants of the United States, there will be some justification for believing that the Negroes are totally lacking in genius, if they have not produced men like Franklin, Rittenhouse, Jefferson, Madison, Washington, Monroe, Warren, Rush, Barlow, Mitchell, Rumford, Barton, [the Virginian who wrote *The English Spy*, the author of the speech to the American armies at the end of the Revolutionary wars who was given the name of "the American Junius,"[7] and thirty others whom I could mention].[8] Then we might say with Gentry, "How could one ever expect genius to spring up in the midst of infamy and deprivation, when there is not a glimpse of recompense and no hope of relief!"[9] [Now that I have argued against an error in Jefferson's mind, I must not leave this topic without rendering homage to his heart. By his speeches and his actions, both as president and as citizen, he has unceasingly called for the liberty and education of the slaves, and for all other measures to better their existence.][10]

In most parts of Africa, civilization and the arts are still in their infancy. If you believe this is because the inhabitants are Negroes, explain to us why white or copper-colored men of other countries have remained savages and even cannibals? Why did the nomadic hunters of North America not even become pastoral tribes before the arrival of the Europeans? Yet no one contests their capacity for improvement. It would be contested, for sure, if there were ever a design to subject them to the slave trade. It can be taken for granted that greed would discover pretexts to justify their slavery.

The arts originate from natural or from artificial needs. Artificial needs are almost unknown in Africa, and as to the natural needs for food, clothing, and shelter, they are minimal on account of the heat of the climate. The first of these needs is quite limited and easily satisfied, because in that region nature is prodigal of her riches. The recent reports by travelers have greatly modified the opinion that the African countries are little more than unfruitful deserts. In that respect James Field Stanfield echoes these travelers in his fine poem *Guinea*.[11]

The Christian religion is an infallible means of extending and securing civilization. Such has been, and will always be its effect. It was by its influence that our ancestors, the Gauls and the Franks, ceased to be barbarians, and that the sacred woods were no longer stained with the blood of human sacrifices. It was this faith that enlightened the African Church, formerly one of the most splendid regions of Catholicity. When Christianity forsook these regions, they were again plunged in darkness. The historian Long reproaches the Negroes for eating wild cats, as if this were a crime, and a circumstance unknown in Europe. This from a man who tries to persuade us that Negroes are incapable of attaining the highest achievements of the human mind, while he himself refutes his own assertions in many passages of his work, as we intend to point out; for instance, in the section concerning Francis Williams. Long also states that Negroes are given to superstition,[12] as though Europe were free of this infection, and particularly the country of that historian. We can find in Grose a long and ridiculous enumeration of the superstitious observances of English Protestants.[13]

While the superstitious are to be pitied, they are at least not inaccessible to sound notions. False glimmering may be dispelled by the splendor of light.[14] Those who are superstitious may be compared to fertile land that produces poisonous or wholesome plants, depending on whether the soil is neglected or cultivated. A completely sterile soil, on the other hand, could be a symbol for anyone who denies all religious principles. Only the belief in a God who rewards and punishes, can assure the probity of a man who is hidden from the eyes of his fellow men, and who could steal or commit any other crime with impunity, since he does not need to fear public vengeance. These reflections enable us to resolve a problem that is so often discussed: namely, Which is worse, superstition or atheism? Even though in many individuals the passions stifle every sentiment of justice and probity, yet as a general principle we cannot hesitate on the choice between an individual who to be virtuous merely needs to act in conformity with his beliefs, and another who must be inconsistent with his general principles if he wishes to avoid becoming dishonest.

Barrow attributes the present barbaric state of certain regions in Africa to the effect of the slave trade. In order to procure slaves, the Europeans created and still perpetuate a state of constant warfare. They have poisoned those regions through their strong liquors, and through every kind of debauchery, rapacity, cruelty, and seduction. Is there a single vice which they do not reenact daily as an example to the Negroes they have brought to Europe or transported into our colonies? I am not surprised to read the following words in Beaver, (who was certainly a friend of the Negroes and, in his *African Memoranda*, gives lavish praise to their native virtues and talents): "I would rather introduce a rattlesnake among them than a Negro who has lived in London."[15] This exaggerated expression is not very flattering to the whites, and it points out what happens to individuals when they are taught every sort of depravity, without being introduced to any form of restraint that might lessen the cruel consequences.

According to Homer, when Jupiter condemns a man to slavery, he deprives him of half his mind. Liberty brings forth all that is sublime in genius and virtue, whilst it is stifled by slavery. What sentiments of dignity or of self-respect can exist in human beings who are considered as though they were cattle, and who are often staked by their masters, at cards or billiards, against barrels of rice or other merchandise? What kind of individuals can they be when they are degraded below the brutes, worked to the bone, covered with rags, worn out by hunger, and at the slightest fault torn by the bloody whip of an overseer?

The worthy Father Sibire, who was a successful missionary in Africa and in Europe before fanatics drove him out of the ministry like so many worthy priests,[16] ridicules the colonial settlers in the following words: "They have described the happiness of their Negroes in such pleasant and attractive colors, that when we admire their fantasies we almost regret being free and wish we could be slaves. . . . I would not wish such happiness on these settlers, although they are only too worthy of it."[17] He also writes in the same book: "Whom can you convince that the eternal wisdom can contradict itself, and that the common father of mankind is its tyrant, as you are? If, by an impossible circumstance, there existed upon earth a man destined to be the prey of his fellow men, this would constitute an invincible argument against Providence."[18] We have not seen one of those white impostors exchange his situation for that of one of his Negroes. If slaves were so happy, why until these last years, were 80,000 blacks transported every year out of Africa to take the place of those who had succumbed to fatigue, deprivation, and despair? For the planters themselves acknowledge that a great number die shortly after their arrival in America.[19]

The colonial settlers endeavor by every means to persuade their slaves that they are happy. The slaves obstinately hold to the contrary opinion. Whom should we believe? Why are their looks and recollections constantly turned toward their country? Whence arise these bitter regrets at being far from home, and this disgust with life? Why are they so cheerful when they attend the funeral of their companions in misery, whom death has freed from bondage without the whites being able to prevent it?[20] Whence this consoling tradition that their happiness in dying shall be to return to their native land? Whence originate these frequent suicides to hasten their return? If Bryan Edwards has thought fit to deny that this opinion is common among the Negroes he is contradicted by a number of authors, among others by his countryman Hans Sloane, who was certainly well acquainted with the colonies,[21] and by Othello, the Negro author.[22]

The inhabitants of Basse-Pointe and of Carbet, two parishes of Martinique, were more truthful than other settlers when they declared, in 1778, that "only religion, which brings hope of a better world, enables the Negroes to support a yoke so contrary to nature, and consoles this people who see nothing in this world but labor and punishment."[23]

In Batavia,[24] the masters take out an annual subscription, at a set price, to arrange a mass flogging of the slaves. Immediately after the flogging, the wounds are covered with pepper and salt to prevent gangrene; this is reported by Barrow.[25] His countryman Robert Percival observes on this occasion, that since the slaves of Batavia and of other Dutch colonies to the East, are cruelly treated and have no defense against the ferocity of their masters, nor any hope of getting justice from the courts, they seek revenge against their tyrants, against themselves, and against the human race, in those homicidal races named Mocks, which are more frequent in those colonies than elsewhere.[26]

One could fill thick volumes with the recital of the crimes by which the slaves have been victimized. When the partisans of slavery find they cannot deny this, they fall back on the argument that this was the past but that nothing of this kind has recently sullied the records of the colonies. To be sure, there are planters who are worthy in every respect and cannot be accused of cruelty. If anyone should protest as though he was being attacked individually, we would answer, with Erasmus, that by protesting he reveals his bad conscience.[27] However, the story is quite recent of the captain of a slave ship, who when he was short of water and saw his cargo ravaged by death, threw the blacks by hundreds into the sea. Not long ago another captain of a slave ship was annoyed by the cries of the child of a Negro woman, dragged it from its mother's bosom, and threw it into the water. Then he was bothered by the groans of the unfortunate mother, and the only reason why she did not experience a similar fate was that this trader hoped to profit by her sale. I am persuaded, says John Newton, that all mothers worthy of the name, will lament her fate. The same author mentions another captain who put down an insurrection and then devoted himself for a long time to devising the most refined tortures in order to punish what he called a revolt.[28]

In 1789, we received the following account from Kingston, in Jamaica: "Besides tearing the flesh of the Negroes with the lash of the whip, they muzzle them to prevent them from sucking the sugarcane which is watered with their sweat, and the instrument of iron with which the mouth is compressed, stifles their cries when they suffer under the lash."[29]

In 1795, the Maroons of Jamaica made the Planters tremble. A colonel Quarrel proposed to the colonial assembly to go to Cuba and seek packs of devouring dogs. His proposal was accepted with enthusiasm. He left and went to Cuba, where the tale of this infernal mission is interrupted by the description of a ball given in his honor by the marchioness of St. Philippe. He returned to Jamaica with his hunters and his dogs: fortunately, neither were of use, since peace had been made with the Maroons. But the intention of those planters ought to be known, who paid the hunters generously, and voted thanks and rewards to Colonel Quarrel, whose name, ever to be execrated, ought to figure with that of Phalaris, Mazentius, and Nero.

I ask the following question with regret, but we must show greater respect to truth than to any individual. Even though there is testimony in favor of the character of Dallas, what can we think of a man who justifies this measure? According to him, only extreme Sophists could denounce it: "Did not the Asians employ elephants in war? Is not cavalry in use among the nations of Europe? If a man were bitten by a mad dog, would he hesitate to cut off the part that had been attacked in order to save his life?" and other such arguments. But who are those who are biting and mad, other than those individuals who are devoured by greed, who trample under foot, in both hemispheres, all human and divine laws, and have dragged unfortunate slaves from Africa, to oppress them in America? So it is true that the thirst for gold and for power turns men into wild beasts, corrupts their reason, and destroys all moral feeling. If circumstances force them to be just, they boast of those acts that are prompted by necessity, as though they were good deeds. Colonists! If you had been dragged from your hearths, to undergo the fate of the slave, what would you say then? What would you do?

Bryan Edwards painted Negroes as tigers: he accused them of having butchered prisoners, women with child, and infants at the mother's breast. Dallas refutes him, and by the facts he offers unintentionally destroys the illogical arguments he advanced to justify the use of blood-hounds.[30]

Oh! that it had pleased God to cause the waves to swallow up these devourers of human flesh, trained and directed by man against his fellow man. I have heard it asserted, that on the arrival of the dogs at Saint Domingue, by way of experiment they were let loose on the first Negro who happened along. The promptitude with which they devoured their prey delighted those white tigers with a human face.

Wimphen, who wrote during the Revolution, declared that in Saint Domingue the strokes of the whip and the groans of sufferers took the place of the crowing of the cock.[31] He mentions a woman who threw her Negro cook into an oven, because he ruined a dish of pastry. A planter named Chaperon did the same thing before her.[32]

The innumerable depositions made at the bar of the British Parliament, have completely revealed the crimes of the planters. New developments have provided additional evidence, by the publication of a work entitled *The Horrors of Slavery*;[33] and more recently by the *Voyages* of Pinckard[34] and of Robin.[35] We learn from reading Robin that many Creole women have renounced the gentleness and modesty that are the patrimonial heritage of their sex. With what singular effrontery do they go to the markets to inspect and buy naked Negroes, whom they take to their workshops without giving them clothes. To cover their nakedness the Negroes have to resort to girdles of moss. Robin reproaches the Creole women for exceeding the men in cruelty. Negroes condemned to the lash are fixed with their face to the earth between four stakes; without emotion the women see the blood flow, and look with indifference at the long stripes of skin torn from the body of these unfortunates. Pregnant Negro women are not exempt from this punishment. The only precaution taken is to excavate the earth where their abdomen is to be placed. The white children, daily witnesses of these horrors, serve an apprenticeship in inhumanity as they amuse themselves by tormenting the Negro children.[36] And yet, even though the cry of humanity rises from all sides against the crimes of the slave trade and slavery, even though Denmark, England, and the United States disown the traffic,[37] there are some among us who argue for its reintroduction.[38] This in spite of the decrees that were published, and in spite of these words in the proclamation by the head of state to the Negroes of Saint Domingue: "You are all equal and free before God and the Republic."[39]

These pamphleteers speak incessantly of unhappy planters, and never of unhappy Negroes. The planters keep repeating that the soil of the colonies has been watered by their sweat, and never utter a word concerning the sweat of their slaves. The colonial settlers are right to describe as monsters those Negroes of Saint Domingue who had recourse to criminal repression and butchered the whites; but they never say that the whites provoked this vengeance by drowning Negroes, or letting dogs devour them. The erudition of the colonials is full of quotes in support of servitude. None are better acquainted than they with the tactics of despotism. They have read in Vinnius, that the air produces slaves; in Fermin, that slavery is not contrary to natural law;[40] in Beckford, that the Negroes are slaves by nature.[41]

Hilliard D'Auberteuil, whom the ungrateful colonists left to perish in a dungeon because he was suspected of being the friend of mulattoes and free Negroes, wrote as follows: "Our interest and safety require that we burden the blacks with so great a contempt that they bear a stain that cannot be effaced into the sixth generation."[42] Barré Saint-Venant regrets that the general belief in the superiority of the whites has been destroyed.[43]

Felix Carteau, author of *Soirées Bermudiennes*, takes as an axiom this "unalterable supremacy of the white race," this "preeminence" that is "the palladium of our species."[44]

He attributes the ruin of Saint Domingue to the "pride and premature claims of the mulattoes," instead of attributing it to the pride and immoderate claims of the whites. The author of *Voyage to Louisiana*, at the close of the last century, wants to perpetuate the convenient prejudice that leads people to hate the Negro because he is destined to be a slave.[45] Armed with these blasphemies, they shamelessly request that new fetters be forged for the Africans. The author who wrote *An examination of slavery in general, and particularly of the slavery of the Negroes in the French colonies*, appears to believe that Negroes receive life only on condition of being slaves, and he claims that they themselves would vote for slavery.[46]

He regrets the time is no more when the shadow of the white man made the Negroes run. A preacher of ignorance, he is unwilling that the people be instructed, and he honors Montesquieu with his criticism, because he dared to ridicule the infallibility of the colonial settlers. Belu, who wishes to restore this abhorrent regime, declares that the Negroes were lacerated by the strokes of the whip, and that the bad effects of this laceration were forestalled by pouring on the wounds a kind of brine, which increased the pain, but brought quick healing.[47] This fact corresponds with what we have read concerning Batavia. But nothing can equal what is written in the *Egaremens du Négrophilisme*[48] by an individual named Lozières, whom, not to believe worse of him, we can only consider as deranged. He assures us "that the inventor of the slave trade merits altars"[49] and that "by slavery we make men worthy of heaven and of earth."[50] Yet he admits that the captains of slave ships, when they have slaves afflicted with disorders of the skin, which might injure their sale, give them drugs to counteract these humors, which at a later time occasion horrible ravages.[51]

Slaves are almost entirely delivered over to the discretion of their masters. The laws have done everything for the latter, and everything against the former. Condemned to legal incapacity, they cannot even be admitted as witnesses against whites. If a Negro endeavors to escape, the Black Code of Jamaica gives the tribunal power to condemn him to death.[52]

A few years ago, less savage regulations were substituted in the code of this island, but this proves how horrible were those that have been annulled. These new regulations are still an outrage against justice, and yet it is not certain that they are carried out. Dallas makes mention of the new regulations, but acknowledges that in practice many improvements remain to be made.[53] This admission makes us wonder whether the recent decisions were anything more than a legislative mockery, intended to silence the protests of philanthropists, for the whites always make a common cause against all those who are not of their color.

Besides, greed will find a thousand ways of eluding the laws. This is the case in the United States where, in spite of the prohibition of the slave trade, traders go out to the coast of Africa and load cargoes of blacks, to be sold in the Spanish colonies. They would even stop, or sell slaves at a port of the Union, if they did not dread the inflexible vigilance of the worthy Quakers, who are always ready to bring to the attention of the magistrates such transgressions that violate the law and the principles of nature.

In Barbadoes, as in Surinam, anyone who willfully and cruelly kills a slave is exonerated by paying the sum of fifteen pounds sterling to the public treasury.[54] In South Carolina the fine is greater: fifty pounds sterling. But an American newspaper informs us that this crime carries no punishment whatsoever since the fine is never paid.[55]

While the lives of the slaves enjoy at best minimal protection, their sense of modesty is totally defenseless against brutish lewdness. John Newton, who was employed for nine years in the slave trade, and then became an Anglican clergyman, makes upright souls shudder as he laments the outrages committed against Negro women, "even though we often admire traits of modesty and delicacy among them of which a virtuous Englishwoman might be proud."[56]

In the French, English, and Dutch colonies, the laws, or public opinion, rejected mixed marriages to such a degree, that those who entered into them were considered to have debased themselves through misalliance. The Portuguese and the Spaniards constitute an honorable exception. In their colonies a Catholic marriage sets the slave free. It is not surprising that Barré-Saint-Venant inveighs against this religious regulation,[57] since he dares to censure the ever-celebrated decree by which Constantine facilitated the freeing of slaves.[58] What has resulted from these legal prohibitions, more particularly those that relate to marriage? Libertinism has eluded the law or has broken through the prejudice. This will always take place when men try to act in contradiction to nature.

I leave to physiologists the task of bringing out the advantages of the mixing of races, with regard to the physical constitution as well as to the energizing of the moral faculties. On the island of St. Helena, for instance, this has produced a magnificent variety of mulattoes. I leave it to moralists and politicians, who ought to start from the same principles, but who often are in direct opposition to each other, to weigh the consequences of a public opinion that considers it a dishonor to have a Negro woman as a legitimate wife, while as a concubine she is no disgrace. Joel Barlow, on the contrary, proposes to encourage mixed marriages by premiums offered for that purpose. Neither Negroes nor mulattoes can ever augment the white caste, whilst the white caste daily augments the number of mulattoes. The inevitable result will be that in the end the mulattoes will become masters. Reasoning from this observation, Robin believes that the distinction of color is a scourge in the colonies, and that Saint Domingue would be still in its splendor, if it had followed the Spanish policy, which does not exclude those of mixed parentage from intermarriage and other social advantages.[59]

The Negroes are accused of a vindictive disposition. What other temper can men possess, who are vexed and deceived continually, and by this treatment are provoked into being vengeful? Of this we could cite a thousand proofs; we shall, however, confine ourselves to a single fact. The Negro Baron, in Surinam, is skilful, educated, and faithful. He is taken to Holland by his master, who promises him his freedom on their return. Notwithstanding this promise, when they arrive back in Surinam, Baron is sold. He obstinately refuses to work and receives a lashing at the foot of a gibbet; he escapes, joins the Maroons, and becomes the implacable enemy of the whites.

This torturing system has been pursued so far as to prevent all development of the mental facilities. By a regulation adopted in the state of Virginia, slaves are not allowed to learn to read. To have been able to read cost one of those black men his life. He demanded, that the Africans should share the benefits promised by American liberty, and he supported this demand by the first article of the Bill of Rights. The argument was unanswerable. In such cases, where refutation is impossible, the Inquisition incarcerates those whom formerly it would have burned. All tyrannies have similar features. The Negro was hanged.

[Thomas Day, that good man, was certainly right when, in dedicating the third edition of his *Dying Negro* to J. J. Rousseau, he criticized the Americans in the South for advocating liberty while they compromised with their conscience, without any feelings of guilt, so as to be able to maintain slavery. He could not be hanged like the Negro, nor could he be refuted. All that could be done was to make harangues and condemn him for writing a "philippic."][60]

In the government of this world, force ought never to intervene except when called upon by reason. But reason is usually forced into silence when confronted by power. "Is it not shameful to speak as a philosopher, and to act as a despot; to make fine discourses on liberty, and to annex as a commentary, an actual oppression. It is a political maxim that the legislative system ought to harmonize with the principles of the government. Does this harmony exist in a constitution reputed free, if slavery is sanctioned by authority?"

Thus William Pinckney expressed himself in 1789, in a discourse delivered before the representative assembly of Maryland, in which sound reasoning is ornamented with erudition and the graces of style, and this does equal honor to his heart and his mind.[61]

It has always been the custom of tormentors to slander the victims. The slave traders and the planters have denied or attenuated the facts of which they are accused. They even tried to make a pretense of being humanitarian by maintaining that all the slaves brought from Africa were prisoners of war, or criminals destined for execution who ought to congratulate themselves that their lives were saved, and that they are permitted to cultivate the soil of the Antilles. They have been refuted by many eyewitnesses, and lately by the worthy John Newton, who lived a long time in Africa. He states: "The respectable author of the *Spectacle de la nature* (Pluche) erred when he declared that fathers sell their children, and children their fathers; I never heard in Africa that this practice existed."[62]

When the truth about the tormenting of the slaves and the barbarity of the masters was substantiated thousands of times, the masters denied that the Negro is capable of morality or of intelligence, and on the scale of all living beings they placed him between man and the animals.

Even if we accepted this hypothesis, we should still inquire whether man has only rights to exercise and no duties to fulfil toward those animals he associates with his labor, and whether he does not offend religion and morality by overworking those unhappy quadrupeds whose life is nothing more than a drawn-out torment. On this subject there are moving statements in the sacred books that Christians and Jews equally revere.[63] A bird pursued by a sparrow-hawk seeks refuge in the bosom of a man who kills it. The court condemns him to death. This punishment was doubtless too severe, but no doubt the moment will come when a justifiably strict administration of justice will punish those barbarous carters who every day, especially in Paris, wear out through fatigue and beatings the most useful of all domestic animals: the horse, which Buffon calls the finest conquest of man. Such actions foster cruel and insensitive behavior in the people who witness it. I recollect with pleasure that in London, at the Smithfield market, I read an official warning of the fines levied on anyone who wantonly abused animals.

This discussion is pertinent to my subject; if the principles of morality cover even the relations that man has with animals, then the Negroes, even if they were lacking in intelligence, would still have grounds for protesting against their condition. But if the most thorough research proves that there is only one human constitution, notwithstanding the different shades of skin color, whether yellow, copper, black, or white. If the presence of virtues and talents among Negroes offers incontrovertible proof that they have the potential for all combinations of intelligence and morality and that, under a differently colored skin, they belong to the same species as we, then how much more guilty do those Europeans appear who scorn enlightened knowledge and the sentiments propagated first by Christianity and then by civilization, as they throw themselves on the bodies of the unfortunate Negroes and suck their blood to extract gold out of it!

Twenty years of experience have taught me what arguments are used by the merchants of human flesh. If they are to be believed, one needs to have lived in the colonies in order to have the right to an opinion on the legitimacy of slavery. As if the immutable principles of liberty and morality varied according to degrees of latitude! When we offer the indisputable authority of men who have inhabited those climates, and have even been engaged in the slave trade, they oppose falsehood and calumny. They may even have succeeded in destroying the reputation of Page, who was one of the fiercest defenders of slavery and then recanted, making such unusual confessions in a work on the restoration of Saint Domingue, which he bases on the freedom of the blacks.[64] The planters obstinately affirm that in the colonies, which are agricultural countries, this first among all the arts must be tarnished by slavery, under the pretext that such work exceeds the strength of Europeans. This is contradicted by the undeniable fact that a colony of Germans was established by Estaing, in 1764, at la Bombarde near the Mole St. Nicholas, whose descendants saw their dwellings surrounded by rich crops, the fruit of their own free labor. Can they be ignorant of the fact that the first cultivation of the colonial soil was made by whites, especially by laborers known as *les engagés de trente-six mois* (i.e., indentured for a term of three years, *Ed.*)? Can it be denied that in our glassworks and foundries the workers support a heat greater than in the Antilles?

Even if it were true that these countries cannot flourish without the assistance of Negroes, we would have to come to a conclusion that is very different from what the colonial settlers advocate. They constantly have recourse to the past in order to justify the present, as if abuses were legitimate because they were long established. If we speak about justice they answer by talking about sugar, indigo, and the balance of trade. If we reason with them, they say we are speechifying. Since they are afraid of discussing the subject, they keep repeating all the irrational arguments, all the platitudes that have so often been refuted, in order to support a bad cause. If we appeal to their compassion, they respond with a sneer. They tell us to consider the poor who besiege the European states, in order to prevent us from directing our attention to those unfortunates who are persecuted out of avarice in other regions of the globe. As if the duty of giving to the one group should forbid us to speak on behalf of the other! What conception do the planters have of the extent of our moral obligations? They claim that we neglect to love human beings because of our love of humanity. Because we can give comfort to those who surround us only in a manner that is inadequate to their number and their needs, we are accused of being guilty when we raise our voice in favor of those who have a different skin color and suffer in distant countries. Such is the argument of the author B. D. in *Voyage to Louisiana.*[65] These gentlemen would forbid us to lament the lot of those whom they torment in Africa and America as long as there is one individual who suffers in Europe. They are indignant because we trouble the pleasure of tigers who are devouring their prey; they have even attempted to vilify the name of philanthropist, or friend of mankind, a name that is borne with honor by those who feel affection for their fellow human beings. They have invented the epithets "Nigger lovers" and "Devourers of Whites,"[66] in the hope that this would leave a stain. They have maintained that all the friends of the blacks[67] were enemies of the whites and of France and were in the pay of England. The author of this book, who was earlier accused of having received 1,500,000 livres for writing in favor of the Jews, was said to have received three million more for constituting himself the advocate of the Negroes. Sarcasm and slander were not the only weapons employed by our antagonists. It is reported that funds were formerly collected in Nantes, for the purpose of assassinating a philanthropist who had been hung in effigy at Cap François and Jérémie.[68] This is an indication of what is to be gained by pleading the cause of justice and misfortune. Fra Paolo Sarpi was right to say that if the plague had rewards and pensions to bestow, it would find people to speak in its favor, while when we defend the poor and the oppressed we must struggle against power, wealth and perversity, and can expect only lies, insults and persecution.

The slave traders clearly have a very bad cause to defend, since they use such means to counter reasoned arguments. Let us avenge ourselves in the only way that is acceptable to religion: Let us seize every opportunity of doing good to the persecutor, as well as to those who are persecuted.

The Negroes have been slandered, first in order to establish the right to enslave them, then to justify keeping them in slavery, and also out of a feeling of guilt toward them. The accusers are both judges and executioners, and yet they call themselves Christians! They have tried many times to distort the sense of the Holy Scriptures, in order to find therein an apology for colonial slavery, although the Scriptures declare that all mortals are children of the Heavenly Father and spring from the same family. Religion admits of no distinction. If we sometimes see blacks and mulattoes relegated, in the churches of the colonies, to seats separate from those of the whites, and even admitted separately to participation in the Eucharist, it is criminal of the pastors to tolerate a custom that is so contrary to the spirit of religion. In the words of Paley, it is particularly in church that the poor man raises his humiliated head and the rich man regards him with respect. It is there that, in the name of Heaven, the minister at the altar reminds his listeners that by their origin they are all equal before a God who declares that for Him there is no respect of persons.[69] There the Heavenly oracle proclaims that we ought to do to others what we wish to be done to us.[70]

It is the glory of the Christian religion alone to have sheltered the weak from the strong. It is this religion that, in the fourth century, established the first hospital in the West.[71] It has constantly labored to console the unfortunate, whatever be their country, their color, or religion. The parable of the Samaritan marks persecutors with the seal of censure.[72] It is a curse laid for all times on anyone who would exclude a single member of the human race from the circle of charity.

I draw the attention of the reader to a fact attested by history: Despotism is usually accompanied by godlessness, and almost all the defenders of slavery are impious, while the defenders of the blacks almost always have a strong religious faith.

The reliable testimony of Protestant authors, among them Dallas, reproaches their clergy for neglecting the religious instruction of the Negroes, and this accusation is directed particularly against the bishops of London, who have the Western colonies under their jurisdiction.[73] But these writers heap praise on the Catholic missionaries, and on some societies of Dissenters, such as the Moravians in Antigua, and the Quakers or Friends, among whom the love of one's neighbor is not a sterile theory. All of these have developed an indefatigable zeal to bring the Negro slaves to Christianity and to freedom. Schools for the education of children of the blacks have been established in Philadelphia and other places by the Friends. These people make up the majority of the committees scattered over the United States for the abolition of slavery. The committees send deputies to a convention or central assembly that meets in January in Philadelphia for the same purpose.[74]

The Quakers have annual meetings composed of representatives who are delegated by their brethren in different regions. At the close of the session they never fail to address a circular letter to all Quakers concerning abuses to be overcome and virtues to be practiced, and the black slaves are always recommended to Christian charity.

To his words of praise for the Catholic priests, Dallas added his correspondence with the present archbishop of Tours. This prelate points out, quite rightly, that the priests do not confine their duties to preaching and reading the liturgy, but include the care of the sick, the education of children, and visits to families.[75] The Catholic religion, more than any other, establishes close and frequent relations between pastors and those who partake of the sacrament. An imposing ceremony speaks to the senses, which are, if I may so express myself, the gates of the soul. Out of these considerations, Protestant writers acknowledge, and Mackintosh[76] has confirmed it to me, that Catholic missionaries are much better suited than those who are not Catholic, to making proselytes of Negroes and affording them consolation.

In order to have the right to butcher the Indians, the first conquerors of America pretended to doubt that they were human. A papal bull condemned this doubt, and the Church Councils of Mexico are in this respect an honorable monument to the clergy of these regions. In another work that I intend to publish[77] the reader will be moved by the decisions against Negro slavery rendered by the College of Cardinals[78] and the Sorbonne.[79] The church has included several blacks in its calendar. There is Saint Elesbaan, who was adopted as patron by the Negroes in the Spanish and Portuguese dominions. Under the date of October 27 we can read his life in Baillet, who is known as a severe critic. But we shall give a few details on another black, whom he does not mention: a lay brother of the order of Recollects.

Benedict of Palermo, also named Benedict of St. Philadelphia, or Santo Fratello, or Benedict the Moor and the Black Saint, was the son of a Negro slave woman and himself a Negro. Rocco Pirri, author of the *Sicilia Sacra*, characterizes him in these words: "Nigro quidem corpore sed candore animi praeclarissimus quem et miraculis Deus contestatum esse voluit." (His body was black, but it pleased God to testify by miracles the innocence of his soul.)[80]

Historians praise in him that assemblage of eminent virtues that conceal themselves from the sight of man, content to have only God as a witness, for real virtues are silent. Only vice creates a loud noise: a great crime usually creates more of a sensation in the world than a thousand good deeds. Nonetheless there are times when men endeavor to remove the modest veil that conceals good deeds, either because they seek edification or out of curiosity. This is what allowed Benedict the Moor or the Holy Black Man to escape oblivion. He died in Palermo, in 1589, where his tomb and his memory are revered. This rite was authorized by the pope in 1610, and more specifically in 1743, by a decree of the Congregation of Church Rites. This is recorded in Joseph Mary Ancona, the continuator of Wadding.[81] The rite will soon gain more solemnity if, as was announced in the Gazettes at the beginning of 1807, his canonization is being considered. Roccho Pirro, Father Arthur,[82] Gravina,[83] and many other writers are full of eulogies concerning the venerable Benedict of Palermo, but in our libraries that have so many gaps, even though they are very extensive, I have never been able to find his life, neither in Italian by Tognoletti, nor in Spanish by Metaplana.

Among the Spaniards and Portuguese, slaves in general have more of a moral sense, because they are allowed to partake of the benefits of civilization, and are not worn out by labor. Religion continually enters into their lives, and almost all the owners reside on their plantations, which they view through their own eyes, and not the eyes of managers. In Brazil, the parish priests are appointed by law as defenders of the Negroes. They can legally force cruel colonists to sell them to someone else, and the slaves thus have at least a chance at a better existence.

Among the Spaniards manumission cannot be refused if a sum is paid that is fixed by law. With their savings the slaves can purchase a day of the week, which facilitates the purchase of a second, of a third, and finally of a whole week, and that gives them complete freedom.

In 1765 the English papers cited as a remarkable event the ordaining of a Negro by Doctor Keppel, bishop of Exeter.[84] Among the Spaniards, and still more among the Portuguese, this is a common occurrence. The history of the Congo gives an account of a black bishop who studied in Rome.[85]

The son of a king and other young noblemen of the Congo were sent to Portugal in the time of King Emmanuel. They distinguished themselves at the universities, and several were admitted to the priesthood.[86] [The Portuguese government has insisted that the secular and regular clergy in their Asian possessions should be composed of blacks. The primatial chapter of Goa was primarily composed of whites and mulattoes and had few blacks when the missionary Perrin, who just published his *Voyage to Hindustan*, visited that city. He took care to note that this was contrary to the expressed wish of the government.][87]

Near the close of the seventeenth century the fleet of Admiral Du Quesne saw, on the Cape Verde islands, a Catholic clergy that was Negro, with the exception of the bishop and the parish priest of Santiago.[88] In our time, Barrow and Jacquemin, consecrated bishop of Cayenne, found that the situation was still the same.[89]

Liancourt and a hundred other Europeans have visited an African church in Philadelphia, where the minister is also a Negro.[90] [Parkinson, who wrote later than Liancourt, states that there are many Negro preachers and that one of them is renowned for his eloquence.][91]

When we consider that slavery supposes all the crimes of tyranny, that it commonly engenders all its vices, and that virtue can scarcely thrive among men who are given no credit for it, who are embittered by misfortune, driven into corruption by the example of all sorts of crimes, excluded from all honorable or bearable ranks in society, deprived of religious and moral instruction, placed in a situation where it is impossible to acquire knowledge without struggling against all the obstacles that stand in the way of the development of their intelligence, we have reason to be surprised that many have become notable for their estimable qualities. In their place we might have been less virtuous than the virtuous among them, and more given over to vice than the worst of them. The same reflections apply to the untouchables of the Asiatic continent, who are vilified by the other castes; to Jews of all colors (for in Cochin there are also blacks among them),[92] whose history since the dispersion is nothing but a bloody tragedy; to the Irish Catholics, condemned, like the Negroes, to a kind of black code, the Popery Laws. These two have already been linked in a manner that is equally insulting to the inhabitants of Africa and of Ireland, by being represented as hordes of brutes who are incapable of self-government and must be subjected for all time to the iron scepter that the British government has held over them for centuries.[93] This infernal tyranny will exist until the time, which should be not far distant, when the brave sons of Erin shall raise the flag of liberty, adopting the sublime invocation of the Americans to the justice of Heaven: "An appeal to Heaven." Irishmen, Jews, and Negroes, your virtues and talents are your own; your vices are the work of nations who call themselves Christian. The more you are maligned, the more these nations are indicted for their guilt.

{ 3 }

Moral Qualities of the Negroes; Their Love of Industry, Their Courage, Bravery, Affection between Parents and Children, Generosity, &c.

What I wrote in the previous chapters is not foreign to my subject, but it contains an excess of proofs. I could have quickly taken up the present topic and substantiated, by a multitude of facts, that the Negroes have an aptitude for virtue and talents. Facts are the best reply.

The Negroes are accused of laziness. Bosman, to prove it, says that they are in the habit of asking, not "How are you?" but "How have you rested?"[1] They have a maxim that it is better to be lying than seated: better to be seated than to stand, and better to stand than to walk. Since we made them so wretched, they have added the Indian proverb, that death is preferable to all this.

The accusation of indolence, which is not without some degree of truth, is often exaggerated. It is exaggerated in the mouths of those who are in the habit of employing a bloody whip to conduct slaves to forced labor; it is true in the sense that men cannot have a great inclination to industry when they own nothing, not even their own person, and when the fruits of their sweat feed the luxury or avarice of a merciless master. Nor are men inclined to be industrious in regions favored by nature, where her spontaneous products, or work that requires no great effort, provide abundantly for man's natural needs. But whether they are black or white, all men are hardworking when stimulated by the spirit of property, by utility, or by pleasure. Such are the Negroes of Senegal, who work with ardor, according to Pelletan, because they are unmolested in their possessions and pleasures. He adds that since the suppression of the slave trade the Moors no longer stage raids upon them, and thus villages are rebuilt and repeopled.[2]

Such are the hard-working inhabitants of Axim on the Gold Coast, whom all travelers love to describe;[3] the Negroes of the country of Boulam, whom Beaver mentions as hardened by work;[4] those of Jagra, celebrated for an industriousness that enriches their country;[5] those of Cabomonte and of Fida or Juida, who are indefatigable cultivators of their soil, according to Bosman who certainly is not prejudiced in their favor: they are so economical of their land that they scarcely leave room for footpaths to get from one property to another; they harvest one day, and the next, they seed the same earth, without allowing it time for repose.[6]

Although the Negroes are too susceptible to pleasure, which they rarely resist, they also know how to bear pain with heroic courage. This may, perhaps, be due in part to their athletic constitution. History is full of traits of their intrepid behavior in the face of the most horrible tortures. The cruelty of the whites has multiplied instances of this. Can life be desirable, when existence itself is a perpetual calamity? After several days of uninterrupted torture, and almost in the grasp of death, slaves have been known to converse calmly among themselves, and even to break out into loud laughter.[7]

A Negro in Martinique was condemned to be burned at the stake. Since he was passionately fond of tobacco, he begged to have a lighted cigar, which was placed in his mouth. According to Labat, he continued to smoke even when his limbs were already burning.

In 1750, the Negroes of Jamaica revolted, with Tucky as their chief: they were defeated and condemned to be burned, and all went cheerfully to their punishment. One of them saw without emotion his legs reduced to ashes; one hand was freed as the flame consumed the cord that bound it. He seizes a brand, and darts it against the face of the executioner.[8]

In the seventeenth century, when Jamaica was still under the dominion of the Spaniards, some of the slaves, under the leadership of John de Bolas, regained their independence. They increased in numbers and became a formidable force after they elected Cudjoe as their chief, whose portrait is included in Dallas's book. Cudjoe, whose bravery was equaled by his skill and enterprise, established in 1730 a confederation of all the

Maroon tribes, made the English tremble, and compelled them to make a treaty, in which they acknowledged the freedom of the blacks and ceded to them for ever a portion of the territory of Jamaica.[9]

The Portuguese historian Barros says, somewhere in his work, that the Negroes were, in his opinion, preferable even to Swiss soldiers, [and this comparison with the Swiss was, for him, the greatest honor and praise he could confer on the Negroes]. Among the traits of bravery that Labat has collected, one of the most remarkable occurred at the siege of Carthagena: all the troops of the line were repulsed as they attacked Fort Bocachique, but the Negroes who were brought from Saint Domingue attacked with such vigor that the besieged were forced to surrender.[10]

In 1703, the blacks took up arms for the defense of Guadeloupe and were more effective than all the rest of the French troops. At the same time they defended Martinique against the English.[11] The honorable conduct of the Negroes and mulattoes at the siege of Savannah and at the taking of Pensacola, is well known. During our revolution, when they were incorporated into the French troops, they shared their perils and their glory.

The African prince Oronoko, sold in Surinam, was a Negro. Madam Behn was a witness to his misfortunes. She saw how the fidelity and courage of the Negroes contrasted with the sordid behavior and treachery of their tyrants. When she returned to England she wrote her *Oronoko*.[12] It is to be regretted that she embroidered a novel on a historical canvas. The simple recital of the misfortunes of this new Spartacus and his companions would have been enough to move the readers.

Henry Diaz, who is extolled in all the histories of Brazil, was a Negro. Brandano[13] (who, to tell the truth, was not a colonist) grants him high intelligence and shrewdness. Once a slave, Diaz became colonel of a regiment of foot-soldiers of his own color. This regiment, composed of blacks, still exists in Portuguese America, under the name of Henry Diaz. The Dutch, who then controlled Brazil, harassed its inhabitants because of this. La Clède took this occasion to reflect on the poor policy of conquerors who, instead of making themselves liked, aggravate their subjects' yoke, foster hatred, and sooner or later bring about a reaction that harms the tyrants but is useful to the people's freedom.

In 1637, Henry Diaz allied himself with the Portuguese in order to drive out the Dutch. They were besieged in the town of Arecise, made a sally and were repulsed with great loss by the Negro general. He took by assault a fort that the Dutch had built at some distance from the town. He combined boldness and courage with a knowledge of military tactics and stratagems that often disconcerted the Dutch generals. Engaged in a battle where the superiority of the enemy's numbers was about to overwhelm him, and perceiving that some of his soldiers were beginning to give way, he rushed into their midst and shouted: "Are these the brave companions of Henri Diaz?" His words and his example inspired them with fresh energy, according to one historian. The enemy, who already thought himself victorious, was attacked with a vigor that forced a headlong retreat into the town. Henry Diaz then forced Arecise to capitulate and Fernanbouc to surrender, and he completely destroyed the Dutch army.

In the midst of these exploits, in 1645, a bullet pierced his left hand. In order to avoid the delay of dressing the wound, he had the hand amputated, saying that each finger of his right was worth an entire hand in combat. It is regrettable that history does not inform us where, when, and how this general died. Menezes praises his consummate experience, and speaks with enthusiasm of these Africans who were suddenly converted into intrepid warriors.[14]

The unfortunate Ogé, worthy of a better fate, was a mulatto. He sacrified himself to ensure that his fellow mulattoes and the free Negroes would derive all the advantages that could be expected from the May 15 decree issued by the Constituent Assembly.[15] This was a decree that would have gradually brought public order to the colonies that was in conformity with justice. Ogé resolved to return to the Antilles because he was indignant at the perversity of the colonists who not only prevented the publication of this law, but also found means to induce the government to forbid the embarkation of Negroes and mulattoes (on boats leaving for France, *Ed.*). The author of this book, who has been so often accused of having advised Ogé to leave for Haiti, argued in vain that it was necessary to play for time, and that the success of so just a cause should not be compromised by acting in haste. Notwithstanding this advice, Ogé found a way, in 1791, to return to Saint Domingue by way of England and the American continent. He asked that the decrees be carried out. His demand was rejected, although it was dictated by reason and supported by the authority of the nation. Both parties became exas-

perated and fighting broke out. Ogé was delivered up by the treachery of
the Spanish government. His trial was prepared in secret, as in the
tribunals of the Inquisition. His request for a defense lawyer was refused:
thirteen of his companions were condemned to the galleys, more than
twenty to the gibbet, and Ogé as well as Chavanne were condemned to
death on the wheel. The colonists carried their animosity so far as to
make a distinction between the place of execution for the mulattoes and
for the whites. In a report where these facts are examined with impartiality, Garran vindicates Ogé and concludes with these words: "We
must shed tears for his ashes but leave his executioners to the judgment of
history."[16]

Saint-George, called the Voltaire of riding, fencing, and instrumental
music, was a man of color. He was recognized as an amateur musician of
the first rank, and placed in the second, or third, rank among composers.
Some of his concertos are still held in esteem. Although he was unusu-
ally talented in gymnastics it is difficult to believe his admirers who say
that he could fire a gun at a ball that was thrown in the air, and strike it.

According to the traveler Arndt, this new Alcibiades was the hand-
somest, strongest, and most agreeable among his contemporaries. Moreover he was generous, a good citizen and a good friend.[17] All people of
social standing or, in other words, frivolous people, considered him an
accomplished man. He was the idol of fashionable social circles.

When he dueled with the Chevalier d'Eon, it was almost an affair of
state, because then the state itself was nothing to the public. Whenever
Saint-George, who was considered the best swordsman of his time, was
about to fence, or to exhibit his musical talents, *La Gazette* (the official
government newspaper, *Ed.*) would announce it to the idlers in the
capital. His violin bow and his fencing foil would draw all of Paris. In the
same manner crowds used to gather in Seville when the Negro brother-
hood, on certain feast days, put on brilliant riding pageants, where they
performed various maneuvers and displays of their skill. This brother-
hood was not disbanded but went out of existence for lack of members.[18]

I do not agree with Malherbe that a good player at ninepins is of equal
importance with a good poet; but are all entertaining talents worth one
that is really useful? What a pity that Saint-George was not directed to
apply his fortunate aptitudes to a purpose that would have brought him
the esteem and gratitude of his fellow citizens! But we should remember

that he enlisted under the banner of the Republic and served in the French army.

Alexandre Dumas was a mulatto who, with four cavalrymen, attacked a post of fifty Austrians near Lille, killed six, and took sixteen prisoners. For a long time he was in command of a legion of cavalry composed of blacks and mulattoes, who were the terror of their enemies.

In the army of the Alps he led a cavalry charge up to the Saint Bernard pass, which was defended by many redoubts, and took possession of the guns, which he immediately directed against the enemy. Others have already related the exploits that brought him renown in Europe and in Africa, for he took part in the expedition to Egypt. On his return he had the misfortune to fall into the hands of the Neapolitan government, who kept him and Dolomieu in irons for two years. The emperor, who called him "the Horatius Cocles of Tirol," named Alexandre Dumas general in command of a division. He died in 1807.[19]

John Kina, of Saint Domingue, was a Negro. He was partisan in a bad cause, for he fought against the freedom of the blacks, but his valor gained him the most flattering reception in London. The British government wanted to entrust him with the command of a company of men of color who were to protect the remote quarters of the colony of Surinam. In 1800 he returned to the Antilles, but he experienced humiliating disdain, which reminded him that he was a freed Negro. Full of indignation, he stirred up an insurrection to protect his brethren against the colonists who worked the Negro women so hard that they miscarried, and who wanted to sell the free Negroes. He was soon apprehended, sent to London, and shut up in Newgate.[20]

Mentor, born in Martinique in 1771, was a Negro. While fighting against the English he was taken prisoner within sight of the coast of Ouessant. He took possession of the vessel that was carrying him to England, and brought her into Brest. He combined a noble physiognomy with an amiable character and a sharp and cultured mind. We saw him occupy a seat in the legislature by the side of the worthy Tomany. Such was Mentor, whose conduct in later years may have sullied these brilliant qualities. He was killed in Saint Domingue.

Toussaint Louverture bore the chains of slavery when he was a herdsman on the plantation of Breda, and yet he sent financial help to its manager. The bravery of Toussaint and of Rigaud, the mulatto general who was his competitor, cannot be disputed, for it was displayed on many occasions. In this respect he may be compared to the Cacique Henry, whose life can be read in Charlevoix.[21]

I have seen a manuscript entitled *Réflexions sur l'état actuel de la colonie de Saint-Domingue, par Vincent, ingénieur.* The following is the portrait he presents of the Negro general:

> Toussaint, at the head of his army, is the most active and indefatigable man one can imagine. One may say, in truth, that he is found wherever sound judgment or danger persuades him that his presence is necessary. He takes particular care to always deceive everyone about the direction of his marches, even the very men whom he needs and who are thought to be in his confidence, which he gives to no one. Consequently he is expected every day in all the chief towns of the colony. His great moderation in food and drink, his unique capacity of never taking a rest, the advantage which he has over others because he is able to take up his desk work after the most tiresome travel, answer daily a hundred letters and make a habit of exhausting five secretaries, all this renders him so superior to all those around him, that most carry their respect and submission to the point of fanaticism. It is certain that no other man, in the present times, has gained such power over a mass of ignorant people, as General Toussaint possesses over his brethren in Saint Domingue.

The engineer Vincent adds that Toussaint is endowed with a prodigious memory; that he is a good father and husband, and that his qualities as citizen are as solid, as his political life is cunning and culpable.

Toussaint reestablished religious worship in Saint Domingue, and on account of his zeal he was named the Capuchin, by a class of men who certainly merited a less flattering name. He was in correspondence with me with the object of obtaining twelve virtuous ecclesiastics. Several set out for that island, under the direction of the estimable Bishop Mauviel, who had been consecrated for Saint Domingue, and who generously devoted himself to this difficult mission. On his arrival Toussaint issued a solemn proclamation, congratulating the colony on its good fortune. Later, however, he was led astray through the influence of some dissident monks, and made difficulties for the bishop. I do not deny that Toussaint may have been cruel, hypocritical, and deceitful, along with the Negroes and mulattoes who accompanied his operations; but as for the whites . . . Let us not judge a cause by hearing from one party only. Some day, perhaps, the Negroes will write and publish in their turn, or the pen of some white author may be guided by impartiality. It is commonly said that recent events are the domain of adulation or of satire. Whilst the Negro general is depicted by many in the most odious colors, Whitchurch, in his poem, pursuing another extreme, has made him a hero.[22] Though Toussaint is dead, posterity, which destroys, confirms, or rectifies the judgments of contemporaries, has not yet passed sentence on his character.

[Let us close this chapter with a very interesting piece of information concerning the courage of a Negro: When Pope Pius II wished to punish Cantelino, duke of Sora, he sent an army against him under the command of General Napoleon, a member of the Ursino family who had already achieved distinction through his exploits as commander of the Venetian troops. Napoleon took the city of Sora, but he encountered stubborn resistance on the part of the citadel, which was protected by its position on a very high rock, on an island of the Garillan. After a siege of several days, one of the towers collapsed under the impact of the bombardment. A Negro, who had been a servant of the general before becoming a soldier, said to his fellow soldiers: "The citadel is ours. Follow me." He threw his lance with all his force onto the ruins of the tower, took his clothes off, swam across the moat, picked up his weapon, and went on the attack. His example was imitated by a crowd of soldiers, two of whom perished as they were carried off by the current. All the others followed him up the slope.

The besieged army was overcome by shame for being beaten by a troop of naked soldiers who were under the command of a Negro. The historian Gobellin affirmed that this exploit, which is assuredly true, will seem unbelievable to posterity.[23] He is to be faulted, like Father Tuzzi,[24] for not mentioning the name of this courageous African, thanks to whom the citadel was taken.]

{ 4 }

Continuation of the Same Subject.

An upright character is the inseparable companion of true bravery. The deeds that follow will, in this respect, place blacks and whites on a parallel. The impartial reader will weigh the scales.

The Negro Maroons of Jacmel have been, for almost a century, the terror of Saint Domingue. Bellecombe, the most imperious of governors, was obliged to negotiate a treaty with them in 1785. Yet there were not more than one hundred and twenty-five men from the French side of the island and five from the Spanish. This is related by the planter Page.[1] Has there ever been any news that those men violated the treaty, even though they were hunted like wolves?

In 1718, when we were entirely at peace with the black Caribs of St. Vincent, who are known to carry their bravery even to rashness, and who are more active and industrious than the red Caribs, an unjust expedition was organized against the black Caribs of Martinique.[2] It proved unsuccessful. Instead of being angered, they showed the forbearance to accept peace in the following year. To quote Chanvalin, we do not find such character traits in the history of civilized nations.[3]

In 1726, the Maroons of Surinam, driven to despair by the savagery of the colonists, gained their freedom by force of arms and forced their oppressors to negotiate a treaty with them. They religiously observed the agreement. Do the colonists merit the same praise? After new clashes the colonists decided to negotiate a peace, and requested a conference with the Negroes, who agreed under the condition that, as a preliminary, they would receive good firearms and ammunition, along with many other useful objects.

Two Dutch commissioners under escort came to the camp of the Negroes. Captain Boston, their commander, noticed that the commissioners brought only trifles, such as scissors, combs, and small mirrors, but neither firearms nor powder. He addressed them with a voice of thunder: "Do Europeans think that Negroes have need only of combs and scissors? One such article is sufficient for us all. But one barrel of powder would have offered proof that the Hollanders have confidence in us."

The Negroes, however, were far from yielding to a sentiment of justifiable indignation against a government that did not keep its commitments. They gave the Dutch a year to deliberate and choose either peace or war. They honored the commissioners with festivities, treated them with the most generous hospitality, and in parting, reminded them that the colonists of Surinam, by their inhumanity to their slaves, were themselves the authors of their own misfortunes.[4] We owe these details to Stedman, who also tells us that the fields of this republic of blacks are covered with yam, Indian corn, plantain, and manioc.

All unprejudiced authors who speak of Negroes, do justice to their happy disposition and their virtues. Even those who are partisans of slavery, are occasionally compelled by truth to make avowals in their favor. Among these there is first of all Long, the historian of Jamaica, who praises several for their excellent character and their affectionate and appreciative heart. He finds that all of them show the highest degree of parental and filial affection.[5]

There is also Duvallon, whose report of the misfortunes of the poor and decrepit Irrouba, cannot fail to move the heart of the reader, and fill him with loathing for the savage colonist, whose foster mother she had been.[6]

The same virtues of Negroes are conspicuous in what is told about them by Hilliard d'Auberteuil, Falconbridge, Granville Sharp, Benezet, Ramsay, Horneman, Pinkard, Robin, and particularly my excellent friend Clarkson who, like Wilberforce, is immortalized by his works and his zeal in the defense of Africans. George Roberts, an English navigator, was pillaged by a compatriot who was a pirate. He sought refuge on St. John, one of the islands in the Cape Verde archipelago, where he was given help by the Negroes. An anonymous pamphleteer, who does not dare to deny this fact, endeavors to diminish its merit, by saying that the condition of George Roberts would have moved a tiger to pity.[7] Durand extols the modesty and chastity of Negro wives, and the good education of the mulattoes of Gorée.[8] Wadstrom, who gives great praise to their friendly welcome, thinks that they are sensitive, gentle, and affection-ate, more so than the whites. Captain Wilson, who lived among them, speaks highly of their constancy in friendship; they shed tears when he left them.

Some Negroes of Saint Domingue, because they were attached to their masters, followed them to Louisiana, where the masters sold them. This and the following fact, taken from Robin, furnish materials for a moral comparison between the blacks and the whites.

A slave had run away; the master promised a reward of twelve dollars to anyone who brought him back. Another Negro brings him and re-fuses to accept the reward. He only asks pardon for the deserter. The master grants it, and keeps the sum he offered. The author of this travel report remarks that the master had the soul of a slave, and the slave the soul of a master.[9]

[After so many other unimpeachable witnesses who speak for the natural goodness of the Negroes, we can still cite the worthy Niebuhr, who comments as follows in the *Deutsches Museum*:[10]

> The character of Negroes, particularly when they are sensibly treated, expresses itself in loyalty toward their masters and benefactors. The Mos-lem traders in Kabira, Djidda, Surate, and elsewhere, like to buy black children, and they have them instructed in writing and arithmetic. Their commerce is directed almost exclusively by these slaves, and they send them out to open their trading posts in foreign countries.
>
> I asked one of these traders how he could turn over entire shiploads to slaves. He answered: "My Negro is faithful, but I would not dare entrust my business to white clerks. They would soon disappear with my fortune."

Blumenbach, who sends me this passage, adds that one could apply to the poor Negroes, our protégés, the following words by Saint Bernard: Felix nigredo, quae mentis candore imbuta est.][11]

Doctor Newton relates that one day he accused a Negro of dishonesty and injustice. The Negro proudly replied: "Do you take me for a white man?"[12] He adds that on the banks of the river Gabaon, the Negroes are the best race of men that he has ever met.[13] Ledyard says the same of the Foulahs, where the ruler acts like a father.[14]

In a history of Loango we read that while those Negroes who inhabit the coast and who associate with Europeans, are inclined to fraud and libertinism; those of the interior are humane, obliging, and hospitable.[15]

This praise is repeated by Golbéry: he inveighs against the presumption with which Europeans despise and slander those peoples whom we blithely call savages, but among whom we encounter men of virtue, who are truly models of filial, conjugal, and paternal affection. They are familiar with all the energies and refinements of virtue, their feelings run very deep, because they are closer to nature than we, and they know how to sacrifice personal interest to the ties of friendship. Golbéry furnishes many proofs of this.[16]

The anonymous author of the *West Indian Eclogues*[17] owes his life to a Negro, who sacrificed his own to save it. The poet relates this circumstance in a note. Why did he not mention the name of his savior?

Adanson, who visited Senegal in 1754, and who describes this country as an Elysium, found the Negroes very sociable and of a fine character. Their amiable simplicity in this enchanting country reminded me, he says, of our conception of earliest man: I thought I saw the world in its infancy.[18] They have generally preserved an estimable simplicity of domestic manners. They are distinguished for their affection for their parents and their great respect for old age, a virtue of olden times that, in our days, is almost unknown.[19]

Those who are Muslims contract a particular alliance with those who were circumcised at the same time, and consider them brethren. Those who are Christians always preserve a particular veneration for their godfathers and godmothers. These words recall to mind a sublime institution for which Philosophy has lately envied Christianity:[20] This type of religious adoption connects children by ties of love and beneficence that in the event of the death of their parents, which unfortunately happens all too often, prepare counselors and shelter for the orphans.

Robin mentions a slave of Martinique who earned enough money for his own ransom, but purchased with it his mother's freedom.[21] The most horrible offense that can be committed against a Negro, is to curse his father or his mother, or to speak of either with contempt.[22] Strike me, said a slave to his master, but curse not my mother.[23] I take this and the following incident from Mungo Park: A Negro woman lost her son and her only consolation was that he had never told a lie.[24] Casaux relates that a Negro who saw a white man abuse his father, quickly took away the child of this brutal fellow, for fear, as he said, that the child might learn to imitate his father's conduct.

The veneration of blacks for the older generation goes beyond the span of life: they are moved to tears at the sight of the ashes of those who are no more. A traveler brought back an anecdote about an African who advised a Frenchman to respect burial sites. What would the African have thought, if he could have believed that one day they would be desecrated throughout the whole of France, a nation that calls itself civilized?[25]

As reported by Stedman, the blacks are so benevolent one to another, that it is not necessary to tell them: Love your neighbor as yourself.[26] Slaves, particularly those from the same country, have a decided inclination to assist each other. Alas! Almost always the wretched can rely only on their associates in misfortune.

Several Maroons were condemned to the gallows: one was offered a pardon, on condition that he act as executioner of his fellows. This he refused, preferring to die. The master than selected one of his slaves to perform this office. Wait, said he, till I get ready. He went into the house, took a hatchet and cut off his hand, then returned to his master, saying: Order me now to be the executioner of my comrades.[27]

We are indebted to Dickson for the following fact. A Negro had killed a white man: another accused of the crime was about to suffer death. The murderer went to the court and confessed his crime, because he could not bear the remorse for having been the cause of the death of two individuals. The innocent man was released and the Negro was sent to the gibbet, where he remained alive for six or seven days.

The same Dickson has verified that of one hundred and twenty thousand Negroes and mulattoes in Barbados, only three have been known to commit a murder in the course of thirty years, although they were often provoked by the cruelty of the planters.[28] I doubt that an inspection of the records of criminal tribunals in Europe would produce a similar result.

According to Stedman, the blacks are often led by gratitude to risk their life in order to save the life of a benefactor.[29] Cowry relates that a Portuguese slave, who had fled into the forest, learned that his master was brought to trial for the crime of murder; the Negro returned in order to go to prison, produced false but legally valid proof of his supposed crime, and suffered execution in place of his guilty master.[30]

The *Journal de littérature*, by Grosier, has recorded touching details on the story of a Negro belonging to du Colombier, who owned property in the colonies but lived near Nantes. This slave obtained his freedom, but his master sank into poverty. The Negro sold all he owned in order to support him. When these funds were exhausted he cultivated a garden and sold the produce in order to continue his good works. Then the master fell ill and the Negro, who was ill himself, declared that he would take care of his own health only when the master was cured. But this good African succumbed to his labors and died in 1776, after twenty years of unpaid service. He bequeathed to du Colombier the little that remained of his possessions.[31]

The anecdote concerning Louis Desrouleaux should be better known. He was a Negro pastry cook, first in Nantes and then in Cap Haïtien, where he used to be the slave of Pinsum, from Bayonne, who was captain of a slave ship. The captain returned to France with great wealth, which he lost. Then he returned to Saint Domingue, where those who called themselves his friends when he was wealthy, now scarcely deigned to recognize him. Louis Desrouleaux, who in the meantime had acquired a fortune, took the place of them all: When he learned of the misfortune of his former master, he hastened to find him, gave him lodging and food, and suggested he return to live in France, where he would not be humiliated by the sight of these ungrateful men. "But I don't have the means to live in France."—"Would 15,000 francs a year be enough for you?" The colonist wept for joy. The Negro signed the contract and the pension was paid until the death of Louis Desrouleaux, in 1774.

If I may be permitted to insert a fact that is foreign to my subject, I would cite the conduct of the Indians toward Bishop Jacquemin, who spent twenty-two years in Guyana as a missionary. The Indians, who felt great affection for him, noted that he was deprived of everything when the clergy were no longer paid (i.e., during the French Revolution, *Ed.*). They went to him and said: Father, you are old, stay with us, we will hunt and fish for you.

And how could these men of nature be ungrateful to their benefactors, when they do good even to their oppressors? During the ocean crossing, the blacks in their chains have been seen to share their scanty and unwholesome rations with the sailors.[32]

A contagious disease carried off the captain, the mate, and most of the sailors of a slave ship. Too few remained to handle the boat. The Negroes helped out and with their aid the boat arrived at its destination. There they allowed themselves to be sold.[33]

The philanthropists of England like to make mention of the good and religious Joseph Rachel, a free Negro of Barbados who grew rich through commerce and devoted his entire fortune to good works. Unfortunates, whatever their color, had a claim on his good heart. He gave to the indigent, lent to those who could repay him, visited the prisoners, gave them advice and tried to persuade the guilty to return to virtue. He died in 1758 in Bridgetown, lamented by blacks and whites.[34]

The French ought to bless the memory of Jasmin Thoumazeau, who was born in Africa, in 1714. He was sold in Saint Domingue in 1736. He gained his freedom, married a Negro woman from the Gold Coast, and in 1756 established a home in Cap Haïtien for poor Negroes and mulattoes. For more than forty years he and his wife devoted themselves to their comfort, and spent all their care and fortune on them. The only sorrow they felt in the midst of those unfortunates who were being helped by their charity, arose from the worry that after their death the hospital might be abandoned. In 1789 the Philadelphian Society of Cap Haïtien and the Agricultural Society of Paris awarded medals to Jasmin,[35] who died toward the end of the century.

Moreau-Saint-Méry and many other writers tell us the Negro and mulatto women deserve praise for their maternal affection and their compassionate charity toward the poor.[36] Proof of this can be found in an anecdote that has not yet received all the publicity it deserves. The traveler Mungo Park was about to perish from deprivation deep in Africa when he was taken by a Negro woman to her home. She extended her hospitality and assembled the women in her family, who passed part of the night in spinning cotton and improvising songs to entertain the white man, whose appearance in that region was a novelty. He was the subject of one of these songs, which calls to mind the following thought of Hervey in his *Meditations*: "I think I hear the winds plead the cause of the wretched."[37]

Here is this song: "The winds howled and the rain fell; the poor white man, overcome with fatigue, comes and sits down under our tree; he has neither a mother to bring him milk, nor a wife to grind his grain." The other women sang in chorus: "Pity the poor white man; he has neither a mother to bring him milk, nor a wife to grind his grain."[38]

Such are the people who are maligned by Descroizilles who, in 1803, published his assertions that social sentiments and religious institutions have no influence on their character.[39]

To these traits of virtue practiced by Negroes, and the honorable testimony they have received from many authors, I could have added a great many more found in the depositions made at the bar of the Parliament of England.[40] What we have given the reader suffices to avenge outraged humanity and truth.

Let us guard, however, against the extravagant exaggeration that we find none but estimable qualities among blacks. But do we whites have the right to condemn them? While I am persuaded that one can rarely count on human virtue and loyalty, whatever the skin color, I have tried to prove that neither race is naturally worse than any other.

It is an almost universal error to call those individuals virtuous who have only a negative morality, if I may put it that way. The form of their character is indeterminate; they are incapable of thinking and acting on their own, since they possess neither the courage to be virtuous nor the boldness to engage in crime; they are equally susceptible to praiseworthy and reprehensible impressions, and their ideas and inclinations are borrowed from others; what in them we call goodness and gentleness is in reality nothing but apathy, weakness, and cowardice. These are the ones who have given rise to the proverb: *There are individuals who are so good that they are not worth anything.*

In the honorable deeds presented here we find, on the contrary, that energy (*vis, virtus*) that brings about sacrifices for the sake of doing good, aiding others, and acting in conformity with moral principles. This practical reason, which is the fruit of a cultivated intelligence, manifests itself also in connection with other situations, even though civilization and the arts are in their infancy with most Negroes. But before I enter upon this subject, I believe I shall please the reader if I insert here the biographical account of a Negro who died twelve years ago in Germany, where he was reputed for his refined virtues and his brilliant qualities.

{ 5 }

[*Biographical Account of the Negro Angelo Solimann*[1]

Although Angelo Solimann did not publish anything,[2] he merits one of the highest places among the Negroes who have distinguished themselves by a high degree of culture, and even more by morality and the excellence of their character.

He was the son of an African prince. The country over which the prince reigned was called *Gangusilang*, and his family *Magni-Famori*. Beside little *Mmadi-Make* (this was Angelo's name in his native country) his parents had another, younger child, a girl. He could recall with what respect his father was treated, and that he was surrounded by a large number of servants. Like all the children of princes in that country, he bore characters imprinted on both thighs, and for a long time he cherished the hope that his people would seek him and recognize him by these characters. Even in his old age his mind often recaptured, with a pleasure mixed with sorrow, memories of his childhood, of his earliest practice of archery, in which he excelled his comrades, of the beautiful sky and the simple manners of his homeland. He was deeply moved whenever he sang his native songs, which he had retained thanks to his excellent memory.

According to the reminiscences of Angelo, it appears that his tribe already possessed some marks of civilization. His father owned many elephants and even some horses, which are rare in that part of the world. Money was unknown among them, but commerce was carried on regularly by barter and auction. They worshiped the stars; circumcision was practiced; two families of whites dwelt in the country.

Authors who have published their travels speak of continual wars between the tribes of Africa, carried on sometimes with the object of vengeance or plunder, and sometimes out of a most shameful sort of greed, because the victor leads his prisoners to the nearest slave market in order to sell them to the whites. Such a war broke out against the tribe of Mmadi-Make, and so unexpectedly that his father had no suspicion of danger. One day the child, then seven years old, was standing next to his mother who was nursing his sister, when suddenly a frightful clashing of weapons was heard, and the shrieking of the wounded. The grandfather of Mmadi-Make rushed into the hut, gripped by fear, and cried: The enemy are here. Fatuma rose in fright, the father hastily sought his weapons, and the little boy, in great fear, fled with the speed of an arrow. His mother called after him: "Where are you going, Mmadi-Make?" The child answered: "Where God wishes." In later years he often reflected on the important meaning of these words. When he left the hut he looked behind him and saw his mother, as well as several of his father's retainers, fall under the enemy's blows. Together with another boy he cowered under a tree and in his fear covered his eyes with his hands. The battle continued. The enemy, believing themselves already victorious, seized and raised him up into the air as a sign of rejoicing. At this sight the compatriots of Mmadi-Make rallied their forces to save the king's son. The battle began again, and as long as it continued the child was held up in the air. In the end the enemy remained victorious and the child was their undisputed prize. His master gave him in exchange for a fine horse to another Negro and he was taken to the place of embarkation. There he found many of his compatriots, who like him were prisoners condemned to slavery. They recognized him with grief in their hearts but they could do nothing for him; they were even forbidden to speak to him.

When small boats brought the prisoners down to the edge of the sea, Mmadi-Make was astonished to see large floating houses. He entered into one of them with his third master. He presumed later that it was a Spanish ship. After having traversed a storm they landed, and the master promised the child that he would take him to his mother. But this hope soon vanished, for he found himself with the master's wife instead of his mother. She received him very well, however, and treated him with affection and much kindness. The husband gave him the name of Andrew and commanded him to take the camels to pasture and to watch over them.

It is not possible to say to what nation this man belonged nor how long Angelo, who died twelve years ago, stayed with him. This account was recently drawn up from information supplied by his friends. We only know that after quite a long stay his master announced his intention to take him to a country where he would be better off. Mmadi-Make was very pleased with this. His mistress parted from him with regret; they traveled by ship and arrived at Messina. He was brought to the house of a wealthy lady who appeared to expect him. She treated him kindly and gave him a teacher from whom he learned the language of the country with great ease. His good nature gained him the affection of the numerous servants, among whom he singled out a Negro woman, named Angelina, for her gentle manner and her kindliness toward him. He fell dangerously ill; the marchioness, who was his mistress, cared for him like a mother, to such an extent that she passed a part of every night at his bedside. She called the most skillful doctors and placed around his bed a great number of persons who awaited his orders. The marchioness desired for a long time to have him baptized. He refused repeatedly, but one day during his convalescence he asked for baptism of his own accord. His mistress was very happy and ordered a great preparation made. A richly embroidered canopy was erected over a bed on which he was to lie in state; the entire family and all the friends of the household attended; Mmadi-Make, who was lying on this bed, was summoned to say the name he wished to bear; out of gratitude and friendship for Angelina he wished to be called Angelo; his wish was granted and Solimann added in place of a family name. Every year on September 11 he celebrated with feelings of devotion his entry into Christianity. He considered that date his birthday.

His goodness, his obliging nature, and his good sense made everyone cherish him. Prince Lobkowitz, who was then in Sicily as general of the emperor, was a frequent visitor to the house where this child lived, and he conceived such an affection for him that he made the most pressing entreaties to obtain him. The fondness which the marchioness felt for Angelo made her reluctant to accede to this request, but in the end she yielded to considerations of self-interest and prudence that urged her to give this present to the general. What tears she shed when parting from the little Negro, who entered with repugnance into the service of a new master!

The duties of the prince did not permit him to reside long in that country. He loved Angelo but the life he led, and perhaps the spirit of the times, caused him to take very little interest in Angelo's education. Angelo became shy and ill-tempered; he spent his days in idleness and childish games. An old steward of the prince, who knew that in spite of his foolishness Angelo had a good heart and excellent talents, gave him a teacher under whom he learned to write German in seventeen days; the child's tender affection, and his rapid progress in all branches of knowledge rewarded the kind steward for his efforts.

Thus Angelo grew to manhood in the household of the prince. He accompanied him on all his journeys and shared with him the perils of war. He fought at the side of his master and once, when the latter was wounded, carried him on his shoulders off the battlefield. Angelo distinguished himself on those occasions as a faithful servant and friend, but also as an intrepid warrior and an officer experienced particularly in tactics, although he never held a military rank. Marshal Lascy, who held him in high esteem, praised his courage in a most honorable manner in the presence of a great number of officers, presented him with a magnificent Turkish saber, and offered him the command of a company, which Angelo refused.

His master died. In his will he left Angelo to Prince Wenceslas von Lichtenstein, who had wanted him for a long time. The prince asked Angelo whether he was satisfied with this arrangement and wished to live in his household. Angelo gave his word and made preparation to change his manner of living. In the meantime the Emperor Francis I made him the same offer with very flattering terms. But Angelo's word was sacred and he remained with Prince Lichtenstein. Here, as with General Lobkowitz, he was a protector of the unfortunate and transmitted to the prince the entreaties of those who had a request. His pockets were always filled with petitions. He neither could nor wished to ask anything for himself, and fulfilled this duty on behalf of others with great zeal and success.

Angelo followed his master on his journeys and even to Frankfurt, when the Emperor Joseph was crowned king of the Romans. One day, at the urging of his prince, he tried his fortune at faro and won twenty thousand florins; he offered a return game to his adversary, who lost another twenty-four thousand florins; Angelo then proposed a third game and arranged it so cleverly, that the loser won back the second sum he had lost. This tactful action brought Angelo wide praise and the admiration of everyone. The passing favor of fortune did not dazzle him; on the contrary, he mistrusted her fickleness and never again wagered a large sum. He delighted in chess and had the reputation of being one of the best players.

He married a widow, Madame de Cristiani, born Kellermann, who was Belgian by birth. The prince did not know of this marriage. It may be that Angelo had good reason to conceal it, and a subsequent event justified his silence. The Emperor Joseph II took a keen interest in all that concerned Angelo and singled him out publicly, even taking his arm when he went walking; one day he revealed Angelo's secret to Prince Lichtenstein, without foreseeing the consequences. The prince had Angelo brought before him and questioned him; Angelo confessed his marriage. The Prince banished him from his house and struck his name from his will. He had intended to leave Angelo diamonds of considerable value, which Angelo used to wear when he accompanied his master on gala occasions.

Although Angelo had so often asked favors for others, he did not say a word on his own behalf. He left the palace and lived in a distant quarter of the city where he had previously bought a house and turned it over to his wife. In this retreat he dwelt with her in the enjoyment of his domestic happiness. To give the most careful education to his only daughter, Baroness von Heuchtersleben, who is no longer living; to cultivate his garden; to pass his time in the society of a few enlightened and virtuous men—such was his occupation and his diversion.

Some two years after the death of Prince Wenceslas von Lichtenstein, his nephew and heir, Prince Franz, came upon Angelo on the street. He stopped his carriage, invited Angelo to enter, told him that he was entirely convinced of his innocence and that he was resolved to repair the injustice of his uncle. Consequently he assigned a salary to Angelo that would convert after his death to an annual pension for his wife. The only request the prince made of Angelo was to oversee the education of his son, Ludwig von Lichtenstein.

Angelo punctually carried out the duties of his new office and went daily to the prince's residence to look after the pupil who had been recommended into his care. When the prince saw that such a long way was arduous for Angelo, especially in bad weather, he offered him lodging. Thus Angelo was for the second time established in the Lichtenstein palace. He brought his family with him, however, and lived as heretofore in retirement in the society of a few friends and of learned men, devoting himself to belles-lettres for which he had a passion. His favorite study was history: he was greatly aided by his excellent memory; he could give names, dates, the year of birth of all famous persons, as well as of the principal events.

His wife had been in ill health for a long time. She continued for a few more years, thanks to the tender care of a husband who lavished on her all the resources of medicine, but at last she succumbed. Thereupon Angelo reformed his household: he no longer invited his friends to dine with him and drank only water, to set an example for his daughter whose education was entirely his work. Perhaps he also wanted to assure the fortune of his only daughter through severe economies.

At an advanced age Angelo still went on several journeys, either for his own affairs or for the affairs of others. He was esteemed and loved everywhere: his acts of helpfulness were recalled and the good deeds he had scattered far and wide, even at a time already far distant. When circumstances led him to Milan the late Archduke Ferdinand, who was governor of the city, showered him with marks of his friendship.

Until the end of his life he enjoyed robust health. His aspect showed scarcely any signs of old age, which occasioned mistakes and friendly disputes; for often persons who had not seen him for twenty or thirty years took him for his own son and treated him accordingly.

At the age of seventy-five he was struck with apoplexy on the street. The help given him proved unavailing and he died on November 21, 1796, mourned by all his friends who still cannot think of him without emotion and without shedding tears. The esteem of all upright men followed him into the grave.

Angelo was of average stature, he was slim and well-proportioned. The regularity of his features and the noble cast of his face contrasted by their beauty with the unfavorable idea that is commonly held of the physiognomy of the Negroes. An extraordinary suppleness in all bodily exercise gave his bearing and his movements grace and agility. He combined tact and virtue with sound judgment, which was heightened by his extensive and thorough learning. He knew six languages, Italian, French, German, Latin, Bohemian, and English, and spoke particularly the first three with purity.

Like all his compatriots he was born with an impetuous character. Consequently his serenity and gentle manner were all the more worthy of respect, because they were the fruit of a difficult struggle, and of many victories he had won over himself. No unseemly expression ever escaped him, even when he had been angered. Angelo was devout without being superstitious; he observed exactly all the precepts of religion and did not believe that it was beneath him to set thereby an example for his family. His word, as well as whatever he had resolved upon after mature reflection, was unalterable, and nothing could turn him from his purpose. He always wore his native costume. This consisted of a kind of very simple suit, in the Turkish manner, almost always in dazzling white, which set off to advantage the brilliant black color of his skin. His portrait, which was engraved in Augsburg, hangs in the Lichtenstein gallery.]

{ 6 }

Talents of the Negroes for Arts and Craftsmanship. Political Societies Organized by the Negroes.

Bosman, Brue, Barbet, Holben, James Lyn, Kiernan, Dalrymple, Towne, Wadstrom, Falconbridge, Wilson, Clarkson, Durand, Stedman, Mungo Park, Ledyard, Lucas, Houghton, Horneman,[1] all of whom know the blacks, and most of whom have lived in Africa, testify to their skill in manufacturing. Moreau St. Méry thinks they are capable of succeeding in the technical and liberal arts.[2] Examine the authors we have cited, consult *L'Histoire générale des voyages* by Prévost, and the *Universal History*, written by English authors, as well as the depositions made at the bar of Parliament. They all mention the dexterity with which the Negroes tan and dye leather, prepare indigo and soap, make cordage, fine fabrics, and beautiful pottery, even though they have no knowledge of the potter's wheel. With the same dexterity they make swords and agricultural instruments of good quality, as well as very fine work in gold, silver and steel: They excel particularly in filigree work.[3] One of the most striking proofs of their talents in this line, is their method of constructing an anchor for a vessel.[4] At Juida, they make canes out of a single piece of ivory nearly two meters in length.[5]

Dickson, who was acquainted with skillful jewelers and watchmakers among the Negroes, speaks with admiration of a wooden lock executed by a Negro.[6]

In a learned dissertation on the floating bricks of the ancients, by Fabbroni, I find this passage: "It is difficult to conceive in what manner the ancient inhabitants of Ireland and the Orkneys were able to construct towers of earth and bake them on the same spot. Yet this is still practiced by some Negroes on the coast of Africa."[7]

Golbéry, who goes into greater detail concerning African industry than other travelers, maintains that the fabrics made by them are of exceptional delicacy and beauty. The most ingenious are the Mandingoles and Bamboukains; their jars and mats are executed with much taste. With the same instruments they produce the coarsest works in iron, and the most elegant in gold; they thin leather in such a manner as to render it as flexible as paper; and the only instrument they employ, in the most delicate workmanship, is a very simple knife.[8]

The same observations apply to the Negroes of Malacca and other parts of India. Black and white slaves are sent from there to Manila. Sandoval, who was there, assures us that they all have great ability, particularly in music, and their women excel in needlework.[9]

While traveling on the continent of Asia, Lescalier found that the Negroes with long hair were well educated, because they have schools. Like the other Indians, they manufacture the fine muslin that this region sends to Europe. France, said another traveler, is full of fabrics made by Negro slaves.[10]

In reading Winterbottom, Ledyard, Lucas, Houghton, Mungo Park, and Horneman, we find that the inhabitants of the interior of Africa are more virtuous and more civilized than those on the coast, and that they surpass them also in working with wool, leather, wood, and metals, as well as in weaving, dyeing, and sewing. Besides work in the fields, which is their main occupation, they work in manufacturing and extract ore from minerals. The inhabitants of the country of Haussa who, according to Horneman, are the most intelligent people of Africa, give cutting instruments a keener edge than the Europeans, and their files are superior to those of France or of England.[11]

These details already indicate what we should think when, in order to degrade the blacks, Jefferson tells us that no black nation was ever civilized. There does exist a problem that has not yet been solved, but which can be solved: How to bring about the development of all intellectual faculties, of every talent, without allowing the germination of the seeds of corruption which are constantly, even if not inevitably, a consequence of the fine arts.

Be that as it may, who could deny the capacity for civilization to blacks, if we limit this term to the meaning conveyed by sociability; that is, the aptitude for living with fellow human beings in a relation of mutual service? This concept of sociability supposes the existence of an ordered society that is characterized by an established form of government and religion, by a social pact that protects individuals and property, and by laws, or customs that have the force of law, that protect work in agriculture, industry, and commerce. This is the case in many black societies. Should we not recognize as civilized the societies described by Leo the African? It is true that those who dwell in the mountains have something of the savage about them, but those in the plains have built cities where they cultivate the sciences and the arts. In a report found in the collection by Prévost, they are described as more advanced than many European nations.[12]

Bosman, who found the country of Agonna well governed by a woman,[13] writes with enthusiasm about the country of Juida, about its many towns, its customs, and industry. More than a century later his recital has been confirmed by Pruneau de Pomme Gouje, who praises the courage and ability of the inhabitants of this country.[14] Their daily life is characterized by a greater complexity of ceremonies and polite conventions than are found in China. Superiority of rank, as it does everywhere, has its claims based on pride; but generally, individuals of equal rank kneel and bless each other when they meet.[15] We do not need to approve this detailed ceremonial, but we must recognize that these are the characteristics of a people that has risen above barbarism.

Deniau, a French consul who resided thirteen years in Juida, has assured me that in crafty diplomacy, the government of this country can rival the European countries that have perfected this pernicious art. We find many proofs of this in the conduct of the celebrated Gingha or Zingha, queen of Angola, who died in 1663, in her eighty-second year. She is assured a place in history because of her exceptional mind and her fierce and bold spirit. Like most great criminals of her rank, she endeavored in her old age to expiate her crimes by remorse, though this did not restore life to the unfortunate individuals whose death she caused.

It is generally accepted among us that a people is not civilized unless it has historians and historical records. I do not claim that the Negroes are on a level with those nations who are heir to the discoveries of all the epochs of the past, and who add their own discoveries. But can it be inferred from this that the Negroes are incapable of becoming partners in the storehouse of human knowledge? If we would argue that those who do not already possess knowledge are therefore incapable of possessing it, then the descendants of the ancient Germans, Helvetians, Batavians, and Gauls would still be barbarians; for there was a time when they did not even have the equivalent of the quipus of Mexico, or the runic sticks of Scandinavia. All they had were vague traditions that had been distorted by the passage of time, just as do all the Negro tribes. Nevertheless these ancient peoples, like all the other Celtic tribes, had an identity and political organization, a regular government, national assemblies, and above all, their freedom.

We agree with the historian of Jamaica (Edward Long, *Ed.*), that in every country the state of legislation is indicative (but only in some respects) of the degree of civilization. For if we apply this standard to his country, England, we might ask him whether an unrepealed law that authorizes a husband to sell his wife is a symptom of a high state of civilization? The same question could be asked about the harsh laws that reduce the Irish Catholics to the level of helots. Notwithstanding these stains that disfigure the British constitution, we cannot deny that it is one of those that best combine the security of the state with individual liberty. In a less complex form the same is true of many black peoples, who in the opinion of Long lack the capacity for reasoning.[16]

In most regions on the coasts of Africa, there are a large number of kingdoms that might be called microscopic, where the chief has no more authority than the father of a family.[17] Gambia, Boudou, and other small states, are governed as monarchies, but authority is tempered by the tribal chiefs, without whose advice the monarch can make neither war nor peace.[18]

The industrious Daccas, who occupy the fertile promontory of Cape Verde, are organized as a republic. Even though they are separated from the king of Damel by an arid expanse of sand, they are often engaged in warfare with him. When the king of Damel had a dispute with the (French, *Ed.*) Government of Senegal, which no longer paid him tribute, and negotiated with the English, who had recently occupied Gorée, he proposed that they help him subjugate this people, arguing that the Daccas were not subject to a chief, like other Negroes, but were free like the French. This trait of African diplomacy was communicated to me by Broussonet.

Here we have peoples who have mastered the complex notions of constitution, government, treaties, and alliances. If they have not developed these political concepts more fully, this is due to the fact that they are young peoples.

The empire of Bornou has an elective monarchy, according to the traveler Lucas, as is also the case in Kachmi. When the chief dies, three elders or notables are entrusted with the right of choosing his successor among the children of the deceased, without regard to primogeniture. The one who is elected is brought by three elders to the dead body of the deceased, who is eulogized or condemned according to his merit; and his successor is reminded that he shall be happy or miserable, according to the good or harm he does to the people. Similar customs prevail among neighboring tribes.[19]

This is the proper place for the following anecdote: the commandant of a Portuguese fort, who expected the arrival of the envoy of an African king, ordered the most sumptuous preparations, in order to dazzle him with opulence. When the envoy arrived he was led into a richly ornamented chamber. The commandant was seated under a canopy, but the Negro ambassador was not even offered a seat. He signaled to his attendants; instantly two of his slaves knelt down with their hands on the floor and he took his seat on their backs. "Is your king as powerful as the king of Portugal?" asked the commandant. "My king," replied the Negro, "has a hundred servants who are the equal of the king of Portugal, a thousand like you, but one like me"—and with that he departed.[20]

It may well be true that there is practically no civilization in several Negro states, where a minor king is only addressed through a speaking tube; where after he has dined, a herald announces that the other potentates of the world may now dine in their turn. The king of Kakongo is no more than a barbarian: he unites all power in his own person, judges all legal cases, swallows a cup of palm wine every time he pronounces sentence, without which it would be illegal, and sometimes settles fifty lawsuits at a single sitting.[21] But the ancestors of civilized whites were also barbarians. Compare fifteenth- and nineteenth-century Russia.

We have already established the fact that there are states in Africa where social organization has progressed. We shall now adduce additional proofs to strengthen this truth.

The Fulahs, whose kingdom is about six hundred kilometers in length, and three hundred and ninety in breadth, have towns with a considerable population. Temboo, the capital, has seven thousand inhabitants. In spreading its errors, Islam has introduced books, chiefly on religion and jurisprudence. In Temboo, Laby, and almost all the towns of the Fulahs and the empire of Bornu, there are schools.[22] According to Mungo Park, the Negroes love learning; they have lawyers to defend the slaves when they are brought before a tribunal,[23] for domestic service is unknown among them, but their form of slavery is very mild. This traveler found splendor deep in Africa, at Sego, a town of thirty thousand souls, although it is in every respect inferior to Jenne, to Tombuctoo and Houssa.[24]

We ought to associate the Boushouanas with these African peoples. They were visited by Barrow, who praises their excellent character, the mildness of their manners, and the happiness they enjoy. They too have crossed the bounds that separate savages from those who are civilized, and they have reached such a high level of morality that Christian missionaries might profitably apply their zeal in this country. Litaku, their capital, is a town of between ten and fifteen thousand souls, located 1,250 kilometers from Capetown. They have a patriarchal form of government. The chief has the right to designate his successor, but in all things he acts according to the will of the people, which is communicated to him by a council of elders, for among the Boushouanas old age and authority are still synonymous, as they were among the ancients.[25]

It is unfortunate that untoward circumstances, related in detail by Barrow, prevented him from going to the Barrolous, who were described to him as being more advanced in civilization, who have no notion of slavery, and in whose country large cities can be found where the arts flourish.[26] I forgot to mention that, according to Golbéry, in Africa one does not see a single beggar, except for the blind, who go about reciting passages from the Koran or singing songs.[27]

The Negro Maroons, those in Surinam and those in the mountains of Jamaica, are blamed by the colonists, who wrongly call them rebels, and claim they have not organized a state that would ensure a free society by limiting individual freedom. Everything written in this chapter already answers this objection. How could the peaceful arts be cultivated by a band of fugitives who are always hiding in forests and marshes, and always occupied with seeking food and defending themselves against their oppressors, who in truth are the real rebels? Yes, rebels against all feelings of justice and of nature.

Some might raise the objection that the Negroes of Haiti have so far not succeeded in instituting a stable form of government and tear each other to pieces. But during the stormy course of our own Revolution, which was sacred in its principles but slandered by those who succeeded in distorting its true nature and consequences, did we not witness all sorts of cruelty? In the words of one member of the National Assembly, did not the Revolution subjugate the nation and activate a volcano that destroyed several generations? Moreover, it is indisputable that foreign hands have often thrown the torch of discord into our midst. As late as 1807 an English writer still condemned the ingenious perversity with which European governments corrupted and "demonized" the spirit of the French Revolution. The Revolution had a praiseworthy goal, according to this writer, but the other governments viewed it in the same way as Satan viewed paradise.[28] Who can doubt that foreign hands were just as active in Saint Domingue?

In former times six thousand Negroes and mulattoes allied themselves with the Caribs who are concentrated in the islands of Saint Vincent and Dominica. These black Caribs are strong and proud of their independence.[29] All the facts about them that have been gathered by those who have been in contact with them, incite us to believe that the condition of their society would show rapid improvement, if they did not have every reason to fear the rapaciousness of the Europeans, and if they could cultivate their land without interference and enjoy in peace the fruits of their fields. For a century they have had to struggle without cease against the elements and against tyrants.

In the province of Fernanbouc, in South America, there existed an organized society formed by Negroes, still referred to as *rebelles* and *révoltés* by Malte-Brun in a strange treatise on Brazil that draws on Barloeus, who was Dutch, and Rochapitta, who was Portuguese, and which he inserted in his translation of Barrow.[30]

Between 1620 and 1630 fugitive Negroes, joined by some Brazilians, formed two free states, the great and the little Palmares, which derived their name from the numbers of palm trees they had planted. Great Palmares was almost entirely destroyed by the Dutch in 1644. The Portuguese historian who, according to Malte-Brun, seems to have been ignorant of the first origins of these states, mistakes their restoration in 1650 for their actual origin.

At the close of the war with the Dutch, the slaves in the surroundings of Fenanbouc, accustomed as they were to suffering and battle, resolved to found a settlement that would guarantee their liberty. It was founded by forty of them, and their number soon increased by a multitude of Negroes and mulattoes. But they had no women and, over a large region of the country, organized raids similar to the rape of the Sabines. Once the Palmarisians were feared in the entire region, they adopted a form of worship that was, in a manner of speaking, a parody of Christianity. They also created a constitution, a set of laws, tribunals, and chose a chief named Zombi, which means powerful, whose office was for life, but elective. They fortified their villages, situated on high points of the terrain, and especially their capital, which had a population of twenty thousand souls. They raised domestic animals and much poultry. Barloeus describes their gardens, their cultivation of sugar cane, sweet potatoes, manioc, and millet. The harvest of these crops was marked by festivities and joyous singing. Almost fifty years passed before they were attacked. But in 1696 the Portuguese organized an expedition in order to surprise the Palmarisians. The latter performed prodigious deeds of valor, led by their chief, Zombi. In the end they succumbed to superior force. Some committed suicide in order not to survive the loss of freedom. Others fell prey to the fury of the victors and were sold and scattered. Thus perished a republic that might have revolutionized the New World and that deserved a better fate.

But while at the end of the seventeenth century iniquity destroyed the settlement of Palmares, at the end of the eighteenth, justice and goodwill created the settlement of Sierra Leone, which we will turn to next.

As early as 1751 Franklin established it as a principle that the labor of a free man costs less and produces more than the labor of a slave. Smith and Dupont de Nemours developed this idea through detailed calculations, the one in his *Wealth of Nations*, the other in the sixth volume of *Les Ephémérides du Citoyen*, published in 1771. He was the first, in this book, to advance the project of doing away with the slave trade and, in its stead, to bring civilization into the heart of Africa by establishing on the coast settlements of free Negroes, where colonial produce would be cultivated.

This idea was taken up by Fothergill and repeated by Demanet, Golbéry, and Postlethwayt who, in the two editions of his *Dictionnaire de commerce* showed himself first an antagonist and then an apologist of the Negroes.[31] It was also repeated by Pruneau de Pomme Gouje who had the misfortune of being engaged in the slave trade, and then asked God and the human race to pardon him; by Pelletan who considered such colonization a sure means of changing the aspect of these forsaken regions; and by Wadstrom, who has published an account of his voyage in Africa with Sparrmann.

By this time Dr. Isert had already tried to put this project into practice at Aquapin, on the banks of the river Volta. In his letters he paints a touching picture of the customs of his Negro colonists. Others have succeeded him in the administration of this settlement.[32] I know nothing of its present condition.

In 1792 the English tried to establish a free colony in Bulam. This attempt failed as the one in Cayenne had failed in 1763, and for the same reasons: faulty planning poorly carried out, and lack of foresight. Beaver published a very detailed report on the settlement in Bulam, in which he proves that success was possible, and indicates the means by which it could have been achieved.[33] Barré-Saint-Venant's doubts as to the viability of such a colony would have been answered by Beaver's book alone, if the existence of the colony established in Sierra Leone had not already done so.

Neither Demanet nor Postlethwayt indicated the place they considered suitable for carrying out this project. It was Dr. Smeathman who chose Sierra Leone, a country with fertile soil and a temperate climate, situated between the eighth and ninth latitude degree North. Two minor neighboring kings ceded a territory of considerable dimensions. Granville Sharp set up a plan together with the London committee for the relief of poor blacks, whose president at that time was the well-known Jonas Hanway. Thus the principal collaborators were:

1. Smeathman, who spent four years in Africa and then returned to Europe in order to take the necessary measures concerning his plan for free colonies. He died there in 1786 without having written anything, but

his conduct was a model of practical virtue and we are indebted to him for the following maxim, which is better than a large book: "If everyone were persuaded that we find happiness in working for others' happiness, the human race would be fortunate."

2. Thornton, who formed the project to transport emancipated Negroes from America to Africa.

3. Afzelius, the botanist, and Nordenskjold, the mineralogist, both of them Swedes. Nordenskjold died in Africa, Afzelius is at present in Europe.

4. Granville Sharp who, in 1788, sent help to Sierra Leone at his own expense on a ship of 180 tons. He had previously published his plan for a constitution and a code of laws for the colonies.[34] To these honorable names must be added those of Wilberforce, Clarkson, and others who assisted with money, writings, and advice in the execution of this plan. These are the same men whose enlightened zeal and imperturbable perseverance finally obtained the bill that abolished the slave trade.

Parliament will doubtless adopt measures for its execution. That this is necessary is made clear by Wilberforce in a letter to his constituents in Yorkshire.[35] The abolition of the slave trade will forever stand as a memorial to the most honorable trait of his public life. It would be worthy of him to turn his attention now to an island that has been martyred for centuries, toward Ireland where four million individuals are politically disinherited, slandered and persecuted because they are Catholic, and this by the government of a nation that has boasted so much about its liberty and tolerance.

If in spite of the political storms that are keeping nations apart in both the Old and the New World,[36] this work should reach the honorable defenders of the human species in other countries, many of them will recall that I had an association with them about which I have fond memories. Thomas Clarkson and Joel Barlow will learn from this book that beyond the seas they have a friend who is as constant in his affection as in his principles. But let us turn back to Sierra Leone.

One of the constitutional articles of the settlement excludes Europeans, for fear of their corrupting influences. Only the agents of the company are admitted. The first shipload, in 1786, consisted of a few whites needed for the management of the settlement, and four hundred

Negroes. This experiment met with very little success. Another took its place, established on better principles, which was incorporated in 1791 by an act of Parliament. The following year 1,131 blacks were brought there from Nova Scotia, who had fought for England in the American Revolutionary War. Many were originally from Sierra Leone. They were moved by the sight of their native soil, from which they had been brutally taken in their childhood, and as the neighboring tribes sometimes came to visit this new colony, an aged mother recognized her son with tears in her eyes and threw herself into his arms. It did not take long for the inhabitants of this coastal region to unite with those who were brought from Nova Scotia. Some of the latter are good gunners; but what is much better is that they are very active and intelligent in agricultural and industrial work. Freetown, the main settlement, ten years ago already had nine streets and four hundred houses, each with its garden. Not far from there lies Granville-Town, named after the worthy philanthropist Granville Sharp.

By 1794 there were some three hundred pupils in the schools, forty of whom were natives, and the great majority were good students. They are taught reading, writing, and arithmetic. Beyond this the girls are instructed in the skills proper to their sex, and the boys in geography and a little geometry.

Most of the Negroes who came from America are Methodist or Baptist. They have meetinghouses for worship, and there are five or six black preachers whose supervision has had a powerful effect on the maintenance of order. The Negroes carry out their civic obligations gently but firmly, in a spirit of justice. They serve on juries, which have been set up in this colony, and they are very jealous of their rights. When the governor ordered punishments on his own authority, those who were sentenced declared that they wanted to be judged by their peers, even after the verdict. In general they are religious, sober, chaste, good husbands, and good fathers. They prove their upright nature in many ways, and in spite of the disastrous events of the war[37] and of the elements that have ravaged this colony, the inhabitants enjoy most of the advantages of an established society. I draw these facts from the yearly reports published by the Sierra Leone Company.[38] These were given to me by the famous Wilberforce. In October 1800 the colony increased through the arrival of Maroons from Jamaica. These were deported to Sierra Leone, contrary to the treaty they had concluded with General Walpole, and in spite of his protests.[39]

All other things being equal, it appears that the countries where one can expect to find the least energy and industriousness are those where excessive heat inclines the people to indolence, and where physical needs, which are limited because of the climate, are easily satisfied by the abundance of products for consumption. These same causes make it appear that slavery ought to be characteristic of very hot climates, and that liberty, whether civil or political, ought to encounter more obstacles within the tropics than in more northerly latitudes. But nevertheless one can only laugh at the serious tone in which Barré-Saint-Venant (of whom I have a high opinion in other respects) assures us that the Negroes, incapable as they are of taking a single step towards civilization, will be "in twenty thousand years what they were twenty thousand years ago: The shame and misfortune of the human race."[40] The many facts we have assembled refute over and over this planter who knows so well what the Negroes were even before they existed, and who gives us such a prophetic revelation of what they will be in twenty thousand years. The natives of Africa and America would long ago have risen to the highest level of civilization if this good purpose would have been supported by a hundredth part of the efforts, the money, and the time that have been given over to tormenting and butchering many millions of these unfortunate people, whose blood calls for vengeance against Europe.

{ 7 }

Literature of Negroes

WILBERFORCE, together with the members of the society concerned with the education of Africans, established for them a kind of college at Clapham, which is about twenty kilometers from London. The first to be placed there were twenty-one young Negroes, sent by the governor of Sierra Leone. I visited this establishment in 1802, in order to examine the progress of the pupils, and I found that between them and European children there existed no difference but their color.[1]

The same observation had been made elsewhere: first, in the *Collège de la Marche* in Paris, where Coesnon, formerly professor at the university, brought together a number of Negro children. Several members of the *Institut national* have, like me, examined and followed the progress of the pupils through all the circumstances of their lives, and have observed them in their own classes as well as in public exercises. They can confirm the truth of my assertion.

Second, this was proved at a school in Philadelphia by Brissot,[2] a man slandered with fury and then judicially assassinated—a true republican of rigid probity, who died poor as he had lived.

Third, the same fact has been confirmed by the French consul in Boston, Giraud, in a school of 400 Negro children who are educated separately from whites. The law authorizes their associating with white children, but because of an inherited prejudice that is not yet totally effaced, the white children used to torment the blacks. Sound reason proves that this conduct disgraces only the whites, and particularly the Masonic lodges in this city. These lodges fraternize with each other but have never once visited the African lodge. The only time this lodge shared equal honors was at the funeral ceremony for Washington, where it formed a part of the procession.

75

Among the innumerable authors who believe that the intellectual faculties of Negroes are susceptible to the same development as those of whites, I forgot to cite Ramsay,[3] Hawker,[4] and Blackford.[5] The honorable Wadstrom claimed that in this respect the blacks are superior,[6] and Skipwith, the former American consul, is of the same opinion.

Clenard found that there were more Moors and Negroes in Lisbon than whites; these blacks, he maintained, were worse than brute animals.[7] Things have changed a great deal: the learned secretary of the Portugal Academy, Corea de Serra, mentions several educated Negroes, lawyers, preachers, and teachers, who have distinguished themselves by their talents, in Lisbon, Rio de Janeiro, and the other Portuguese possessions. In 1717 the Negro Don Juan Latino taught the Latin language in Seville. He lived 117 years.[8] The brutishness of the Africans, mentioned by Clenard, was merely the consequence of oppression and extreme poverty; besides, he himself acknowledges their native ability and states: "I am teaching literature to my Negro slaves. One day I shall free them and, like Crassus, I shall have my *Diphilus*, or my *Tyro* like Cicero. They already write very well and are beginning to understand Latin. The best of them reads to me at table."[9]

Lobo, Durand, Demanet, who all spent a long time in Africa, Lobo in Ethiopia, the other two in Guinea, found that the Negroes have a keen and penetrating mind, good judgment, good taste, and refinement.[10] Various writers have collected brilliant repartees and really philosophical answers by blacks. Such is the following, reported by Bryan Edwards: A slave who was asleep was woken up by his master, who said: "Don't you hear your master calling?" The poor Negro opened his eyes, immediately shut them again and said: "Sleep has no master."

Their intelligence in business is well known in the Levant. This was the case with Farhan. He was sold to the prince of Yemen, who appointed him governor of Loheia. His talents, his prudence, and his domestic virtues were praised by Niebuhr, who knew him personally. The elder Michaud told me that in various ports of the Persian Gulf he saw Negroes who were at the head of large commercial companies, received incoming consignments, and sent out ships to all the coasts of India. In Philadelphia he bought a young Negro from the interior of Africa, who had been taken from there at an age when some geographic notions regarding his native land were already inscribed in his memory.

The naturalist Michaud took him to France where he raised him with care, intending to send him back to his native country, once his education was completed, to travel through and explore regions that were scarcely known. But when Michaud died on the shores of Madagascar his Negro, who had gone with him, was cruelly sold. Michaud's son protested against this act of inhumanity, but I do not know whether his protests were of any avail.

Among the Turks the Negroes sometimes rise to the highest offices. Various writers mention Kislar-Aga, who in 1730 was chief of the black eunuchs, and describe him as a man of profound wisdom and great experience.[11]

Adanson was astonished to hear the Negroes of Senegal name a great many stars and reason with pertinence concerning the heavens. He is certain that they would become good astronomers if only they had good instruments.[12]

In various places on the African coast there are Negroes who know two or three languages and who act as interpreters.[13] In general they grasp very quickly what is said, and have an astonishingly good memory. Villaut, Barbot, and other travelers have remarked on this.[14]

Stedman met a Negro who knew the Koran by heart. The same is told about Job-ben-Salomon, son of the Muslim king of Bunda, on the river Gambia. Salomon was captured in 1739, taken to America and sold in Maryland. A series of extraordinary adventures, recorded in the *Morelack*, brought him to England, where he won friends by his dignified appearance, his gentle character, and his talents. Among these was Hans Sloane, baronet, for whom he translated various Arab manuscripts. He was received with honors at the Court of Saint-James, and the Africa Company sent him back to Bunda in 1734, since they were interested in that country. An uncle said to Salomon as he embraced him: "You are the first in sixty years whom I have seen return from the American islands." Salomon wrote letters to his friends in Europe and the New World, which were translated and read with interest. Since his father had died, he succeeded him and was beloved by his subjects.[15]

The son of the king of Nimbana came to England for his studies. He mastered different sciences with remarkable success and learned Hebrew in order to read the Bible in the original. This young man of great promise died soon after his return to Africa.

Ramsay, who spent twenty years among the Negroes, says that they possess the art of mime to such a degree that they could rival our modern star actors. Labat assures us that they are naturally eloquent. Poivre was often astonished by the gift for eloquence of the Malagasy, and Rochon felt it necessary to insert into his *Voyage à Madagascar* a speech by one of their chiefs that may be read with pleasure, even after the speech by Logan.[16]

Stedman believes they have the capacity to make great progress and puts particular stress on their poetic and musical genius. He lists eighteen string and wind instruments,[17] yet does not include the famous balafon[18] that consists of about twenty pipes of hardwood, arranged in decreasing order in length, and has the sound of a small organ.

Grainger describes a kind of guitar invented by the Negroes, on which they play tunes that express a gentle and sentimental melancholy, the music of afflicted hearts.[19] The Negroes' passion for singing is no proof that they are happy, as Benjamin Rush observes, who points out the illnesses that are a consequence of their state of distress and misfortune.[20]

Dr. Gall used to assure me that the Negroes lack the organs for music and mathematics. When I objected that one of their most salient characteristics is their incomparable taste for music, he would agree but argued that they lacked the capacity to improve this fine art. But surely the strength of their penchant is an indisputable indication of their talent. We know from experience that men succeed in those studies toward which they are driven by an evident propensity and a strong urge of their will. Who can foretell to what degree the Negroes will excel in this art, once they have acquired the knowledge of Europe? They may produce musicians of the rank of Gluck and Piccini. Already Gossec has not considered it beneath him to transpose a tune of the Negroes of Saint Domingue into his composition, *Le Camp de Grand-Pré.*

Once upon a time France had its *Trouvères* and *Troubadours*, as Germany had its *Minnesinger* and Scotland its *Minstrels.* Among the Negroes these are called *Griots*, and they also attend the royal courts in order to do what is done at all courts, that is to praise and lie with wit. Their wives, known as *Griotes*, have more or less the same function as the *Almées* in Egypt and the *Bayaderes* in India.[21] This forms another trait of resemblance between them and the traveling women of the Troubadours. But these *Trouvères*, *Minnesinger*, and *Minstrels* were the forerun-

ners of Malherbe, Corneille, Racine, Shakespeare, Pope, Gessner, Klop-
stock, Wieland, and others. In all countries genius is a spark that is
hidden within the flint and only bursts forth when struck by steel.

In the sixteenth century there was Louise Labbé, from Lyon, who was
given the name *la belle Cordière* (the beautiful ropemaker, *Ed.*), which
was an allusion to her husband's trade.

In the seventeenth century, Billaut, who was known as *maître Adam*,
was a carpenter in Nevers.

Hubert Pott, a simple laborer in Holland, and Beronicius, a chimney-
sweep in the same country, exemplified poetic talent linked to profes-
sions generally considered alien to our conception of a cultured mind.
Yet even the most critical taste assigns them a place on Parnassus, although not at the summit. The traveler Pratt proclaims Pott to be the
father of elegiac poetry in Holland,[22] and in the edition of Beronicius's
works published in Middleburg, the engraving that serves as frontispiece
shows Apollo placing a crown of laurel on the head of the chimney
sweep.[23]

In our day, a domestic servant from Glatz, in Silesia, has come to
public attention through his novels.[24] Bloomfield, a fieldhand, has published poetry that has been reprinted several times, and some of which
has been translated into our language.[25] Greensted, a female servant in
Maidstone, and Anne Yearsley, a milkmaid from Bristol, have joined the
ranks of the poets. The latter has written about the suffering of the Negroes, and her work has gone through four editions. Similarly, in the case
of those Africans who have been treated with such iniquity that they
seem destined to be scorned, we have seen that a few have overcome all
the obstacles due to their condition and have cultivated their mind.
Several have become authors.

When Toderini published three volumes on the literature of the
Turks,[26] many people who doubted that the Turks had any literature at
all were surprised to learn that Constantinople has thirteen public libraries. Will there be any less surprise when it is revealed that there exist
works authored by Negroes and mulattoes? Among the mulattoes I
could name Castaing, who has given evidence of poetic talent and whose
poems can be found in various anthologies; also Barbaud-Royer, Bois-
rond, and the author of *Précis des gémissements des sang-mêlés*;[27] and Milscent, one of whose works has appeared under the pseudonym Michel

Mina. All these are mulattoes from the Antilles. There is also Julien Raymond, a mulatto who is an associate member of the section on moral and political sciences, in the subsection on legislation, of the Institut. While we do not intend to justify the conduct of Raymond in all respects, he is to be praised for the energy with which he came to the defense of the mulattoes and free Negroes. He has published a great number of short pieces that taken as a whole form an important source for the history of Saint Domingue and can serve as an antidote to the lies spread by the colonists.[28]

I could also add the name of the Negro woman Belinda. She was born in a delightful region of Africa, then stolen when she was twelve and sold in America. Although I have been servant to a colonel for forty years, she says, my labors have not brought me any comfort. I am seventy years old and have yet to enjoy the benefits that creation bestows on us. Together with my daughter I drag out the remainder of my days in slavery and destitution. For her and for myself I ask for freedom at last. That is the essence of the petition she addressed in 1782 to the Massachusetts legislature. The authors of the *American Museum* (1:538) have preserved this piece of writing that shows no art but is dictated by the eloquence of suffering, and therefore moves the reader all the more.

I could also mention Caesar, a Negro from North Carolina, who is the author of various poems that have appeared in print and have become popular songs, like those of the fieldhand Bloomfield.

There are more Negro than mulatto writers, and in general they have defended their African compatriots more zealously. This will appear in the articles on Amo, Othello, Sancho, Vassa, Cugoano, and Phillis Wheatley. My research has made it possible for me to make known other Negroes, some of whom have not written anything but who gained fame through their superior talents and their great knowledge. Among these there are only one or two mulattoes. Marcel, the director of the imperial printing press who published an edition of Loqman in Cairo,[29] believes that this slave author of fables was an Abyssinian or Ethiopian. Marcel concludes, therefore, that Loqman was one of those Negroes with thick lips and curly hair who were brought from the interior of Africa, and that he was sold to Hebrews and was a shepherd in Palestine. The editor presumes that Aesop (*Aisopos* in Greek, which is nothing more than a corruption of *Aidioph*, Ethiopian) could be Loqman.[30] This conjecture is too vague. Among the fables attributed to him, the seventeenth and the twenty-third concern Negroes, but was the author a Negro? That is doubtful.

If we start from this hypothesis, we might include with Loqman all the distinguished Ethiopians whose names have been preserved by history, above all the Father Grégoire who came to Europe in the mid-seventeenth century. He visited Italy and Germany, he was very well received at court in Gotha, and he died in a shipwreck on his return home. He may have been praised too highly by Fabricius, la Croze, and Ludolph.[31] Ludolph was repaying a debt of gratitude to a man who had been very helpful in teaching him the language and history of Ethiopia. He inserted into his commentary on the history of Ethiopia the portrait of Father Grégoire, engraved by Heiss in 1691. It is clearly the face of a Negro.[32] Such was also the case with the painter Higiemond.

Sonnerat maintains that the Indian painters know neither perspective nor chiaroscuro, even though their work has a perfect finish. Yet Higiemond or Higiemondo, who was commonly referred to as The Negro, was recognized as a skillful artist whose compositions were characterized less by art than by natural talent. This is the opinion of Joachim von Sandrart in his *Academia nobilissimae artis pictoriae*.[33] He calls him very famous (*clarissimus*) and is gratified to own several good paintings by him, but he does not indicate the period when the painter lived. The epithet *nigrum*, in Sandrart's Latin text, would not be sufficient proof that Higiemond was a Negro, since many whites in Europe bore the name Black. But there is no doubt when we consider the face of Higiemond, engraved in 1693 by Kilian, which was inserted into the two works by Sandrart: into the one we have just mentioned,[34] and into his German treatise, published under an Italian title, *Academia Tedesca delle architettura, scultura, pittura*.[35]

The scholar von Murr doubts the existence of Higiemond. He states that this name is foreign to African languages. According to him the name is taken from a passage by Pliny the Elder, author of *Natural History*: "Apparet multo vetustiora, picturae principia esse, eosque qui monochromata pinxerint (quorum aetas non traditur) aliquanto ante fuisse Higiemonem, Diniam, Charmodam, etc."[36] Various manuscripts have *Hygienontem*, and Sandrart himself lists a Hygiaenon among the earliest portrait painters. Von Murr concludes from this that Sandrart, who was then in Holland, was taken in by some secondhand dealer who sold him Chinese paintings and decided to attribute the best of these to a certain Higiemond, although this name is also foreign to Chinese, and although there are no Negroes in China.[37]

I thank this scholar for his observations, but doubt that they are anything more than conjectures. To judge by the little knowledge we possess of Negro languages, I can see nothing, absolutely nothing that would rule out the name Higiemond. An art dealer might have alleged for no reason at all that a man was Chinese and given him a name that happened to be almost identical to the name of a painter of antiquity. This explanation would be just as plausible as the conjecture of a second-hand dealer who was sufficiently familiar with classical authors to borrow from Pliny the name of Higiemond, rather than forging some other name.

Talent is not linked exclusively to any country or variety of mankind. In 1805 we saw in Paris the chief painter of the court of Baden, who is a Kalmuck named Fedor, and I have before me a poem in English that celebrates the talents of a Negro painter in the United States.[38] This may be the moment to recall that in Rome slaves were forbidden to practice the art of painting. That is why, according to Pliny the elder, no slaves are known to have distinguished themselves in this art, nor in toreutics.[39]

{ 8 }

Negroes and Mulattoes Distinguished by Their Talents and Their Writings.

Hannibal[1]

In the course of his travels, Peter the Great made the acquaintance of the Negro Annibal or Hannibal, who had received a good education. Under this monarch he became lieutenant general in Russia and chief of the corps of engineers. He was decorated with the red ribbon of the order of St. Alexander Nevski. Bernardin de St. Pierre, Colonel de La Harpe, and Lévêque, the historian of Russia, knew his son, a mulatto, who was reputed for his talents. In 1784, he was lieutenant general in the artillery corps. It was he, who under the command of Prince Potemkin, the minister of war, initiated the building of the harbor and fortress at Cherson, near the mouth of the Dnieper.

Amo

Antony William Amo, born in Guinea, was brought to Amsterdam when very young, in 1707. He was given to the Duke of Brunswick-Wolfenbüttel, Anton Ulrich,[2] who gave him to his son, August Wilhelm. The latter sent him to study at the universities of Halle, in Saxony, and Wittenberg. At Halle, in 1729, he defended a thesis, in the presence of Chancellor von Ludwig, and published a dissertation *De jure Maurorum*.[3] Amo was versed in astronomy and spoke Latin, Greek, Hebrew, French, Dutch, and German.[4]

He so distinguished himself by his good conduct and his talents that the rector and council of the University of Wittenberg felt obliged in 1733 to offer him a public tribute in a congratulatory letter. They recall in this letter that Terence was also an African, and that many martyrs, doctors, and church fathers were born in the same region, where learning once flourished, and which, by losing the Christian faith, has again fallen back into barbarism.

Amo had success with giving private courses, and these are highly praised in the congratulatory letter. In a list of courses published by the dean of the Philosophical Faculty, this learned Negro is described as a man who examined the systems of the ancients and of the moderns, and selected and taught all that was best in both of them.[5]

Amo received his doctorate and in 1744 defended a thesis at Wittenberg. He also published a dissertation on the sensations that are absent from the soul, but present in the human body.[6] In a letter that the president of the university addressed to him, he is named *vir nobilissime et clarissime* (most noble and famous man, *Ed.*). This shows that, as concerns differences in color, the University of Wittenberg did not share the absurd prejudices of so many who claim to be enlightened. The president declared that he made no changes in the dissertation by Amo, because it was well executed. Indeed, the work gives evidence of a mind trained in reflection. The author endeavors to ascertain the differences in phenomena that occur in beings that merely exist, and in those endowed with life: a stone exists, but it is without life.

It appears that our author had a particular predilection for abstruse discussions: when he was appointed professor, he defended a similar thesis, that same year, on the distinction between the operations of the mind and those of the senses.[7] The royal court of Berlin bestowed the title of state councillor on him.[8] However, after the death of his benefactor, the prince of Brunswick, Amo fell into a deep state of melancholy. He decided to leave Europe, where he had lived for thirty years, and to return to his native Axim, on the Gold Coast. In 1753 he was visited, in Axim, by the learned physician and traveler David Henry Gallandat, who mentions this in the proceedings of the Academy of Vlissingen, in which he held membership.

Amo was then about fifty years old and led a solitary existence. His father and his sister were still living, and his brother was a slave in Surinam. Some time after this he left Axim and settled in Chama, in the fort of the Dutch Company of Saint Sebastian.[9] I have sought in vain to discover whether Amo published any other works, and when he died.

Lacruz-Bagay

The original inhabitants of the Philippines were black, if we are to believe the authors who have written about these islands, and particularly Gemelli Carreri. Even if it should be true that he only traveled in his chamber, as some believe, his work is based on good material, and he is known to be truthful. Many blacks with frizzled hair, enamored of freedom, still inhabit the mountains and forests of those islands. They have even given their name to the island of Negros, one of those that make up this archipelago. Although the population has mixed with Chinese, Europeans, Indians, and Malays, the general color is black, and when it is not sufficiently deep, the women, who in all countries call upon art to assist nature and attain this objective in a variety of ways, deepen their color by the use of various drugs.[10]

Among the varieties produced by this mixture of different races, the Tagals are particularly noteworthy. They resemble the Malays in stature, color, and language. If this observation applies to Bagay, of whom we shall give some account, it may be doubted whether he was entirely black, or merely of mixed race. I must acknowledge my own uncertainty on this subject. Carreri cites the Tagal language as the first of the six languages that are in greatest use in these islands. He also cites a Tagal dictionary made by a Franciscan friar.[11] Another Tagal vocabulary is printed in the works of Father Navarette. A third was published in Vienna, in 1803.[12]

In general we know little about the Philippines. It appears that the Spanish government has tried to conceal this portion of the globe from Europe, while maintaining colleges and printing-offices, a regular administration, and a numerous clergy on these islands. But at least we have a very interesting and valuable large-scale map of this country, drawn by Father Murello Velarde, a Jesuit, and engraved in Manila by Nicholas de la Cruz Bagay, a Tagal Indian.[13] This is the Bagay I wanted to mention. A note attached to the map states that the natives of this country have a great aptitude for painting, sculpture, embroidery, and all forms of design. The productions of Bagay may be presented as a proof of this assertion. This map has been published in a reduced size in 1750, by Lowitz, professor of mathematics in Nuremberg. I would be ungrateful if I ended this article without thanking Barbier du Bocage, who very obligingly provided me with these maps, as well as the dictionary of the Tagal language.

Lislet Geoffroy

Lislet Geoffroy, a mulatto, is an officer in the corps of engineers and in charge of the depository of maps on the Ile de France.[14]

On August 23, 1786, he was named a correspondent of the Academy of Sciences. He is acknowledged as such in the *Connoissance des temps ou calendrier et éphémérides du lever et coucher du soleil, de la lune et des autres planètes pour l'année* 1791, published in 1789 by this learned society, to whom Lislet regularly transmitted meteorological observations and sometimes hydrographical journals. The section of physical and mathematical sciences of the National Institute, considered it their duty to enrol the members of the Academy of Sciences as correspondents and associates.[15] By what fatality is Lislet the sole exception? Is it owing to his color? Let us banish a suspicion that would be an outrage against my colleagues. Certainly, during the last twenty years, Lislet has not lost reputation. In fact he has gained a greater claim on the esteem of scientists.

His map of Ile de France and Réunion was drawn on the basis of the astronomical observations and the geometrical operations of La Caille, as well as from detailed surveys of the islands. It was published in 1797, year 5, by order of the minister of the navy, and given to me by Buache. A new edition, corrected from drawings sent in by the author, was published in 1802, year 10. It is the best map of those islands that has yet appeared.

In the *Almanach de l'Ile de France*, which I have not been able to find in Paris, Lislet has inserted several reports, among them the description of Pitrebot, one of the highest mountains of the island. This fact was communicated to me by a distinguished botanist, Aubert du Petit-Thouars, who resided ten years in this colony.

The Institut administers the legacy of the various Parisian Academies, and it will doubtless publish a precious collection of manuscript reports deposited in its archives. One of these is the report of a voyage by Lislet to the Bay of St. Luce on the island of Madagascar, which Malte-Brun has just published in his collection of voyages. A map of this Bay

and of the Coast accompanies the report. Lislet points out the commodities that should be brought for trading and the resources offered by
this region, which would increase, in his opinion, if the natives were not
incited to war against each other for the sake of obtaining slaves, but
instead were encouraged to greater industry by the expectation of profit-
able commerce. He gives very interesting information on the customs of
the inhabitants of Madagascar. His descriptions are those of a man
versed in botany, physics, geology, and astronomy: and yet this man
never set foot in Europe in order to acquire knowledge and cultivate his
intellect. He had to struggle against the obstacles put in his way by the
prejudices of his island. It is reasonable to suppose that he would have
accomplished more if in his youth he had been brought to Europe and
had lived in an atmosphere of learning. This environment would have
powerfully stimulated his curiosity and stimulated his genius.

A member of the expedition of Captain Baudin informed me that
Lislet established a scientific society on the Ile de France, but that some
whites refused to become members, merely because its founder was a
black. Have they not proved by their conduct that they were unworthy of
the honor of membership?

James Derham

James Derham, originally a slave in Philadelphia, was transferred by his
master to a physician who employed him to prepare drugs. During the
American Revolutionary War he was sold by this physician to a surgeon,
and by the surgeon to doctor Robert Dove, of New Orleans. Derham,
who had never been baptized, had this ceremony performed and was
received into the Episcopalian church. He speaks English, French, and
Spanish with ease. By 1788, at the age of twenty-six, he had become the
most distinguished physician in New-Orleans. "I conversed with him on
medicine," says Dr. Rush, "and found him very learned. I thought I
could give him information concerning the treatment of diseases, but I
learned more from him than he could expect from me." In 1789 the
Pennsylvania society, established in favor of the Negroes, took it upon
itself to publish these facts, and they are also reported by Dickson.[16] In
the *Home Medicine* of Buchan,[17] and in the *Médecine du voyageur* by
Duplanil we find an account of the cure for rattlesnake bite. I do not

know whether it was discovered by Derham, but it is an established fact that we owe the cure to a Negro who received his freedom from the general assembly of Carolina, which rewarded him with an annuity of a hundred pounds sterling.[18] [When Blumenbach traveled in Switzerland he encountered a Negro woman in Yverdon who was reputed to be the most accomplished midwife of the region. This reminded him of the fact that Boërhave and de Haen praised several Negroes for their medical talent. The name of Derham is worthy of being added to this list.]

Thomas Fuller

Thomas Fuller, who was born in Africa and lived four miles from Alexandria, in Virginia, did not know how to read or write but gained admiration for the prodigious facility with which he performed the most difficult calculations. The following is one example among many of the various ways in which his talent was tested: one day he was asked to give the number of seconds lived by a man aged seventy years, seven months, and as many days. He answered the question in a minute and a half. One of those who had put the question took a pen, and after a lengthy calculation claimed that Fuller had made a mistake and given too high a number. No, replied the Negro, the mistake is yours, for you forgot the leap years. His answer was found to be correct. Thomas Fuller was then seventy years old. We are indebted for this information to Dr. Rush, whose letter is quoted in the Travels of Stedman,[19] and the facts can also be found in the fifth volume of *The American Museum*[20] which appeared several years ago. Brissot met him in Virginia and gives the same testimony of his talents.[21] There are examples of other Negroes who performed the most difficult calculations in their head, while Europeans had to have recourse to the rules of arithmetic.[22]

Banneker

Benjamin Banneker, a Negro from Maryland who is a resident of Philadelphia, has applied himself to astronomy without any other encouragement than his passion for acquiring knowledge, and without books, except for the works of Ferguson and the tables of Tobias Mayer. He published astronomical almanacs for the years 1794 and 1795 that contain calculations of the different aspects of the planets, a table of the motions of the sun and moon, their rising and setting, and other calculations.[23] Banneker has received his freedom. [In a letter of congratulation sent by the president of the United States,[24] Jefferson retracts, in a sense, what he wrote in his *Notes on Virginia*, and expresses his pleasure at seeing that nature has bestowed talents on his black brothers that are the equal of those bestowed on men of another color. He draws the conclusion that their apparent lack of genius is only due to their degraded condition in Africa and in America.]

Imlay states that in New England he knew a Negro who was knowledgeable in astonomy, and who had composed astronomical tables.[25] He does not mention his name. If it be Banneker, it is another testimony to his talents. If it be some other, it is another piece of evidence in favor of the Negroes.

Othello

In 1788, Othello published an "Essay on Negro Slavery."[26] "The European powers (he said) should have made a united effort to abolish this infernal commerce, yet it is they who have brought desolation to Africa. They declaim against the inhabitants of Algiers and they vilify the Barbary pirates, who inhabit a corner of that continent to which ferocious Europeans go in order to buy and carry away men, for the purpose of torturing them. It is so-called Christian nations that act as vile torturers. Is not your conduct, continues Othello, a sacrilegious irony when compared with your principles? When you dare talk of civilization and the gospel you pronounce your own condemnation. In your case superior power produces nothing but superior brutality and barbarism. Weakness, which calls on us for protection, appears to incite your inhumanity. Your fine political systems are sullied by the offenses committed against human nature and divine majesty."

"When America rose up against England, it declared that all men have the same rights. Can it be that, after having proclaimed hatred of tyrants, America has betrayed its principles? We ought to bless the measures taken in Pennsylvania on behalf of the Negroes, but we must execrate South Carolina, which recently forbade teaching slaves to read. To whom shall these unfortunates then have recourse? The law either ignores or chastises them."

Othello depicts in fiery words the grief and the sighs of children, relatives, and friends who are dragged far away from their country of birth—a country that will always be dear to their hearts through the memory of their family and the impression left by their homeland. Their land is so dear to them that in their superstitious credulity they imagine they will return to it when they die. Othello contrasts the happiness they enjoyed in their native land with their horrifying condition in America, where they are naked, hungry, bereft of education, and see all the evils of life heaped upon their heads. It is his hope that their cries will rise up to Heaven, and that Heaven may be propitious to their prayers.

Few works can be compared to Othello's essay in force of reasoning and fiery eloquence; but what can reason and eloquence achieve against greed and crime?

Cugoano

Ottobah Cugoano, born on the coast of Fantin, in the town of Agimaque, relates that he was carried off from his country, with twenty other children of both sexes, by European robbers who brandished their pistols and sabers, and threatened to kill them if they attempted to escape. They were confined with others, and soon, he reports, he heard nothing but the clanging of chains, the sound of the whip, and the howling of his fellow prisoners. He served as a slave in Grenada, and owed his freedom to the generosity of Lord Hoth, who brought him to England. In 1788 he was in the service of Cosway, the foremost painter of the Prince of Wales. Piattoli, the author of a treatise in Italian on the location and the dangers of burial grounds (translated into French by Vicq D'Azir at the request of d'Alembert) came to know Cugoano particularly well during a long residence in London. Cugoano was then about forty years of age, and his wife was an Englishwoman. Piattoli has high praise for this African and speaks in strong terms of his piety, his mild character and modesty, his integrity and talents.

Since he lived for a long time in slavery, Cugoano had shared the fate of those unfortunates who are corrupted and slandered by the iniquity of the whites. Like Othello, he paints the heartrending spectacle of the Africans who were forced to bid an eternal farewell to their native soil. He depicts fathers, mothers, husbands, brothers, and children who invoke Heaven and earth, throw themselves, bathed in tears, into each others' arms, embrace each other for the last time, and are instantly torn from all that the heart holds dear. Cugoano states that this spectacle would move the heart of monsters, but has no effect on the colonists.[27]

In Grenada he saw Negroes slashed by the whip because they had been to church on Sunday, instead of going to work. He saw others whose teeth were broken because they had sucked sugar cane.[28] Out of the many instances contained in the registers of the courts of justice, he cites the following: when the captains of slave ships ran short of provisions, or when the cargo was too great, their custom was to throw those Negroes overboard who were sick, or those whose sale would bring the least profit.

In 1780, a slave trader who was detained by contrary winds on the American coast, and was in distress, selected one hundred and thirty-two of his sickest slaves and had them thrown into the sea, tied together in pairs so that they would not escape by swimming. He hoped that the insurance company would indemnify him for his loss. During the trial occasioned by this crime he stated that "Negroes cannot be considered in any other light than as beasts of burden, and to lighten a vessel it is permitted to throw the least valuable merchandise overboard."

Some of these unhappy wretches escaped from the hands of those who were tieing them up, and threw themselves into the waves. One of them was saved by ropes thrown by the sailors of another vessel. The barbarous assassin of these innocents had the audacity to claim him as his property, but the judges rejected his claim.[29]

Most of the authors who attacked the trade in human beings, used only the weapons that reason supplies. Then a voice was raised that rang with the cry of outraged religion and set out to prove by the authority of the Bible, that the stealing, sale, and purchase of human beings, and keeping them in a state of slavery, are crimes that merit capital punishment. This was the voice of Cugoano, whose *Thoughts and sentiments on the evil and wicked traffic of the slavery and commerce of the human species* was published in English and is available in a French translation.

His work is not very methodical. There are repetitions, because grief vents itself in many words. He is a man whose feelings run deep, who is always afraid that he has not said enough and that he will not be understood. His talent lacks cultivation, and it would have been much more highly developed if he had benefited from a good education.

After some observations on the causes of the differences in color and complexion in the human species, such as climate, the physical configuration of a country, and diet, he asks whether[30] "being black or white is more of a crime than wearing a black or white coat. Whether color and bodily shape justify enslaving men whose vices are the work of the colonists. A state of freedom and a Christian education would lead them to all that is good, useful, and just; but since the colonists are blinded by avarice and greed, every slave has the inalienable right to free himself from their tyranny."

"The Negroes have never crossed the seas to steal white men. If they had done this, the European nations would have accused them of robbery and murder. The Europeans complain about the pirates of the Barbary Coast, while their conduct toward the Negroes is much worse. The European trading posts in Africa are nothing but dens of thieves and murderers. To steal men, to rob them of their liberty, is worse than to plunder them of their goods. In Europe, which claims to be civilized, thieves are put in chains or hanged, and murderers are executed after being tortured. If the slave traders and colonists escape such punishment, this is only because the people and the governments are their accomplices, since the laws encourage the slave trade and tolerate slavery. On occasion Heaven will inflict national punishments on national crimes. Moreover, injustice is sooner or later fatal to those who perpetrate it." This idea is in conformity with the basic tenets of religion, and its consequences are brought out very well in this book. The author predicts that the wrath of Heaven will be directed against England, which by itself carries on two-thirds of the trade that supplies the colonies with eighty thousand slaves every year.

The argument is made that there have been slaves at all times. But there have also been criminals at all times. Bad examples can never render evil actions legitimate. Cugoano draws the comparison between ancient and modern slavery, and proves that the latter, which prevails among Christians, is worse than slavery among the pagans, and especially worse than among the Hebrews, who did not steal men to enslave them, who did not sell them without their consent, and who did not put a price on the head of those who had run away. In Deuteronomy it is stated explicitly, "Thou shalt not deliver up to thy master a fugitive slave, who, in thy house, had sought an asylum."[31] At the expiration of the seventh year, which was jubilee, a man was given back his freedom. In a word, slavery among the Hebrews was nothing more than a temporary vassalage.

From the Old Testament the author then passes on to the New. He discusses its facts and principles, and the reader senses the superior force that his arguments derive from the celestial morality that commands us to love our neighbor as ourselves, and to do to another that which we wish he would do to us. He writes: "I would wish for the honor of Christianity, that the odious art of kidnapping had already been known to the pagans."[32] He ought to have said for the honor of the Christians. The trading and enslaving of Negroes is the greatest of all the iniquities that dishonor the name of Christian, but even though religion suffers under this iniquity, no guilt attaches to religion itself, just as the idea of justice cannot be blamed for the dishonest acts of some judges.

"By its very establishment the clergy brings the message of justice: it ought to watch over society, expose its errors and bring it back to truth and virtue. If the clergy do not carry out this mission, they will bear the guilt for the sins of society. But it is clear that the men of the church either do not know truth, or dare not reveal it. Consequently they bear their share in the crimes of the nation."

He might have added that flattery and cowardice are vices against which the clergy have in recent centuries almost never offered instruction to the faithful. In fact they have often set the example for these vices. We know the conduct of Saint Ambrose and his answers to Theodosius, and the answers Saint Basil gave to the prefect Modestus.[33] Others have occupied their seats, but they have rarely had a successor. Although it is the general opinion that Bossuet was not a prelate of the court, but a prelate at court, these saints might well have thought that in his answer to the question by Louis XIV concerning theater, he showed himself too much a courier, and not enough of a bishop.

Wherever he went, the worthy Cugoano saw temples erected to the God of the Christians, and saw ministers who were charged with repeating His precepts. How could he believe that the children of the Gospel would trample under foot the morality contained in the book that is the depository of the divine oracles? He had too good an opinion of the Europeans, and this error, which does honor to his heart, adds to the shame of the Europeans.

Capitein

James Eliza John Capitein, born in Africa, was bought at seven or eight years of age, on the banks of the river St. André, by a Negro trader who gave him as a present to one of his friends. The latter named him Capitein, had him instructed and baptized, and brought him to Holland. There Capitein learned the language of the country and at first devoted his time to painting, in which he showed a great interest. He began his studies at the Hague. Miss Roscam, a pious and learned lady who, like Miss Schurman, was very interested in languages, taught him Latin, and the elements of Greek, Hebrew, and Chaldean. From The Hague he went to the University of Leyden, and found everywhere zealous protectors. He devoted himself to theology under able professors, with the intention of returning home and preaching the Gospel to his countrymen. After four years of study he took his degrees, and in 1742 was sent as a Calvinist missionary to Elmina, in Guinea. An English newspaper, on the authority of Metzère, a minister of the Gospel in Harlem, printed as a vague rumor that Capitein, after his return to Guinea, had taken up again idolatrous worship.[34] In a letter addressed to me, de Vos is less categorical concerning this anecdote. This Mennonite minister in Amsterdam, who is the author of some good writings against Negro slavery and duelling, states that Capitein, who was so much praised before his departure, and whose portrait, engraved by Tanjé after the manner of Van Dyck, was circulated throughout Holland, did not live up to his reputation: on his return to Europe troubling rumors spread concerning the immorality of his conduct. It was even asserted that he was not far from abjuring Christianity.[35] This is quite likely if the news about his conduct is true. Like so many others, he probably proclaimed his loss of faith to ease his conscience about disregarding the moral teachings of the Gospel. But are these bad reports well founded?

De Vos himself weakens the force of the information, by the doubtful manner in which he expresses himself. Blumenbach, who had Capitein's portrait engraved in his collection of the varieties of the human face, has written me to confirm that his research did not bring to light any negative information on Capitein.

The first work of Capitein was an elegy in Latin verse, on the death of Manger, who was a minister at the Hague and his preceptor and friend. I shall quote its beginning and provide a translation:[36]

> The arrows of inexorable death fall on the globe, and no one can escape them. Death enters the palaces of kings and demands that they take off their crown. It takes trophies out of the warriors' hands and closes their eyes to the spectacle of the victory celebration. The treasures of the wealthy and the huts of the poor fall prey to death. Youth and old age succumb equally to its scythe and are death's harvest.
>
> Covered with a somber veil, Death crossed the threshold of the house of Manger. The celebrated city of the Hague moans in sorrow at the sight of the cypress that has been raised before his door. His beloved wife tears at her bosom and sheds her tears on his coffin with the same deep sorrow as Noemi, when the death of Elimelech condemned her to widowhood. Her sobs increase and invoke the spirit of her husband, and sorrow speaks through her quivering lips:
>
> You who were my happiness and who will always be my pride, you have disappeared from my eyes, as the sun conceals its rays from the earth behind dark clouds. I do not envy you for having preceded me into eternal happiness. You are always present, whether night brings repose to the earth, or whether it flees at the return of light, and my memories accuse death as they call you back to my lonely bed. When will come the day that renews our marriage vows? I weep at the sight of the funereal decorations draped around the room where you sought refuge in prayer and study, and my soul expires at the sight of the tears shed by the children, the pledges of our love. When the shepherd has been killed by the bloodthirsty wolf, his scattered flock call in vain for their leader and fill the air with their pitiful bleating. That is the cry that echoes through our home at the sight of your lifeless body. These cries of the widow and her children mingle with the recital of poetry that laments your disappearance.
>
> This mortal man is no more, who brought honor to the clergy and to his wife, who was beloved equally by a pious nation and by the powerful. The lips are stilled that brought us the wisdom of faith, and that consoled me in my troubles. How quickly vanished the voice that had been endowed by Heaven with the most soothing eloquence! Let the ancients

vaunt the eloquence of old Nestor. In Manger Nestor would have found his match.

For his admission to the University of Leyden, Capitein published a Latin dissertation on the calling of the Gentiles, divided into three parts.[37] In this dissertation he bases himself on the authority of the Bible and affirms the certainty that this promise was given to all nations, even though the Gospel will only become manifest to them in gradual succession. He proposes that in order to carry out the designs of the Almighty, the study of the languages of these nations should be fostered, and also that missionaries should be sent out to them who, by the mild voice of persuasion, would gain their affection and dispose them to receive the light of the Gospel.

The slaves are undoubtedly treated better by the Spaniards, and even more so by the Portuguese, than by other nations. The Christian religion inspires them with a paternal attitude that brings the slaves closer to their masters. They have not made skin color a sign of nobility, they do not disdain marriage with Negro women, and they make it easier for slaves to regain their freedom.

In other colonies the planters have often prevented their Negroes from being instructed in a religion that proclaims that all men are equal, since all come from a common stock and all partake of the benefits granted by the Father of us all, who makes no exception of anyone. A countless number of writers have demonstrated these consoling truths. In our times we need only mention Robert Robinson,[38] Hayer, Roustan, Ryan, who was translated into French by Boulard, and Turgot in a magnificent speech that Dupont de Nemours brought to my attention, and that he proposes to publish. Political tyranny and slavery are an outrage against the teaching of the Gospels. The base flattery practiced by a great number of bishops and priests only succeeded in introducing contrary maxims by distorting the Christian religion.

Dutch planters, who stifled the voice of conscience, probably instigated Capitein to become the apologist of a bad cause. He believed, or pretended to believe that supporting slavery would favor the propagation of the faith, and he wrote a politico-theological dissertation, to prove that slavery is not opposed to Christian freedom.[39] This scandalous assertion was revived in America a few years ago. A minister, named John Beck, dared to preach and publish in 1801 two sermons in order to justify slavery.[40] We owe thanks to Humphrey for having affixed the name of John Beck to the post of infamy.[41]

Capitein fully realizes the difficulty of his undertaking, most particularly when it comes to finding an explanation for the text by Saint Paul: *"you have been redeemed: be slaves to no person."*[42] He supposes (I do not say he proves) that this refers only to commitments made with pagan masters, such as to become gladiators and fight in the arena with wild beasts,[43] as was the custom among the Romans. He is contradicted, but does not discuss this point, by the famous edict of Constantine that authorized the freeing of slaves, as well as by the Christian usage, mentioned in the writings of the church fathers, of giving freedom to slaves, particularly at Easter. From all quarters we hear the cry of history in favor of the freeing of the slaves. The formal procedures for this are mentioned in Marculf,[44] but because the law made freeing optional, Capitein infers the lawfulness of slavery. This is clearly a forced conclusion.

He draws on the testimony of Busbec and asserts that the abolition of serfdom had great disadvantages. He argues that if the practice of serfdom had continued, we would not see so many crimes committed, nor so many scaffolds erected to control individuals who have nothing to lose.[45] But slavery that is imposed as a legitimate punishment does not legitimize the slavery of the Negroes; moreover the authority of Busbec does not prove anything.

This Latin dissertation of Capitein, which is rich in erudition, though very poor as a piece of rational argument, was translated into Dutch by Wilhelm[46] and has gone through four editions. The most reasonable conclusion we can draw from the fallacious arguments of this Negro, who will assuredly not get a vote of thanks from his compatriots, is that nations and individuals who have been unjustly enslaved, ought to resign themselves to their unhappy lot, when they are unable to break asunder their chains. Gallandat, author of a treatise on the slave trade in the proceedings of the Academy of Vlissingen, shows poor judgment when he praises Capitein's writings on this topic.[47]

Capitein also published a small volume in 4to. of sermons in the Dutch language, which he preached in different towns, and which were printed in Amsterdam in 1742.[48]

Francis Williams

The information concerning this Negro poet has been taken partly from the *History of Jamaica,* by Edward Long, who cannot be suspected of being too partial to Negroes.[49] His prejudice against them is manifest even in the words of praise that truth forced him to utter.

Francis Williams was born in Jamaica, toward the end of the seventeenth or the beginning of the eighteenth century, since he died at the age of seventy, not many years before Long's book appeared in 1774. The duke of Montague, governor of the island, was struck by the young Negro's precocious talents and decided to try whether with a liberal education, he would become equal to a white man who was placed in the same circumstances. Francis Williams was sent to England, commenced his studies in private schools, and afterward entered the University of Cambridge, where, under able professors, he made considerable progress in mathematics. During his stay in Europe he published a ballad that began with the following line: "Welcome, welcome, brother debtor." This ballad was so much in vogue in England, that certain individuals, irritated to see such merit in a black, attempted, but without success, to claim it as their own.

When Francis Williams returned to Jamaica, his protector, the duke of Montague, tried to obtain a place for him in the government council, but the council refused. Williams then opened a school, in which he taught Latin and mathematics. He trained a young Negro as his successor, who unfortunately became deranged. Long cites this fact as a demonstrative proof that African minds are incapable of abstruse research, such as problems in advanced geometry, although he supposes that creole Negroes have a greater aptitude than those born in Africa. To be sure, if an isolated fact could be the basis of a general induction, then we might conclude that no class in society is capable of profound thoughts, since the exercise of the intellectual faculties has proportionally deranged more heads among the learned and men of letters, than in any other class of society. In any case Long refutes himself: Since the facts obliged him to acknowledge that Francis Williams had a talent for mathematics, he might with as much justice have come to precisely the opposite conclusion.

He maintains that Williams had no respect for his parents, and that he was harsh, almost cruel with his children and his slaves. He wore unusual clothing and a long wig in order to gain respect for his knowledge. He described himself as a white man under his black skin, for he despised men of his color, *and often said, shew me a negro, and I will shew you a thief.*[50] He was also of the opinion that both the Negro and the white man, each of whom is perfect in his species, are superior to mulattoes, who are formed of a heterogeneous mixture. This portrait of Williams may be true, but we must recollect that it was not executed by a friendly hand.

It appears that Williams wrote many pieces in Latin verse. He loved this type of composition, and he was in the habit of presenting addresses of this kind to a new governor. The one he wrote for Haldane is included in Long's book. Long criticizes it all too severely, even though he believed it appropriate to make a translation, or rather to paraphrase it in English verse. Since Williams gave his muse the name Nigerrima, Long indulges in low pleasantry about this new addition to the nine sisters, and calls her Madam Aethiopissa. Since there are three or four lines in the poem that are a reminiscence or an imitation of Latin poets, Long accuses Williams of plagiarizing not ideas but certain expressions, while these can be found in the works of good poets. Since these can also be found in the dictionaries, he is in effect blaming Williams for making Latin verses with Latin words.

Long also criticizes Williams for low flattery of the new governor, when he compares him to the heroes of antiquity. This accusation is more justified, but unfortunately it applies to almost all poets. Have they not always flattered power? Did they not carry adulation of one of the most criminal men of Rome to such a degree that the name of Maecenas has become a classic? If we except Churchill, Akenside, Pope, Joel Barlow, and a few other poets, are they not, in this respect, all Wallers?[51]

Nickolls, who was full of indignation against the colonists because they compared blacks to apes, exclaimed in reference to this Latin poem: "I have never heard of an orangutan composing an ode. Among the defenders of slavery we do not find one half of the literary merit of Phillis Wheatley and Francis Williams."[52] In order to make it possible for the reader to appreciate the talent of Williams, we insert his Latin poem with a translation:[53]

TO
THAT MOST UPRIGHT AND VALIANT MAN,
GEORGE HALDANE, ESQ.
GOVERNOR OF THE ISLAND OF JAMAICA:
UPON WHOM
ALL MILITARY AND MORAL ENDOWMENTS ARE
ACCUMULATED.

An Ode.

AT length revolving fates th' expected year
Advance, and joy the live long day shall cheer,
Beneath the fost'ring law's auspicious dawn
New harvests rise to glad the enliven'd lawn.[54]
With the bright prospect blest, the swains repair
In social bands, and give a loose to care.
Rash councils now, with each malignant plan,
Each faction, that in evil hour began,
At your approach are in confusion fled;
Nor while you rule, shall raise their dastard head.
Alike the master and the slave shall see
Their neck reliev'd, the yoke unbound by thee
Till now, our guiltless isle, her wretched fate
Had wept, and groan'd beneath the oppressive weight
Of cruel woes; save thy victorious hand,
Long form'd in war, from Gallia's hostile land,
And wreaths of fresh renown, with generous zeal
Had freely turn'd, to prop our sinking weal.
Form'd as thou art, to serve Britannia's crown;
While Scotia claims thee for her darling son.
Oh! best of heroes, ablest to sustain
A falling people, and relax their chain.
Long as this isle shall grace the western deep
From age to age, thy fame shall never sleep.
Thee, her dread victor, Guadaloupe shall own,
Crush'd by thy arm, her slaughtered chiefs bemoan,
View their proud tents all levell'd in the dust,
And while she grieves, confess the cause was just.
The golden iris the sad scene will share,
And mourn her banners scatter'd in the air,
Lament her vanquish'd troops with many a sigh,
Nor less to see her towns in ruins lie.
Favorite of Mars! believe, the attempt were vain,

It is not mine to try the arduous strain.
What! shall an Aethiop touch the martial string
Of battles, leaders, great achievements sing?
Ah no! Minerva, with the indignant nine,
Restrain him, and forbid the bold design.
To a Buchanan does the theme belong,
A theme, that well deserves Buchanan's song.
'Tis he should swell the din of war's alarms,
Record thee great in council, as in arms:
Recite each conquest by thy valor won,
And equal thee to great Peleides son.
That bard, his country's ornament and pride,
And who with Mars might e'en the bays divide:
Far worthier he, thy glories to rehearse,
And paint thy deeds in his immortal verse.
We live, alas! where the bright God of day,
Full from the zenith whirls his torrid ray:
Beneath the rage of his consuming fires,
All fancy melts, all eloquence expires.
Yet may you deign to accept this humble song,
Tho' wrapt in gloom, and from a falt'ring tongue
Tho' dark the stream on which the tribute flows,
Not from the skin, but from the heart it rose.
To all of human kind, benignant heaven,
(Since nought forbids) one common soul has giv'n,
This rule was 'stablish'd by the eternal mind;
Nor virtue's self nor prudence are confin'd
To color, none imbues the honest heart;
To science none belongs, and none to art:
Oh! muse of blackest tint, why shrinks thy breast,
Why fears to approach the Caesar of the West!
Dispel thy doubts, with confidence ascend
The regal dome, and hail him for thy friend:
Nor blush, altho' in garb funereal drest
Thy body's white, tho' clad in sable vest.
Manners unsullied, and the radiant glow
Of genius, burning with desire to know;
And learned speech, with modest accent worn
Shall best the sooty African adorn.
A heart with wisdom fraught, a patriot flame,
A love of virtue, these shall lift his name
Conspicuous, far beyond his kindred race,
Distinguished from them by the foremost place.

In this prolific isle I drew my breath
And Britain nurs'd, illustrious thro' the earth.
This my lov'd isle, which never more shall grieve
Whilst you, our common friend, our father live.
Then this my prayer, "May earth and heaven survey
A people ever blest beneath thy sway."

FRANCIS WILLIAMS

Vassa

Olaudah Equiano, better known by the name of Gustavus Vassa, was born in 1746, at Essaka, a beautiful and charming valley far distant from the coast and capital of Benin. It is considered a part of Benin, although it is largely self-governing under the authority of elders or chiefs, one of whom was his father.

At the age of eleven, Vassa was carried off together with his sister, by robbers who stole children to take them into slavery. These barbarians soon deprived him even of the consolation of mingling his tears with those of his sister. He was forever separated from her and thrown into a slave ship. After his passage across the ocean, under terrible conditions which he relates, he was sold in Barbados, and resold to a lieutenant commander of a vessel who brought him to England. He accompanied him to Guernsey, to the siege of Louisbourg in Canada by Admiral Bascaven, in 1758, and to the siege of Belle-isle, in 1761.

When events brought him back to the New World he was, through treachery, again put in irons. Sold into slavery in Montserrat, Vassa became the plaything of fortune, sometimes free, sometimes a slave or a domestic servant. He made many voyages to most of the Antilles and to different points on the American continent. He often returned to Europe, visited Spain, Portugal, Italy, Turkey, and Greenland. The love of freedom, whose first fruits he had tasted in his childhood, increasingly tormented his mind because of the obstacles that prevented him from recovering freedom. He hoped in vain that a consistent zeal for the interests of his masters would be a sure means to this end. Justice would have found in his zeal another reason for breaking his chains, but for greed it was a motive for riveting them tighter. He saw that with men possessed by the thirst for gold he had to have recourse to other means. Then he forced himself to live as economically as possible, and with three pence he began small trade that brought him a modest nest egg, in spite of the many losses he sustained through the thievery of the whites. Finally in 1781, having escaped the dangers of the sea and several shipwrecks, and having survived the cruelty of his masters, one of whom, in Savannah, almost murdered him, Vassa, after thirty years of a wandering and stormy life, was restored to liberty and settled in London, where he married and published his memoirs,[55] which have been reprinted several times in both hemispheres. It is proven by the most respectable testimony that he was the Author. This precaution is necessary against a class of individuals who are always disposed to slander the Negroes in order to extenuate the crimes of their oppressors.

The book is written with the naïveté, (I could almost say the roughness) of a man of nature. His manner is that of Daniel Defoe in his *Robinson Crusoe*, or that of Jamerai Duval, who rose from a cowherd to hermit to librarian of Emperor Francis I, and whose unpublished memoirs, so worthy of publication, are in the hands of Ameilhon.[56]

We share the feelings of surprise that Vassa experienced at the shock of an earthquake, the appearance of snow, a painting, a watch, and a quadrant, and we follow him as he questions his reason about the use of those instruments. The art of navigation had an inexpressible attraction for him: He also saw it as a way of one day escaping from slavery. He made an agreement with the captain of a vessel to give him lessons. They were often interrupted, but his initiative and intelligence made up for this. While he was a servant to Dr. Irving, he learned from him the method of desalting sea water by distillation. Some time afterward Vassa was a member of an expedition to find a passage to the North. When the expedition found itself in distress he used the doctor's procedure to provide drinking water for the crew.

Although he was taken from his country when he was quite young, he retained a rich store of recollections, thanks to his affection for his family and a good memory. We read with interest the description he has given of his country, where luxuriant nature has been prodigal of her bounties. Agriculture is the principal occupation of the inhabitants, who are very industrious, although they are passionately fond of poetry, music, and dancing. Vassa remembers clearly that the physicians of Benin drew blood by means of cupping glasses, and that they excel in the art of healing wounds and overcoming the effect of poisons. He draws an interesting picture of the superstitions and customs of his country, which he contrasts with those of countries where he has traveled. Thus, in Smyrna he finds that the Greeks have dances that are common in Benin; he compares the customs of the Jews and those of his fellow countrymen, among whom circumcision is generally practiced. In his country anyone who touches a dead body is considered to have become impure, according to law, and the women are subject to the same purifying rites as among the Hebrews.

Adversity often has the effect of strengthening religious sentiment. When we are struck by misfortune and abandoned on earth by our fellow men, we turn our eyes toward Heaven where we seek consolation and a father. Such was the case with Vassa; he did not sink under the unending load of evils that pressed upon him. Imbued with the presence of the Supreme Being, he directed his view beyond the bounds of life, toward a new land.

He hesitated a long time on his choice of a faith, and he gives a striking description of his anguish in a poem of 112 lines, written in English, that he inserted into his memoirs. He was shocked to see that in all Christian groups there were so many individuals whose actions are in direct opposition to their principles and who blaspheme the name of God, whom they profess to worship. For example, he felt indignant that the king of Naples and his court went every Sunday to the opera. He saw that some observed four precepts of the ten commandments, others six or seven, and he could not conceive how anyone could be half-virtuous. He did not realize that, in the words of Nicole, we cannot deduce the doctrine from conduct, nor conduct from the doctrine. He was baptized in the Anglican church and, after a long period of uncertainty, turned Methodist and was almost sent as missionary to Africa. In the school of adversity Vassa had become very sensitive to the misfortunes of others, and no one could more justifiably claim the maxim of Terence (*Homo sum: nil humani alienum mihi puto*, I am a man and consider nothing human foreign to me, *Heautontimoroumenos*, line 77. *Ed.*). He deplored the fate of the Greeks, who were treated by the Turks in almost the same manner as the Negroes by the colonists. He even felt pity for the galley slaves of Genoa, because their punishment went beyond the bounds of justice.

He saw his African countrymen fall victim to all the tortures that

greed and rage could invent. He contrasted this cruelty with its antith-
esis, the morality of the Gospel. He proposed a plan of commerce between Europe and Africa, which at the least would not wound justice. In
1789 he presented to the Parliament of England a petition for the suppression of the slave trade. If Vassa is still living, the bill that was lately
passed, must be a consolation to his heart and to his old age. Anyone is to
be pitied, for sure, who does not feel affection for Vassa, after reading his
memoirs.

His son, who is expert in bibliography, became assistant librarian to
Sir Joseph Banks, and is also secretary to the committee for vaccination.

Sancho

The mother of Ignatius Sancho was thrown into a slave-trading vessel
on the coast of Guinea that was destined for the Spanish possessions in
America. She was delivered of Sancho during the voyage, in 1729. When
they arrived in Cartagena he was baptized by the bishop and named
Ignatius. The change of climate soon conducted his mother to the tomb,
and his father, delivered up to the horrors of slavery, killed himself in a
moment of despair.

Ignatius was not two years of age when he was taken to England by
his master, who made a present of him to three young sisters residing in
Greenwich. He was compared in character to the squire of Don Qui-
xote, and this brought him the name Sancho. The young Sancho was
fortunate enough to attract the attention of the duke of Montague, who
resided at Black-Heath. This gentleman admired in him a frankness that
was neither degraded by servitude, nor corrupted by a false education.
He often called for him, lent him books, and advised the three sisters to
cultivate his mind. But in living with them Sancho had the opportunity
to discover that ignorance is one of the means of enslaving Africans and
that, in the opinion of the planters, to instruct the Negroes is to emanci-
pate them. The sisters often threatened to send him back to slavery. The
love of freedom that seethed in his soul, rose to an even higher pitch
through study and meditation. He conceived a violent passion for a
young woman, and this brought down upon him another kind of re-
proach from the sisters. He then resolved to leave their house. But the
duke, his patron, was no more. Sancho, now destitute, spent his last five

shillings to purchase an old pistol, with which to terminate his days as his father had done. Then the duchess, who received him coldly when he first came, but who nonetheless esteemed him, took him on as a butler. He remained in this situation till the death of his patroness. By saving his money, and through a legacy left him by this lady, he found himself with seventy pounds sterling, plus thirty as an annuity.

For some time he combined his passion for study with other passions, for the theater, for women, and for gambling. He renounced cards after a game in which a Jew won all his clothes. He then spent his last shilling at Drury Lane to see Garrick, who later became his friend. He tried to become an actor and to play Othello and Oroonoko, but a poor pronunciation prevented him from succeeding in a profession he viewed as a resource against adversity. He then went into the service of the chaplain of the family of Montague, and his conduct, which had become very respectable, obtained for him the hand of a woman of means, who was born in the West Indies.

Around 1773 he would have again descended into poverty, due to attacks of gout and the smallness of his fortune, if the generosity of his protectors and his economical habits had not provided him with the means of taking up an honest trade. Through his own and his wife's industry he raised a large family. His domestic virtues brought him general esteem. He died December 15, 1780. After his death, a fine edition of his letters was published for the benefit of his family, in 2 volumes, 8vo., which were well received by the public. There was a second edition in 1783, with the life of the author, as well as his portrait engraved by Bartolozzi, and painted by Gainsborough. Some articles he had published in the newspapers were included in this edition.[57]

Jefferson criticizes him for yielding too much to his imagination, whose eccentric motion, in Jefferson's words, can be compared to those fugitive meteors that dart across the firmament. Nevertheless he acknowledges that Sancho has an easy style, with well-chosen expressions, and that his writings breathe the sweetest effusions of sentiment. Imlay declares that he has not had the opportunity to read them, but he observes that since Jefferson generally errs in his opinions concerning Negroes, all he says about Sancho is suspect.[58]

Letters are a type of literature that is not really subject to analysis, either because they cover such a variety of topics, or because the author takes liberties in grouping several topics in the same letter, examining some in depth while barely touching on others, and often going far afield from his subject so that the letter ends in digressions. We read the letters of Madame de Sévigné, but no one has ever attempted to analyze them. We certainly cannot compare the African author to her, but in the genre that has made Madame de Sévigné so illustrious there remain many honorable places to be filled by other authors. The epistolary style of Sancho resembles, in its positive and negative qualities, the style of Sterne, with whom Sancho was acquainted. The third volume of the letters of Sterne includes a very fine letter addressed to Sancho, in which he tells him that the natural variations in the human species in no way contradict the fact that they all share the same blood, and also expresses his indignation that certain men want to degrade a large number of their fellow men to the rank of animals, in order to be able to treat them as such with impunity.[59]

Sometimes Sancho descends to a rather common style, at other times he becomes inspired by his subject and is poetic, but in general he has the grace and light touch of the epistolary style. He is witty and playful as he portrays a man of the world who hesitates over the choice between the tyrannical empire of fashion on the one hand, and health and happiness on the other. His style is serious as he discusses the motives of a Providence that has made poverty the companion of genius. His writing is lofty when he addresses nature, which reveals to him on all sides the work and the hand of the Creator.

He writes that "according to the plan of the Deity, commerce should make the products of each country available to the entire globe. It should unite the nations through the awareness of reciprocal needs as well as the bonds of brotherly friendship, and it should facilitate the general propagation of the benefits of the Gospel. But those poor Africans, whom Heaven has favored with a rich and luxuriant soil, are the most unhappy segment of humanity because of the horrible traffic in slaves; and it is the Christians who carry on this traffic."[60]

The tragic end of Dr. Dodd is memorable. He was condemned to death for forgery, while his entire previous life was a model of wisdom. We regret his punishment, when we read the letter in which Sancho expounds the reasons that made a case for his pardon.

Some of his moral assertions might be disputed if his writings generally did not present a repeated homage to virtue. He inspires love of virtue when he describes the remorse of the duchess of K—— as she is tormented by conscience, which he calls *the high chancellor of the human heart*: "Act then always in such a manner as to gain the approbation of your heart—to be truly brave, one must be truly good. We have reason as a rudder, religion for our anchor, truth for our polar star, conscience as a faithful monitor, and perfect happiness as a recompense."

In the same letter, as he drives away recollections that might expose his virtue to a new shipwreck, he exclaims, "why bring to mind these combustible matters, while rapidly glancing over my past years, I approach the end of my career? Have I not the gout, six children, and a wife? O Heaven, where art thou? You see that it is much easier to preach than to act. But we do know how to separate good from evil; let us arm ourselves against vice and act like a general in his camp, who ascertains the force and position of the enemy, and places advance guards to avoid surprise. Let us act thus even in the ordinary course of human life; and believe me, my friend, that a victory gained over passion, immorality and pride, is more deserving of a *Te Deum*, than the victories won on the fields of ambition and of carnage."[61]

I invite the reader not to limit himself to these extracts, which give only an imperfect idea of the author. Since the authority of Jefferson is so impressive and worthy of respect, it is all the more important to contest his judgment, which is much too severe, and to give Sancho the esteem that is his due.

Phillis Wheatley

Phillis Wheatley was stolen from Africa when she was seven or eight years old, taken to America and sold, in 1761, to John Wheatley, a wealthy merchant in Boston. Her amiable manners, exquisite sensibility, and precocious talents, made her so beloved by the family, that they not only freed her from the burdensome labors reserved for slaves, but even from the care for the household. She was passionately fond of reading, and especially of reading the Bible, and she soon learned Latin. In 1772, at nineteen years of age, Phillis Wheatley published a small volume of thirty-nine poems. This work has run through several editions in England and in the United States. In order not to leave ill-will any pretext for saying that she was not the author, the authenticity of her authorship was confirmed on the first page of the volume, by a declaration from her master, the governor and lieutenant governor of the state, and fifteen other respectable persons in Boston, to whom she was known.

In 1775 she received her freedom from her master. Two years later she married a man of her color, who in the superiority of his mind, compared to other Negroes, was also very unusual. It was therefore no surprise to anyone that her husband rose from a grocer to a lawyer, under the name of Doctor Peter, and defended the cause of the blacks in courts of law. The reputation he enjoyed procured him a fortune.

Phillis, a woman of sentiment who was brought up like a spoiled child, as the common saying goes, knew nothing about running a household, but that is what her husband wanted her to do. He began with reproaches and followed this up by maltreating her. This continued and affected her so much, that in 1787 she died of a broken heart. Her husband, by whom she had a child that died when very young, survived her only by three years.[62]

Jefferson, who appears unwilling to acknowledge the talents of Negroes, even those of Phillis Wheatley, maintains that the heroes of the *Dunciad* are divinities, when compared with this African muse.[63] If we wanted to quibble, we might say, that such an assertion needs only to be confronted by a contrary assertion, and we would appeal to the judgment of the public, which received the poetry of Phillis Wheatley with praise. But we can refute Jefferson's opinion more directly by selecting some samples of her writings, and that will give an idea of her talents.

It was doubtless her acquaintance with the works of Horace that induced her to begin, as he did, with an ode to Maecenas,[64] whose protection poets secured by flattery. Their base words made readers forget the vileness of Maecenas. It was the same procedure by which Augustus buried in oblivion the horrors of the Triumvirate. This poem is not without merit, but let us proceed to subjects more worthy of being treated in poetic form.

Almost all her poems have a religious or moral theme, and almost all express a sentimental melancholy. Twelve treat the death of persons who were dear to her. Of particular note are her odes on the works of Providence, on virtue, and on humanity; the ode to Neptune, and the verses addressed to a young painter of her own color on viewing his paintings. As we might expect she expresses her grief over the sorrows of her compatriots.

I am including three of her poems. The reader should remember that indulgence is mere justice when judging the writings of a Negro slave woman who is nineteen years old.

(Remember, Christians, Negroes black as Cain
May be refin'd and join the Angelic train).⁶⁵

On the death of J. C. an infant.

No more the flow'ry scenes of pleasure rise,
Nor charming prospects greet the mental eyes,
No more with joy we view that lovely face
Smiling, disportive, flush'd with ev'ry grace.

The tear of sorrow flown from ev'ry eye,
Groans answer groans, and sighs to sighs reply
What sudden pangs shot thro' each aching heart,
When, *Death*, thy messenger dispatch'd his dart!

Thy dread attendants, all destroying Pow'r,
Hurried the infant to his mortal hour.
Could'st thou unpitying close those radiant eyes?
Or fail'd his artless beauties to surprise?
Could not his innocence thy stroke control,
Thy purpose shake and soften all thy soul?

  The blooming babe, with shades of *Death* o'erspread,
No more shall smile, no more shall raise its head;
But like a branch that from the tree is torn,
Falls prostrate, wither'd, languid, and forlorn.
"Where flies my *James*," 'tis thus I seem to hear
The parent ask, "Some angel tell me where
"He wings his passage thro' the yielding air?"
Methinks a cherub bending from the skies
Observes the question and serene replies,
"In heav'n's high palaces your babe appears:
"Prepare to meet him, and dismiss your tears."

Shall not th' intelligence your griefs restrain,
And turn the mournful to the cheerful strain?
Cease your complaints, suspend each rising sigh,
Cease to accuse the Ruler of the sky.
Parents, no more indulge the falling tear:
Let *Faith* to heav'n's refulgent domes repair,
There see your infant like a seraph glow:
What charms celestial in his numbers flow.
Melodious, while the soul-enchanting strain
Dwells on his tongue, and fills th' etherial plain?
Enough—forever cease your murm'ring breath;
Not as a foe, but friend, converse with *Death*,
Since to the port of happiness unknown
He brought that treasure which you call your own.
The gift of heav'n intrusted to your hand
Cheerful resign at the divine command;
Not at your bar must sov'reign *Wisdom* stand.

An hymn to the Morning.

ATTEND my lays, ye ever honour'd nine,
Assist my labors, and my strains refine;
In smoothest numbers pour the notes along,
For bright *Aurora* now demands my song.

    Aurora, hail, and all the thousand dyes,
Which deck thy progress through the vaulted skies:
The morn awakes, and wide extends her rays,
On ev'ry leaf the gentle zephyr plays;
Harmonious lays the feather'd race resume,
Dart the bright eye, and shake the painted plume

    Ye shady groves your verdant gloom display
To shield your poet from the burning day:
Calliopie, awake the sacred lyre,
While thy fair sisters fan the pleasing fire:
The bow'rs, the gales, the variegated skies
In all their pleasures in my bosom rise.

    See in the east th' illustrious king of day!
His rising radiance drives the shades away—
But Oh! I feel his fervid beams too strong,
And scarce begun, concludes th' abortive song.

To the right honorable William, Earl of Dartmouth,
his Majesty's principal Secretary of State for North America, etc.

HAIL, happy day, when, smiling like the morn,
Fair *Freedom* rose *New-England* to adorn:
Long lost to realms beneath the northern skies
She shines supreme, while hated *faction* dies:
Soon as appear'd the *Goddess* long desir'd,
Sick at the view, she languish'd and expir'd:
Thus from the splendors of the morning light
The owl in sadness seeks the caves of night.
No more, *America*, in mournful strain
Of wrongs, and grievance unredress'd complain,
No longer shalt thou dread the iron chain,
Which wanton *Tyranny* with lawless hand
Had made, and with it meant t' enslave the land.

Should you, my lord, while you peruse my song,
Wonder from whence my love of *Freedom* sprung,
Whence flow the wishes for the common good,
By feeling hearts alone best understood:
I, young in life; by seeming cruel fate
Was snatch'd from *Afric's* fancy'd happy seat:
What pangs excruciating must molest,
What sorrows labor in my parents' breast?
Steel'd was that soul, and by no misery mov'd,
That from a father seized his babe belov'd:
Such, such my case: And can I then but pray
Others may never feel tyrannic sway? etc. etc.

{ 9 }

Conclusion

Of all the countries where letters are cultivated, I doubt whether there is any that is less familiar with foreign literature than France. We need not therefore be surprised that in our historical dictionaries, which are little more than financial speculations, no mention is made of any Negro author. They contain tiresome listings of ephemeral romances and theatrical pieces long forgotten. A place is given to Cartouche,[1] while no mention is made of Raikes, the founder of the Sunday Schools, nor of William Hawes, the founder of the Humane Society that cares for individuals struck with apparent death, nor of men such as Hartlib, Maitland, Long, Thomas Coram, Hanway, Fletcher of Salton, Ericus Walter, Wagenaar, Buckelts, Meeuwis-Pakker, Valentyn, Eguyara, François Solis, Mineo, Chiarizi, Tubero, Jerusalem, Finnus Johannaeus, etc. We do not even find the name of Suhm, the Pufendorf[2] of the last century, nor of many national writers who merit distinction, such as Persini, Blaru, Jehan de Brie, Jean des Lois, de Clieux, and the good Quaker Benezet, born at San Quentin, the friend of all mankind, the defender of the oppressed who, during his whole life, combatted slavery by reason, religion, and example. He established, in Philadelphia, a school for black children, and he taught them himself. During those moments of leisure that this work allowed, he sought out unfortunates to give them comfort. At his funeral, which was honored with the solemn attendance of an immense number of people, an American colonel who had served as engineer in the war of independence, exclaimed: "I would rather be Benezet in his coffin, than George Washington with all his fame." This was no doubt an exaggeration, but it honors Benezet. Yvan Raiz, a Russian traveler, said about Benezet: "The Academies of Europe resound with the praise of famous names, and the name of Benezet is not found on their lists. For whom then do they reserve their crowns?"[3] This Frenchman, who so powerfully stirred the admiration of foreigners, is not even known in France. He has not been granted even the smallest space by those who make a business of publishing dictionaries. But Benjamin Rush and many others from England and America have made up for this omission.

Men who listen only to their common sense, and who have paid no attention to the discussions concerning the colonies, may well have difficulty believing that the Negroes have been degraded to brute animals, and that their moral and intellectual capacities have been put in doubt. This doctrine is as absurd as it is abominable, and yet it is insinuated or professed openly in many writings. It cannot be disputed that the majority of Negroes combine ignorance with absurd prejudices and vulgar vices, especially those vices that are characteristic of slaves of all kinds and all colors. You who are French, English, or Dutch: What would you have become if you had been placed in the same circumstances? I maintain that you have no right to blame them for even the stupidest error, nor the most hideous crime.

For a long time the whites in Europe have, in various ways, engaged in trading other whites as slaves. Can we give any other name to the use of press-gangs in England, to the conduct of sellers of souls in Holland, and the conduct of German princes who sold their regiments for service in the colonies? But, if ever the Negroes should break out of their chains and (Heaven forbid) land on European shores, in order to tear whites of both sexes away from their families, put them in chains and take them to Africa, branding them with a red-hot iron; if those whites who had been stolen, sold, and bought by criminals, were placed under the surveillance of merciless managers and ceaselessly forced to work, under the lash, in a climate injurious to their health, with no other consolation at the end of each day than the thought that they had come a step closer to the tomb, no other prospect than to suffer and die in utter despair; if destined to ignominious destitution, they were excluded from all the privileges of society, declared legally incapable of any recourse to the law, and had their witness declared inadmissible even against other blacks [*sic*]; if, like the slaves of Batavia, these whites, now enslaved in their turn, were not permitted to wear shoes, if driven from the sidewalks, they were compelled to mingle with the animals in the middle of the street, if people took out subscriptions to participate in mass whippings, and would cover the backs of the slaves with salt and pepper in order to prevent gangrene; if the fine for killing them was only a trifling sum, as is the case in Barbados and Surinam, if a reward was offered for apprehending those who escaped from slavery, if those who escaped were hunted by a pack of hounds expressly trained to tear them to pieces; if, blaspheming the Divinity, the blacks claimed that their priests were the emissaries of Heaven when they preached passive obedience and resignation to the white slaves; if greedy hireling writers betrayed liberty by maintaining that it is nothing more than an "abstraction" (such is now the fashion in a nation that goes from fashion to fashion); if these writers justified the taking of reprisals against the "rebellious" whites, and that in any case the white slaves were happy, happier than the peasants in Africa itself— in a word, if all the arts of cunning and calumny, all the strength and fury of greed, all the inventions of ferocity were directed against you by a coalition of beings with a human face, in whose eyes justice has no meaning because nothing matters except money, what cries of horror would echo throughout our countries! To express this horror our language would have to find new epithets; innumerable writers would wear themselves out producing eloquent lamentations (provided, of course, that they had nothing to fear and could expect to reap some profit).

Europeans, reverse this hypothesis, and see what you are! During the last three centuries, tigers and panthers have been less terrible for Africa than you. For three centuries Europe, which calls itself Christian and civilized, has tortured, without pity and without remorse, the peoples of Africa and America whom Europe calls savages and barbarians. In order to obtain indigo, sugar, and coffee, Europe has brought them debauchery, desolation, and disregard of all natural sentiments. Africa cannot even breathe freely when the European powers are at war with each other. Yes, let me repeat it, there is no vice, no form of criminal conduct for which Europe does not set an example and bears the guilt in its relations with Negroes. Avenging God! suspend thy thunder, exhaust thy compassion, and give Europe the time and the courage to repair, if that is possible, these horrors and atrocities.

I took on the task of proving that the Negroes are capable of virtues and talents. This I have done through reasoning and even more by supplying facts. These facts do not announce sublime discoveries, and the works I mention are not masterpieces, but they furnish irrefutable arguments against those who vilify the Negroes. I do not maintain, like Helvetius, that all individuals are born with equal aptitudes, and that human beings are merely the product of their education. I consider this assertion false as a generalization, but it is true in many respects. A conjunction of fortunate circumstances developed the genius of Copernicus, Galileo, Leibniz, and Newton. Others might perhaps have surpassed them if unfortunate circumstances had not prevented their mental development. Every country has its Boeotia (region of dim-witted people, *Ed.*), but we can say that in general virtue and vice, wisdom and foolishness, genius and stupidity, characterize all varieties of regions, nations, skulls, and colors.

In order to draw a comparison between the people of different countries, we must place them in the same situation and circumstances. What parity can be found between the whites, who are enlightened by the truths of Christianity (which lead to almost all other truths), enriched by the discoveries and the learning of all centuries, and urged on by every type of encouragement, and on the other hand the blacks, who are deprived of all these advantages, and who are the victims of oppression and destitution? If not one of them had given evidence of any talent, that would not have been surprising. What is truly astonishing is that so many *have* displayed talent. What could they be if the dignity of being free were restored to them and they occupied the place in society that nature assigns and tyranny refuses them?

Sudden revolutions in the political realm may be compared to the great convulsions of nature, on account of the disasters they occasion. It is another of the lies spread by the planters that they blurred the distinction between emancipation and the problem of the slave trade, by asserting that the Friends of the Blacks wanted a sudden and general freeing of the slaves. This was not the case: they were in favor of progressive measures that would introduce betterment without turmoil. Such was the opinion of the author of this work when he addressed an epistle to free Negroes and mulattoes that brought upon him so much abuse, in which he predicted (and he still predicts) that one day, on the shores of the Antilles, the sun will shine on free men only, and that its rays will no longer fall on chains and slaves.[4] But the French planters rejected with fury all the decrees by which the Constituent Assembly proposed to introduce salutary reforms *gradually*. Their pride lost them the colonies of the New World, which (as Genty pointed out) will flourish only under the sign of personal freedom. The revolting traffic to which men in that region dare to subject their fellow men, will never lead to a durable prosperity.

The American continent, that sanctuary of liberty, is advancing toward a state of things that will be shared by the Antilles, a course of progress the combined powers will be unable to arrest. When the Negroes are reinstated in their rights by the irresistible force of events, they will owe no debt of gratitude to the colonial settlers, who might have found it equally easy and useful to win their affection.

Paid piecework, which in Brazil and the Bahamas has already been recognized as a useful alternative to slavery, as well as the successful introduction of the plow in Jamaica,[5] would suffice to overturn or modify the colonial system. This revolution will spread more quickly once the leaders of industry and politics have a better understanding of their interdependence. They will then call in the aid of the steam engine and other mechanical inventions that shorten labor and facilitate practical work. When an energetic and powerful nation, which in every way holds the promise of a great destiny, stretches her arms over the Atlantic and Pacific Oceans, and speeds her ships from one ocean to the other by a shorter route, either by cutting the isthmus of Panama, or by building a canal of communication, as has been proposed, through the river St. John and the lake of Nicaragua, then this will change the world of commerce and the shape of empires. Who knows whether America will not then avenge herself for the outrages she has suffered, and whether old Europe, reduced to the rank of a secondary power, will not become a colony of the New World?

There is nothing useful and lasting but what is just: there is no law of nature that makes one individual the dependent of another, and all laws that reason disavows have no force. Every person brings with him into the world his title to freedom.[6] Social conventions have circumscribed its use, but its limits must to be the same for all the members of a community, whatever their origin, color, or religion. Price stated that if you have the right to make another man a slave, he has the right to make you a slave; and if no one has the right to sell him, then no one has the right to purchase him.[7]

May the European nations finally expiate their crimes against the Africans! May the Africans raise their heads, freed from humiliation; may they give free rein to all their faculties, compete with the whites only in talents and virtues, forget the crimes of their tormentors, avenge themselves only by good deeds, and in a burst of fraternal affection enjoy at last freedom and happiness! Even if this prospect is only a dream in the brief life of an individual, it is at least a consolation to carry to the tomb the certainty to have made every possible effort to procure a better life for others.

P.S. Two men of letters who are distinguished by their talents and their writings, one Swiss and the other American, have translated the original manuscript, one into German and the other into English. These will soon be published, the one in Germany and the other in the United States of America.[8]

NOTES

Notes followed by (G) are by Grégoire himself. Those followed by (W) are by Warden. Those followed by an (E) are by the present editors.

Dedication

1. Names followed by an asterisk were omitted by Warden. (E)

2. Name added by Warden. Author of *Travels in the Interior Districts of Africa*, London 1799. (E)

3. *The Crisis of the Sugar Colonies* (London, 1802; repr. New York: Negro Universities Press, 1969). *The Sorrows of Slavery: A Poem, Containing a Faithful Statement of Facts Respecting the African Slave Trade*, by the Rev. Jamieson. (London: J. Murray, 1789). We were unable to identify *Indian Eglogues*. (E)

4. That is, in Spain and Portugal. (E)

5. *Analyse sur la justice du commerce du rachat des esclaves de la côte d'Afrique*, by J. J. d'Acunha de Azeredo Coutinho, in 8vo. (London). (G)

6. *O Poddanych polskich, i.e. Concerning the Peasants of Poland*, by Joseph Paulikowski, 8vo. (Roku, 1788). (G)

7. *Kazania X. Michala Karpowicza, W. Roznych okolicznosciach Miane*, i.e., *Sermons of Father Karpowicz*, 3 vols. in 12 (W. Krakovie, 1806). See particularly vols. 2 and 3. (G)

8. Peter Lotharius Oxholm (1753–1827), author of a book on the Virgin Islands. (E)

Chapter 1

1. See Jer. 13:23. Flavius Josephus, *Jewish Antiquities* I.8.chap. 7. Theophrastus, 22d character, Herodotus, &c. (G)

2. Pliny, book 5, chap. 9. Terence, *Eunuchus*, act 1, scene 1. (G)

3. See *Annals of Commerce* by Macpherson, in-40. (London, 1805), 1:51 and 52. Frontin, *Straiagemata*, book 1, chap. 2. (G)

4. "Subito flens Africa nigras procubuit lacerata genas" states Sidonius Apollinaris in the *Panegyric on Maiorianus*. (G)

5. See Gibbon's *History*, reviewed by the Rev. Whitaker, in 8vo. (London, 1791), 182ff. (G)

6. William of Malmesbury, folio 84. (G)

7. 4to. (Argentorati, 1778). (G)

8. *Voyage d'Ethiopie*, by Poncet, 99, &c; and *Histoire du Christianisme d'Ethiopie* by La Croze, 77ff. (G)

9. *Idées sur les relations politiques et commerciales des anciens peuples de l'Afrique* by Heeren, 8vo. (Paris, an 8 [i.e., 1799, *Ed.*]), 2:10 and 75. (G)

10. Ibid., 1:134, 156, 160. (G) Cerne is thought to be one of the Canary Islands. (E)

11. *Asiatic Researches*, 3:355. (G) This was a periodical published in Calcutta between 1788 and 1822 in 14 volumes: *Asiatic Researches or Transactions of the Society instituted in Bengal for Enquiry into the History and Antiquities, the Arts, Sciences and Literature of Asia.* (E)

12. 3:41, plate 35. (G)

13. *Recueil d'Antiquités*, 5:247, plate 88; 7:285, plate 81. (G)

14. J. Ch. Jahn, *Archaeologica biblica* (Vienna), 389. (G)

15. Josephus, *Antiquities*, book viii, chap. 7, p. 2. Hudson in his Latin translation, says: "AEthiopes in Mancipia" (i.e., slaves). This is suggested by the Greek text, but not stated explicitly. (G)

16. P. 85. (G)

17. *Modern Geography*, 4to. (London, 1807), 2:2; 3:820 and 833. (G)

18. Book 3, para. 3. (G)

19. Herodotus, book II, no. 104. (G)

20. *New Voyage into Upper and Lower Egypt*, by Browne, 1:chap. 12, and Walkenaer in the *Archives Littéraires*. (G)

21. *Voyages en Syrie et en Egypte*, by Volney, nouvelle édition, 1:10ff. (G)

22. Ledyard, 1:24. (G) This is probably *Voyages de Ledyard et Lucas en Afrique, entrepris et publiés par ordre de la Société anglaise d'Afrique* (Paris: an xii [1804]). (E)

23. *Mémoire sur le commerce des Nègres au Caire*, by Louis Franck, in 80. (Paris, 1802). (G)

24. Jobi Ludolf, *Historia AEthiopica*, in-fol. (Francofurti ad Moenum, 1681), 3:chap. 1. (G)

25. *De Generis humani varietate nativa*, 8vo. (Göttingen, 1794). (G)

26. Browne, *New Voyage*. (G)

27. *Voyage dans l'Empire ottoman, l'Egypte, la Perse, &c* by Olivier, 3 vols. 4to. (Paris, 1804–7), 2:82ff. (G)

28. Volney, *Voyages*. (G)

29. George Gregory (1754–1808), *Essays Historical and Moral*, (London, 1785; 2d augmented edition, 1788). (E)

30. *Dissertation sur la préjugé qui attribue aux Egyptiens la découverte des sciences*, by Cailly, 8vo. (Caen). (G)

31. *History of Jamaica*, 3 vols., 4to. (London, 1774), 2:355ff., and 371ff. (G) It is not clear why Grégoire referred to Long as an "anonymous" author, since Edward Long is the author's actual name. (E)

32. Ibid., 2:352. (G)

33. *Adversaria Anatomica*, decad. 3, p. 26, no. 23. (G) Most probably by Frederik Ruysch, though we could not find the exact title. (E) *Dissert. de sede et causa coloris AEthiopum et caeterorum hominum*, Lugd. Bat. 1707. (G) By Bernhard Siegfried Albinus. (E) *Mémoires de l'Académie des Sciences, 1702. Observations anatomiques, 1724.* Venet. (G) By Giovanni Domenico Santorini. (E) *Exposition anatomique, 1743.* Amsterdam 3:278. (G) By Jacques Bénigne Winslow. (E) *De habitu et colore AEthiopum*, Kilon, 1677. (G) By

Johann Nicolas Pechlin. (E) *Discours sur l'origine et la couleur des Nègres*, 1764. See his works translated by Herbel (1784), 1:24. (G) We could not find the exact reference, but this is probably a work by the Dutch scientist Petrus Camper, since some of his writings were translated into German by Herbel (see *General Catalogue of Printed Books of the British Museum*, vol. 32, column 1027). (E) *Histoire de l'Afrique française*, 2 vols., 8vo. (G) The reference is to: abbé Demanet *Nouvelle histoire de l'Afrique française* (Paris, 1767). (E) *Sur la différence physique qui se trouve entre les Nègres et les Européens*, para. 48 (G) This seems to be a French translation of Samuel Thomas von Soemmerring, *Über die Körperliche Verschiedenheit des Negers vom Europäer* (Frankfurt a.M., 1785). (E) *De Generis Humani varietate nativa*, 3d ed., 8vo. (Göttingen, 1785). (G) By Blumenbach. (E) *An Essay on the Variety of Complexion and Figure in Human Species*, by the Rev. S. Stanhope-Smith, 8vo. (Philadelphia, 1787). I call the reader's attention to this work, which merits reflection. (G)

34. *De l'Unité du Genre humain*, by Blumenbach, trans. Chardel. (G)

35. *The Progress of civil Society, a didactic Poem*, by Richard Payne-Knight, 4to. (London, 1796), book 5, line 227ff. (G)

36. *A Topographical Description of the Western Territory of North America*, by George Imlay, 8vo. (London, 1793), letter 9. (G)

37. *Voyage dans les départements méridionaux de la Russie*. See 600n. (G)

38. It is said, as a joke, that the shipowners in Liverpool, where many grow wealthy through the slave trade, pray God daily not to change the color of the Negroes. (G)

39. *The Natural and Civil History of Vermont*, by S. Williams, 8vo. (Walpole, N.H., 1794), 391ff. (G)

40. *An Essay, &c.* by Stanhope-Smith, 20, 23, 34, 58, 77, &c. (G) See note 33 for complete title. (E)

41. *An Essay, &c*, 43. (G) This seems to refer to the work by Stanhope-Smith cited in note 33, not to any book by Soemmerring. (E)

42. *Dissertation sur les variétés naturelles qui caractérisent la physionomie des hommes des divers climats et des différents âges*, by Camper, trans. Jansen, in 4to. (Paris, 1791), 18. (G)

43. *Transactions of the American Philosophical Society*, 4to., 287ff. (G)

44. *Monthly Review*, 38:20. (G)

45. *Opuscules*, 1:16, and *Dissertation physique sur la différence réelle que présentent les traits du visage chez les hommes de divers pays*. (G)

46. *Descriptio thesauri ossium morbosorum Hoviani* (1785), 133. (G)

47. *Epigrammata in complures musaei anatomici res*, by Fr. B. Osiander, 8vo. (Göttingen, 1807), 45 and 46. (G)

48. See 20 in Chardel. (G) See Chapter 1, note 34. (E)

49. *Relazione del reame di Congo*, 6. (G)

50. *History of the Maroons, from their origin to the establishment of their chief Tribe in Sierra Leone*, by R. C. Dallas, 2 vols., 8vo. (London, 1803), 1:88ff. (G)

51. Soemmerring, para. 74. (G) Samuel Thomas von Soemmerring, *Über die Körperliche Verschiedenheit des Negers vom Europäer* (Frankfurt a.M., 1785). (E)

52. 5:part 2. (G) This is undoubtedly a reference to the *Memoirs of the Literary and Philosophical Society of Manchester* (London: Cadell, 1785–1802). (E)

53. Bosman, *Voyage en Guinée* (Utrecht, 1705), letter 8. (G)

54. *Voyage* of Ledyard and Lucas, 2:338. (G) See Chap. 1, note 22. This is a reference to the Djolof kingdom in Senegal. (E)

55. *Relation historique de l'Abyssinie*, by Lobo, 4to. (Paris, 1726), 68. (G)

56. Adanson, *Voyage au Sénégal*, 22. (G)

57. Cossigny, *Voyage à Canton*. (G)

58. *Histoire de l'île des Barbades*, by Richard Ligon, in *Recueil de divers voyages faits en Afrique et en Amérique*, 4to. (Paris, 1764), 20. (G) This is a translation of *A true and exact History of the Island of Barbados*, by Richard Ligon, (repr. London: Frank Cass, 1970). "Santiago" refers to one of the Cape Verde islands. (E)

59. *Journal d'un voyage aux Indes orientales, sur l'escadre de du Quesne*, 3 vols., 12mo. (Rouen, 1721), 1:202. (G)

60. *Voyage* of Leguat, 2:136. (G)

61. Ulloa, *Noticias americanas*, 92. (G)

62. Isert, *Reis na Guinea* (Dordrecht, 1790), 175. (G)

63. P. 182. (G) We have not been able to identify the title of the book (E).

64. By the Baron de Beauvois, 6 and 24. See also *Rapport sur les troubles de Saint-Domingue*, by Garran, 8vo. (Paris an 5 [1797]). (G)

65. *L'Institut*, the collective name of the national literary and scientific Academies in France. See Introduction. (E)

66. *Lois et constitution des colonies*, by Moreau-Saint-Méry, 6:144. (G)

67. *Voyage à la Cochinchine*, by Barrow, 2 vols., 8vo. (Paris, 1807), 2:68ff. (G) Grégoire is referring to the French translation of *Voyage to Cochin China* by Sir John Barrow (London, 1806). (E)

68. Henry Home, Lord Kames (1696–1782). Grégoire is probably referring to *Sketches in the History of Man* (1774) but we have not been able to trace down the exact reference. (E)

69. See *De generis humani varietate nativa*. Nevertheless, Desfontaines maintains that the female of the *pithèque* (simia pithecus) has a slight periodical discharge. (G)

Chapter 2

1. David Hume, *Essays, Moral, Political and Literary*, part 1. Grégoire refers to note 1 in chapter 21, "Of National Characters": "I am apt to suspect the negroes, and in general all the other species of men (for there are four or five different kinds) to be naturally inferior to the whites. There never was a civilized nation of any other complexion than white, nor even any individual either in action or in speculation. No ingenious manufactures amongst them, no arts, no sciences. On the other hand the most rude and barbarous of the whites such as the ancient Germans, the present Tartars, have still something eminent about them, in their valour, form of government, or some other particular. Such a uniform and constant difference could not happen, in so many countries and ages, if nature had not made an original distinction betwixt these breeds of men. Not to mention our colonies, there are negroe slaves dispersed all over Europe, of which none ever discovered any symptoms of ingenuity; tho' low people, without education, will start up amongst us, and distinguish themselves in every profession. In Jamaica indeed they talk of one negroe as a man of parts and learning; but 'tis likely he is admired for very slender accomplishments, like a parrot, who speaks a few words plainly." (E)

2. *Considerations on the Negro Cause*, by Estwick. (G)

3. Barré-Saint-Venant, *Des colonies sous la zone torride, particulièrement celle de Saint-Domingue*, 8vo. (Paris, 1802), chap. 4.

4. *Notes on the State of Virginia*, by T. Jefferson, 8vo. (London, 1787). (G) The "two Negro writers" referred to in the next sentence are Phillis Wheatley and Ignatius Sancho. (E)

5. *A Topographical Description of the Western Territory of North America*, by G. Imlay (London, 1793), letter 9. (G)

6. It does not correspond to present-day Mauritania, but to Morocco, Algeria, and Tunisia. (E)

7. We were unable to identify the author of *The English Spy*. The writer Arthur Lee (1740—92) was known as "The American Junius," but there is no evidence that he gave a speech to the American armies. According to Sidney Kaplan, Grégoire probably refers to Thomas Paine, a personal acquaintance during the French Revolution. On April 19, the day after Washington proclaimed the cessation of hostilities, a pamphlet by Paine was published in Paris, with the title *Thoughts on Peace and the probable Advantages Thereof.* (E)

8. [The dawn of fine arts in America has already shown brilliant promise. West, Copely, Vanderlyn, Stewart, Peale, and Allston are considered distinguished painters. Even women have made a successful start on a literary career. We can mention, among others, Mrs. Warren, who has just published her *History of the American Revolution*, and Miss Hannah Adams, who among other works has published *La vérité et l'excellence du Christianisme prouvées par les écrits des laïcs.* This list by itself dispels Paw's fantasies about the inferior talent of the citizens of the New World.] (G)

Editorial note: The above note was omitted by Warden, but the names of painters were integrated into the text, and Warden added the following names: Putnam, Hancock, Miller, Trumbull, Smith, Fulton, Edwards, and Ramsay. Warden, however, omitted Madison and Monroe from Grégoire's original list, as well as the passage in square brackets. "Paw" refers to Cornelius de Pauw, author of *Recherches philosophiques sur les Américains* (Berlin, 1765—68) and subsequent editions. "Mrs. Warren" is Mercy Otis Warren, author of *History of the rise, progress and termination of the American Revolution* (Boston, 1805). The American title of Hannah Adams's book is *The truth and excellence of the Christian religion exhibited in two parts* (Boston, 1804). (E)

9. Louis Genty, *Influence de la découverte de l'Amérique sur le bonheur du genre humain* (Paris, 1787), 167. (G)

10. The passage in square brackets was omitted by Warden. (E)

11. *The Guinea Voyage, a Poem in 3 Books*, by James Field Stanfield, 4to. (London, 1789). I beg leave to cite the beginning of the 2d book:

> High where primeval forests shade the land
> And in majestic solemn order stand,
> A sacred station raises now its seat,
> O'er the loud stream that murmurs at its feet—
> Of Niger rushing thro' the fertile plains,
> Swelled by the Cataract of tropic rains:
> Long ere surcharged, his turgid flood divides,
> To burst an ocean in three thundering tides. (G)

12. Long, 2:420. (G) See Chapter 1 note 31. (E)

13. *A Provincial Glossary with a Collection of Local Proverbs and Popular Superstitions*, by Francis Grose, 8vo. (London, 1790). (G)

14. Grégoire uses the word *lumière*, which for his generation had the double meaning of "artificial light" and "enlightenment." (E)

15. *African Memoranda, relative to an attempt to establish a British settlement in the island of Boulam*, by Capt. Philip Beaver, 4to. (London, 1805). "I would rather carry thither a rattlesnake," 397. (G)

16. Grégoire is referring to priests, like himself, who rallied to the Revolution and were excluded from the ministry after Napoleon concluded a concordat with the pope. (E)

17. *L'Aristocratie négrière*, par l'abbé Sibire, missionaire dans le royaume de Congo, 8vo. (Paris, 1789), 93. (G)

18. *Ibid.*, 27. (G)

19. *Practical rules for the management and medical treatment of Negro slaves in the sugar colonies*, by a professional planter, 8vo. (London, 1805), 470. (G)

20. *Notes on the West Indies*, by G. Pinckard, 3 vols., 8vo. (London), 1:273, and 3:67. (G)

21. *Voyage to the Islands of Madeira, Barbadoes, and Jamaica*, by Hans Sloane, 2 vols. fol. (London, 1707), 48. (G)

22. His *Essay Against Public Slavery* (Baltimore, 1788). (G)

23. *Lettre d'un Martiniquais à M. Petit, sur son ouvrage intitulé: Droit public du gouvernement des colonies françaises*, 8vo. (1778). (G)

24. Former name of Djakarta, now capital of Indonesia. (E)

25. *Voyage à la Cochinchine*, 2:98–99. (G) See Chapter 1, note 67. (E)

26. *Voyage à l'île du Ceylan*, by Robert Percival, trans. P. F. Henry (Paris, 1803), 1:222 and 223. (G) This is a translation of Percival's *An Account of the Island of Ceylon.* (E)

27. Qui se laesum clamabit is conscientiam suam prodet. (G)

28. *Thoughts upon the African Slave-trade*, by John Newton, 2d ed., 8vo. (London, 1788), 17 and 18. (G)

29. *American Museum*, 8vo. (Philadelphia, 1789), 6:407. (G)

30. See the horrible details of this in Dallas, 2:letter 9, p. 4, &c. (G) The reference is to Robert Charles Dallas, *The History of the Maroons* (London, 1803). (E)

31. Wimphen, 1:128. (G) The reference is to the book by François Alexandre Stanislaus, baron de Wimpffen, *Voyage à Saint-Domingue pendant les années 1788, 1789 et 1790* (Paris, 1797). (E)

32. *Voyage aux Indes occidentales*, by Bossu (Amsterdam, 1769), 14. (G)

33. *The Horrors of the Negro Slavery existing in our West-Indian Islands, irrefragably demonstrated from Official Documents recently presented to the House of Commons*, 8vo. (London, 1805). (G)

34. *Notes on the West-Indies*, by George Pinckard. London 1806. (G)

35. *Voyages dans l'intérieur de la Louisiane, de la Floride, &c.* by Robin, 3 vols., 8vo. (Paris, 1807). (G)

36. 1:175, and following. (G)

37. The original "repoussent l'une et l'autre" suggests that the three countries rejected slavery as well as the slave trade. Grégoire probably meant to refer to the abolition of slavery in the northern states of the Union. It is not clear why he mentions England here. (E)

38. An anonymous author has even published a pamphlet with the following title: *De la nécessité d'adopter l'esclavage en France, comme moyens de prospérité pour les colonies, de*

punition pour les coupables, etc., 8vo. (Paris, 1797). (G) Translation of the title: Concerning the necessity of instituting slavery in France, as a means of creating prosperity, punishing those guilty of crimes, etc. (E).

39. This is an allusion to the *Proclamation aux citoyens de St. Domingue*, addressed to the citizens of Saint Domingue by Napoleon Bonaparte, as first consul, on December 25, 1799, not long before he decided to reimpose slavery on the colony. (E)

40. *Dissertation sur la question, s'il est permis d'avoir en sa possession des esclaves, et de s'en servir comme tels dans les colonies de l'Amérique*, by Philippe Fermin, 8vo. (Mastrich, 1776). (G)

41. Will. Beckford, *Descriptive Account of the Island of Jamaica*, 2 vols., 8vo. (London, 1790), 2:282. (G)

42. *Considérations sur l'état présent de la colonie française de Saint-Domingue*, par H. D. L. (Hilliard D'Auberteuil), 8vo. (Paris, 1777), 73ff. (G)

43. *Colonies modernes.* (G) I.e., *Des colonies modernes sous la zone torride* (Paris, 1802). (E)

44. *Les Soirées Bermudiennes, ou entretien sur les événemens qui ont opéré la ruine de la partie française de Saint-Domingue*, par F.C., *un de ses précédens colons*, 8vo. (Bordeaux, 1802), 60 and 66. (G)

45. *Voyage à la Louisiane et sur le continent de l'Amérique*, by B. D., 8vo. (Paris, 1802), 147 and 191. (G)

46. *Examen de l'esclavage en général, et particulièrement de l'esclavage des Nègres dans les colonies françaises* by V. D. C. formerly lawyer and settler in Saint Domingue, 2 vols., 8vo. (Paris, 1802). (G)

47. *Des colonies et de la traite des nègres*, par Belu, in 8vo. (Paris, an 9).

48. 8vo. (Paris, 1803). (G)

49. *Egaremens du négrophilisme*, 8vo. (Paris, 1803), 22. (G)

50. Ibid., 110. (G)

51. Ibid., 102.

52. Long, 2:489. (G) See Chapter 1, note 31. (E)

53. Dallas, 2:416 (G) Robert Charles Dallas, *The History of the Maroons* (London, 1803). (E)

54. *Remarks on the Slave Trade*, 4to. (1788), 125. (G)

55. *Literary Magazine and American Register*, 8vo. (Philadelphia, 1803), 36.

56. *Thoughts upon the African Slave Trade*, 20 and following. (G)

57. Barré-Saint-Venant, 92. (G) See Chapter 2, note 43. (E)

58. Ibid., 120 and 121. (G) Cf. Raynal, *Histoire philosophique des Indes* (1780), 1:12. (E)

59. 1:231. (G)

60. "The Dying Negro" in *Portfolio*, 4to. (1804), vol. 4, no. 25, p. 194. (G)

61. *American Museum, or Repository of Ancient and Modern Fugitive Pieces*, 8 vols. (Philadelphia, 1789), 6:74, and following. (G) The quotation renders the spirit but not the actual words of Pinckney. Grégoire seems to have quoted from memory. (E)

62. *Thoughts*, 31. (G)

63. *Deuteronomy* 26:6. 1 Timothy 5:18. "Non alligabis, etc." (G)

64. Page, Pierre-François, *Traité d'économie politique et de commerce des colonies*, part 1 (Paris, year 7 [1798]); part 2 (year 10 [1801]). (G)

65. 103f. I believe the author is Berquin Duvallon. (G)

66. The terms used by Grégoire are *négrophile* and *blancophage*. (E)

67. Grégoire is referring to the Société des Amis des Noirs. See Introduction for information on this organization. (E)

68. Grégoire is referring here to himself. Cf. Grégoire, *Mémoires* (Paris: Editions de la santé, 1989), 83. Jérémie and Cap François are two towns in Haiti, and Nantes was one of the principal French slave-trading ports in the eighteenth century. (E)

69. 2 Paral. 19, Eccles. 7:20, Rom. 24:2, Ephes. 11:6, Coloss. 9:3, James 25:2, 1 Peter 1:13. (G)

70. Matthew 7:12. (G)

71. *Mémoire sur différents sujets de littérature*, by Mongez (Paris, 1780), 14; and *Commentatio de vi quam religio christiana habuit*, by Paetz, 4to. (Göttingen, 1799), 112ff. (G)

72. The colonial settlers and their friends are in the habit of constantly repeating the same accusations. That they are false has been demonstrated in a manner that admits of no reply. Thus Dupont, author of a *Voyage à la Terre Ferme*, (1:308), and Bryan Edwards (*The History civil and commercial of the British colonies* [London, 1801], 2:44) mention that Las Casas, bishop of Chiappa, usurped the honors of celebrity while voting for the enslavement of the Negroes. I demolished that lie six years ago: my *Apologie de Las Casas* was printed in the *Mémoires de l'Institut National, classe des sciences morales et politiques*, 4:45ff. I refer Dupont to this, and invite a reply. The author of the *Voyage à la Louisiane*, B. D., has just repeated the same lie: see 105ff. (G)

73. Dallas, 2:427ff. (G) See Chapter 2, note 53. (E)

74. It is with pleasure that I take this occasion to express my gratitude: first, to the presidents and secretaries of the conventions, who for many years sent me the minutes of their proceedings; second, to Mr. Philips, a Quaker and a bookseller in London, who, during my stay in England, procured me many rare and useful works on the freedom of the blacks; third, to the excellent and learned Vanprat, librarian of the Imperial Library. Everyone who knows him holds him in high esteem. (G)

75. Ibid., 430ff. (G) See Chapter 2, note 53. (E)

76. Most likely Sir James Mackintosh (1765–1832), a writer on philosophical and historical subjects and a Whig member of Parliament (see the *Dictionary of National Biography*). But we have not been able to find any correspondence between him and Grégoire, nor any evidence that the two met during Grégoire's visits to London. (E)

77. *Histoire de la liberté des Nègres*, read in the sessions of *la classe des sciences morales et politiques de l'Institut national* (the section of moral and political sciences in the National Institute) in 1797. (G) These lectures were never published. (E)

78. In the collection of the *Voyages* of Astley, 2:154; and in Benezet, 50, etc. (G) The references are to Thomas Astley, *Collection of Voyages and Travels*, in 4 vols. (London, 1745–47); and Anthony Benezet, *Some Historical Account of Guinea, with an Inquiry into the Rise and Progress of the Slave Trade, its Nature and lamentable Effects* (1780: repr. London: Frank Cass, 1968). Grégoire refers to the following quote from Astley, reprinted by Benezet: "Carinal Cibo, one of the Pope's principal ministers of state, wrote a letter on behalf of the College of Cardinals, or great council at Rome, to the missionaries in Congo, complaining that the pernicious and abominable abuse of selling slaves was yet continued, requiring them to remedy the same, if possible; but this the missionaries saw little hopes [*sic*] of accomplishing, by reason that the trade of the country lay wholly in slaves and ivory." (E)

79. Labat, 4:120. (G) This is probably *Nouvelle relation de l'Afrique occidentale* by

Jean-Baptiste Labat (Paris, 1728). The reference is to the prerevolutionary Sorbonne, which was under the direction of the Catholic Church. (E)

80. *Sicilia Sacra disquisitionibus et notitiis illustrata.* Editio tertia emendata et continuatione aucta, cura et studio Antonini Mongitore, 2 vols. folio (Panormi, 1733), 1:207. (G)

81. *Annales Minorum, etc. continuati a F. Jo Maria di Ancona,* fol. (May 20, 1745), 19:201 and 202. (G)

82. *Martyrologium franciscanum cura et labore Arturi,* fol. (Paris, 1638), 32. (G)

83. *Vox turturis seu de florenti ad usque nostra tempora sanctorum Benedicti, dominici, francisci, etc., religionum statu* (Coloniae Agrippinae, 1638), 88. (G)

84. *Gentleman's Magazine* 25 (1765): 145. (G)

85. Abbé Prévost, *Histoire générale des voyages,* 5:53. (G)

86. *Histoire du Portugal,* by La Clede, 2 vols., 4to. (Paris, 1735), 1:594, 595. (G)

87. *Voyage dans l'Indostan,* by Perrin, 8vo. (Paris, 1807), 1:164. (G) This paragraph was omitted by Warden. (E)

88. *Journal d'un Voyage aux Indes orientales, sur l'escadre de Du Quesne, en 1690,* 3 vols. in 12mo. (Rouen, 1721), 1:193. Also, *Relation du Voyage et retour des Indes orientales, pendant les années 1690 et 1691,* by Claude-Michel Ponchot-de-Chantassin, of the naval guard on board the Du Quesne. 12mo. (Paris, 60). (G)

89. Barrow, *Voyage à la Cochinchine,* 1:87. (G)

90. *Voyage dans les Etats-Unis d'Amérique,* by La Rochefoucauld-Liancourt, 8vo. (Paris, year 8), 6:334. (G)

91. *A Tour in America,* by William Parkinson, 2 vol. 8vo. (London 1805), 2:459. (G)

92. On this subject there exists a noteworthy dissertation in Dutch, that can be found in volume 6 of the Proceedings of the society of Vlissingen: *Verhandelingen uitgegeven door het zeeuwsch, genootschap der wetenschappen te Vlissingen, etc.* (G)

93. In *Pieces of Irish History,* an interesting work, published by MacNeven, 8vo. (New York, 1807), there is an interesting essay by his friend Emmet, entitled "Part of an Essay towards the History of Ireland," 2. See also the *Memoirs* of William Sampson, 8vo. (New York, 1807). (G) William James MacNeven, *Pieces of Irish History, illustrative of the Condition of the Catholics of Ireland; of the Origin and Progress of the Political System of the United Irishmen; and of their Transactions with the AngloIrish Government* (New York, 1807). (E)

Chapter 3

1. *Voyage en Guinée* (Utrecht, 1705), 131. (G)

2. *Mémoire sur la colonie française du Sénégal,* by Pelletan, 8vo. (Paris, year 9), 69 and 81. (G) The Moors referred to in this passage are the inhabitants of the region to the north of Senegal now known as Mauritania. (E)

3. Prévost, 4:17. (G) See Chapter 2, note 85. (E)

4. Beaver, 383. (G). *African Memoranda.* See Chapter 2, note 15. (E)

5. Ledyard, 2:332. (G) See Chapter 1, note 22. (E)

6. Bosman, letter 18. (G) See Chapter 1, note 53. (E)

7. Labat, 4:183. (G) Jean Baptiste Labat, *Nouveau voyage aux isles de l'Amérique* (Paris, 1723). (E)

8. Bryan Edwards, *History of the West Indies*, and the *Bibliothèque Brittanique*, 19: 495ff. (G)

9. Dallas, 1:25, 46, 60, &c. (G) See Chapter 2, note 53. (E)

10. Labat, 4:184. (G) See Chapter 3, note 7. (E)

11. *Le mémoire pour le nommé* Roc, *Nègre, contre le sieur Poupet*, by Poncet de la Grave, Henrion de Pancey and de Foisi, 8vo. (Paris, 1770), 14. (G)

12. Aphra Behn, *Oronoko, or the royal slave* (London, 1688). A critical edition with introduction by Adelaide P. Amore was published in 1987 by the University Press of America. (E)

13. Alessandro Brandano, *Historia della guerra di Portugallo succedata per l'occasione della separazione di quel Regno dalla Corona cattolica*, Venice, 1689. (E)

14. *Nova Lusitania, istoria de guerras Brasilicas*, by Francisco de Brito Freyre, fol. (Lisbon, 1675), book 8, p. 610; and book 9, no. 762. Alessandro Brandano, 4to. (Venice, 1689), 181, 329, 364, 393, &c.

Istoria delle guerre del regno del Brasile, &c. by P. F. G. Jioseppe, di santa Theresa Carmelitano, fol. (Rome, 1698), part 1, 133 and 183; part 2, 103ff.

Historiarum Lusitanarum libri, &c. autore Fernando de Menezes, comite Ericeyra, 2 vols., 4to. (Ulyssippone, 1734), 606, 635, 675, &c. La Clède, *Histoire du Portugal*, &c, passim. (G)

15. That is, in 1791. This was the decree that granted political rights of citizenship to free Negroes and mulattoes. See the Introduction for information on Ogé. (E)

16. *Rapport sur les troubles de Saint-Domingue*, by Garran, 4 vols. in 8vo. (Paris: year 6 [1798]), 2:52ff., 78. (G)

17. *Bruch-Stücke einer Reise durch Frankreich im Frühling und Sommer 1799*, by Ernst Moritz Arndt, 3 vols., 8vo. (Leipzig, 1802), 2:36 and 37. (G)

18. Note communicated by my friend de Lasteyrie, who has made several scientific voyages in Spain. We await their publication, which will justify the expectations of the public. (G)

19. He was the father of the writer Alexandre Dumas, author of *The Count of Monte Cristo* and *The Three Musketeers*. (E)

20. Book entitled *Paris*, 31:405ff. (G)

21. Pierre-François-Xavier de Charlevoix, *Histoire de l'île espagnole ou de S. Domingue*. 2 vols. (1730–31). The Cacique Henry (1:book 6), was a leader in the Indian resistance against Spanish rule of Hispaniola in the sixteenth century. (E)

22. *Hispaniola, a Poem*, by Samuel Whitchurch, 12mo. (London, 1805). (G)

23. See *Pii secundi, pontificis maximi, commentarii, etc.*, a Joan. Gobellino compositi, etc, 4o. (Rome, 1584), book 5, 259; and book 12, 575 et seq. It is claimed that these commentaries were composed by Pius II himself and that Gobellin only lent his name. (G)

24. *Memorie istoriche massimamente sacre della città di Sora*, dal padre Fr. Tuzzi, 4to. (Rome 1727), part 2, book 6, 116 et seq. (G)

Chapter 4

1. *Traité d'économie politique et de commerce des colonies*, by Page, 8vo. (Paris, 1802), part 2, 27. (G)

2. Red Caribs: the original Indian tribe on the Lesser Antilles. Black Caribs: The offspring of the intermarriage of the red Caribs with people of African origin. (E)

3. *Voyage à la Martinique*, by Chanvalin, 4to., 39ff. (G)

4. Stedman, 1:88ff. (G) *Narrative of a five years expedition against the revolted Negroes of Surinam*, by Capt. T. G. Stedman, 2 vols. 4to. (London, 1796). (E)

5. Long, 2:416. (G) See Chapter 1, note 31. (E)

6. *Vue de la colonie espagnole du Mississippi ou des provinces de Louisiane et Floride occidentale, en l'année 1802* by Berquin-Duvallon, 8vo. (Paris, 1803), 268ff.: "Let us visit the old woman, who has seen her hundredth year, says someone of the company; and we went to the door of a little hut, where an old Negro woman from Senegal appeared. She was so decrepit that she was bent toward the ground, and obliged to lean against the side of her hut to receive the company assembled at the door. She was almost deaf, but her sight was still quite good. Every thing around her shewed that she was destitute and wretched. She had scarcely rags enough to cover her nakedness, and just a few brands to give warmth, in a season when the cold is so keenly felt by the old, and more particularly by those of the black race. We found her occupied boiling a little water and rice for her supper. For she received not from her master that regular subsistence which her great age and former services required. Moreover, she was alone and left to herself, in a state of freedom that owed more to her exhausted nature than to her masters.

The reader needs to know that over and above her long service, this woman, now in her hundredth year, had formerly nourished, with her milk, two white children, whom she saw reach full growth, and afterwards accompanied to the tomb; and these were the brothers of one of the masters who was accompanying us. The old woman saw him and called him by his name, addressing him with *tu* (according to the custom of the Negroes of Guinea), with an air of kindness and simplicity that was truly affecting. When, she said, wilt thou repair the roof of my hut? the rain falls as freely inside as outside. The master raised his eyes toward the roof; it was no higher than the hand could reach. I shall take care of this, he said. Thee always tells me so, but nothing is ever done. Hast thee not thy children (two Negroes of the workshop who were her grandchildren) who can mend the hut? —And thee, art thee not their master, and art thee not thyself my son? Come, said she, taking him by the arm and leading him into the Cabin, come and see thyself these openings. Have pity then, my son, on the old Irrouba, and repair at least that part of the roof which is above my bed, it is all I ask, and God will bless thee. And what was her bed? Alas three boards that were roughly joined, and on which was disposed a bundle of a parasite plant of the country, named Spanish Beard.

The roof of thy hut is almost uncovered, the sleet and the rain beat against thy miserable bed; thy master sees all this; and yet has no compassion. Poor Irrouba!" (G)

7. *De l'esclavage en général, et particulièrement, etc.*, 180. (G) We have not found any information on this anonymous pamphlet. (E)

8. *Voyage au Sénégal*, by Durand, 4to. (Paris, 1802), 568ff. (G)

9. See Robin, 2:203ff. (G) See Chapter 2, note 35. (E)

10. *Deutsches Museum* (1787), 1:424. (G)

11. Letter from Mr. Blumenbach, on February 6, 1808, to Bishop Grégoire, senator. (G) Translation of the Latin quotation: "A blackness that is blessed because it is imbued with the luster of the mind." The entire section in brackets was omitted by Warden. (E)

12. *Thoughts upon the African slave trade*, 24. (G) See Chapter 2, note 28. (E)

13. *An Abstract of the evidence, &c*, 91ff. (G) See Chapter 4, note 40. (E)

14. Ledyard, 2:340. (G) See Chapter 1, note 22. (E)

15. *Histoire de Loango*, by Proyart (1776), 8vo. (Paris), 59ff. and 73. (G)

16. *Fragments d'un voyage en Afrique*, 2 vols., 8vo. (Paris, 1802), 2:391ff. (G)

17. In 4to. (London, 1787). (G)

18. Adanson, 38 and 118. (G) See Chapter 1, note 56. (E) See also, Lamiral, *L'Afrique et le peuple africain*, 64. (G)

19. Demanet, 11. (G) *Voyage de l'abbé Demanet a l'île de Gorée, au Sénégal et à la Gambie en 1763 et 1764*. (E)

20. Philosophy here clearly refers to the philosophers of the Enlightenment. (E)

21. Robin, 1:204. (G) See Chapter 2, note 35. (E)

22. Long, 2:416. (G) See Chapter 1, note 31. (E)

23. *Voyage into the Interior of Africa*, by Mungo Park, 2:8 and 10. (G)

24. Ibid., 11. (G)

25. Grégoire is referring to the period in the French Revolution (1793–94), when the radical Jacobins tried to eradicate Christianity in France and many graves were desecrated. (E)

26. Stedman, 3:66. (G) See Chapter 4, note 4. (E)

27. *Le bonnet de nuit* by Mercier, vol. 2, article "morale." (G)

28. William Dickson, *Letters on Slavery* (1789), 20ff. (G) Reprinted 1970 by Negro Universities Press. (E)

29. Stedman, 3:70 and 76. (G) See Chapter 4, note 4. (E)

30. Cowry, 27. (G) We were not able to identify this reference. (E)

31. Abbé Jean-Baptiste Grosier, *Journal de littérature, des sciences et des arts* (Paris, 1779–83), 3:188. (G)

32. Stedman, 1:270. (G) See Chapter 4, note 4. (E)

33. Stedman, 1:270. (G) See Chapter 4, note 4. (E)

34. Dickson, 180. (G) See Chapter 4, note 28. (E)

35. *Description de la partie française de Saint-Domingue*, by Moreau-Saint-Méry, 1: 416ff. (G)

36. Saint-Méry, 44. Three pages earlier he praises them for a remarkable love of cleanliness. (G)

37. Hervey, *Meditations*, 151. (G)

38. *Voyage of Discovery in the Interior of Africa*, by Houghton and Mungo Park, 180. (G) P. 198 in Mungo Park, *Travels in the Interior Districts of Africa* (New York: Arno, 1971). (E)

39. *Essai sur l'agriculture et le commerce des îles de France et de la Réunion*, 8vo. (Rouen, 1803), 37. (G)

40. Among other works we may consult *An Abstract of the Evidence Delivered Before a Select Committee of the House of Commons, in the Years 1790 and 1791*, 8vo. (London, 1791); see in particular 91ff. (G)

Chapter 5

1. This entire chapter was omitted by Warden. (E)

2. I acquit myself of a duty in revealing to the public the names of the persons to whom I owe the biography of this worthy African, who was first mentioned to me by Dr. Gall. At the request of my fellow citizens d'Hautefort, who is connected here with the Ministry of Foreign Affairs, and Dodun, first secretary of the French legation in Austria, everything was done to satisfy my curiosity. Two respectable ladies of Vienna, Frau von

Stief and Frau von Picler, did so with the greatest zeal. Information furnished by the friends of the late Angelo was collected with care. The interesting account which the reader has before him is based on this material. It loses in elegance of style when translated into French; for Frau von Picler, who drew it up in German, possesses the talent of writing equally well in prose and in verse. It is with pleasure that I express my gratitude to these obliging persons. (G)

Chapter 6

1. *Abstract of the evidence*, 89. (G) See Chapter 4, note 40. (E); Clarkson, 125. (G) Thomas Clarkson, *An Essay on the slavery and commerce of the human species* (London, 1788). (E); Stedman, chap. 26. (G) See Chapter 4, note 4. (E); Durand 368ff. (G) See chapter 4, note 8. (E); *Histoire de Loango*, by Proyart, 107. (G) See Chapter 4, note 15. (E); Mungo Park, 2:35, 39 and 40. (G) See Chapter 4, note 23. (E)

2. *Description topographique de Saint-Domingue*, 1:90. (G)

3. Prévost, 1:3, 4, and 5, etc., 4to.; and *Histoire universelle*, 17:chap. 7; Beaver, 327. (G) For Prévost, see Chapter 2, note 85; for Beaver, see Chapter 2, note 15. (E)

4. Prévost, 2:421. (G) See Chapter 2, note 85. (E)

5. *Description de la Nigritie*, par P. D. P. (Pruneau de Pomme Gouje), 8vo. (Paris, 1789). (G)

6. Dickson, 74. (G) See Chapter 4, note 28. (E)

7. *Le Magazin encyclopédique*, no. 2 (Ier brumaire an. 7): 335. (G)

8. *Fragments d'un voyage en Afrique*, 2 vols., 8vo. (Paris, 1802), 1:413ff.; 2:380, &c. (G)

9. Sandoval, part 1, book 2, chap. 20, p. 205. (G) We were unable to identify this reference. (E)

10. *Journal d'un voyage aux Indes, sur l'escadre de du Quesne*, 2:214. (G) See Chapter 1, note 59. (E)

11. Mungo Park, 2:35, 39, 40. (G) See Chapter 4, note 23. (E) *The Journal of Frederic Horneman's Travels*, 4to. (London, 1802), 33ff. (G)

12. Prévost, 4:283. (G) See Chapter 2, note 85. (E)

13. Bosman, letter 5. (G) See Chapter 1, note 53. (E)

14. *Description de la Nigritie*, par D. P., 8vo. (Paris, 1789). (G) See Chapter 6, note 5. (E)

15. Bosman, letter 18. (G) See Chapter 1, note 53. (E)

16. Long, 2:377 and 378. (G) See Chapter 1, note 31. (E)

17. Beaver, 328. (G) See Chapter 2, note 15. (E)

18. Mungo Park, 128. (G) See Chapter 4, note 23. (E)

19. Lucas, 1:190ff. (G) See Chapter 1, note 22. (E)

20. Anecdote related by Bernardin St. Pierre. The author of the *Anecdotes africaines* relates the same thing about Zingha. He adds that when she got up, the slave remained in the same posture. When this was pointed out to her, she replied: "The sister of a king never sits twice on the same seat; it remains in the house in which she sat on it." (G)

21. *Histoire de Loango, &c.* (G) See Chapter 4, note 15. (E)

22. Lucas and Ledyard, 1:190ff. See also *Substance of the Report*, 136. (G) For Lucas and Ledyard, see Chapter 1, note 22; for *Substance of the Report*, see Chapter 6, note 38. (E)

23. Mungo Park, 13 and 37. (G) See Chapter 4, note 23. (E)

24. Warden added the following sentence at this point: It became necessary to pay no attention to narratives in other respects concordant, which we have till the present time obtained concerning these three towns. (E)

25. *Voyage à la Cochinchine*, 1:289ff. (G) See Chapter 1, note. 67 (E)

26. Ibid., 319ff. (G)

27. *Fragments d'un voyage en Afrique fait pendant les années 1786 et 1787, dans les contrées occidentales de ce continent*, (Paris, 1802), 2:400. (G)

28. *Critical Review* (April 1807): 369. (G)

29. *De l'influence de la découverte de l'Amérique sur le bonheur du genre humain*, by Genty, 8vo. (Paris, 1788), 74ff. (G)

30. Gaspari Barlaei, *rerum per Octennium in Brazilia gestarum historia*, folio (Amsterdam, 1647), 243, etc. Rochapitta, *America portugueza*, book 8. *Voyage à la Cochinchine* by Barrow, trans. Malte-Brun 8. (Paris, 1807), 1:218ff. (G)

31. Grégoire is referring to the 1766 and 1774 editions of *The Universal Dictionary of Trade and Commerce* by Malachy Postlethwayt. (E)

32. Grégoire is referring to Paul Erdmann Isert, *Reise nach Guinea und den Caribäischen Inseln in Columbien* (Copenhagen, 1788), which he probably read in the French translation *Voyages en Guinée et dans les îles Caraïbes en Amérique* (Paris: Maradan, 1793). The book is now available in English: *Letters on West Africa and the Slave Trade: P. E. Isert's Journey to Guinea and the Caribbean Islands in Columbia* (Oxford: Oxford University Press, 1992). (E)

33. *African Memoranda*, 402. (G) See Chapter 2, note 15. (E)

34. *A Short Sketch of Temporary Regulations for the intended Settlement on the Green Coast of Africa*. (G)

35. *A Letter on the Abolition of the Slave Trade, addressed to the Freeholders and Other Inhabitants of Yorkshire*, by W. Wilberforce 8vo. (London, 1807). (G)

36. A reference to the ongoing conflict between Britain and the Napoleonic Empire, and to the blockade that Britain had imposed on the European continent. This sentence and the rest of the paragraph were omitted by Warden. (E)

37. In 1794 a French squadron charged with destroying the English settlements on the coast of West Africa, partly destroyed the colony of Sierra Leone. This led to serious accusations. In 1796 I read a report before the Institut, based on my examination of the registers of the commander of the squadron, in which I proved that his attack on Sierra Leone was due to an error. He believed that this was a purely commercial enterprise, rather than a philanthropic settlement. This report was published in the *Décade philosophique*, and then reprinted separately. The colony of Sierra Leone, which was destroyed a second time during the war, has overcome its misfortune and has recovered. (G)

38. *Substance of the Report delivered by the Court of Direction of the Sierra Leone Company*, particularly the one dated 1794, 55ff. (G)

39. Dallas, 2:78. (G) See Chapter 2, note 30. (E)

40. Barré-Saint-Venant, 119. (G) See Chapter 2, note 43. (E)

Chapter 7

1. Grégoire is referring to the sons of Sierra Leone chiefs who were brought to England by Zachary Macaulay, the governor of the Sierra Leone Colony, to be educated as missionaries and leaders of their people. Wilberforce and the circle of friends who

supported him lived in Clapham, and they sent their sons to school together with the African boys. Cf. John Pollock, *Wilberforce* (London, 1977), 183–84. (E)

2. *Voyages*, 2:2. (G) The reference is to Brissot's translation (published 1786) of William MacIntosh, *Travels in Europe, Asia, and Africa: describing characters, customs, manners, laws, and productions of nature and art; containing various remarks on the political and commercial interests of Great Britain; and delineating in particular, a new system for the government and improvement of the British settlements in the East Indies; begun in the year 1777, and finished in 1781* (London, 1782), 2 vols.
Brissot was tried during the Terror and condemned to death, a fate Grégoire here qualifies as "judicial assassination." See our Introduction for more on Brissot. (E)

3. *Objections to the Abolition of the Slave Trade, with Answers*, by Ramsay, in 8vo. (London, 1788). (G) Grégoire's French text, as well as the Warden translation, mistakenly give the date of publication as 1778, while the National Union Catalog gives 1788. (E)

4. *Sermon*, 4to. (1789). (G)

5. *Remarks upon the situation of the Negroes in Jamaica*, 8vo. (London, 1788), 84ff. (G)

6. *Observations on the Slave Trade*, 8vo. (London, 1789). (G)

7. *Variétés littéraires*, 8vo. (Paris, 1786), 1:39. (G)

8. This fact was communicated by de Lasteyrie. (G)

9. *Variétés littéraires*, 88. (G)

10. Durand, 58. (G) See Chapter 4, note 8. (E) Demanet, *Histoire de l'Afrique française*, 2:3. Lobo, *Relation historique de l'Abyssinie*, 4to. (Paris, 1728), 680. (G)

11. *Observations sur la religion, les loix, les moeurs des Turcs, traduit de l'anglais par M. B.* (London, 1769), 98. (G)

12. *Voyage au Sénégal*, 149. (G) See Chapter 1, note 56. (E)

13. Clarkson, 125. (G) See Chapter 6, note 1. (E)

14. Prévost, 4:198. (G) See Chapter 2, note 85. (E)

15. *Le More-lack*, by Le Cointe-Marcillac, 8vo. (Paris, 1789), chap. 15. (G) The complete reference for this work is *Le More-lack, ou essai sur les moyens les plus doux et les plus équitables d'abolir la traite et l'esclavage des nègres d'Afrique, en conservant aux colonies tous les avantages d'une population agricole* (London and Paris, 1789), xxxii and 288p. (E)

16. *Voyage à la Madagascar et aux Indes occidentales*, by Rochon, 3 vols., 8vo. (Paris); see 1:173ff. (G)

17. Stedman, chap. 26. (G) See Chapter 4, note 4. (E)

18. Some call it *balafat* or *balafo* and compare it to a spinet. (G)

19. *The Sugar Cane, a Poem in Four Books*, by James Grainger, 4to. (1764). (G)

20. *American Museum*, 4:82. (G)

21. Golbéry, op. cit. (G)

22. Pratt, 2:208. (G) We were unable to identify this reference. (E)

23. Beronicius wrote poems in Latin. His poem in two volumes, entitled *Georgarchontomachia*, or Battle between Peasants and Nobles, has been translated into Dutch verse, and the entire work was reprinted at Middelburg in 1766. (G)

24. See in *La Prusse littéraire*, by Denina, the article on Peyneman. (G)

25. *Contes et chansons champêtres*, by Robert Bloomfield, trans. de la Vaisse, 8vo. Paris, 1802). (G)

26. *Letteratura turchesca dall'abate Giambatista Toderini*, 3 vols. 8vo. (Venice, 1787). (G)

27. By P. M. C., sang-mêlé, 8vo., chez Baudoin. (G)

28. Cf especially *La véritable origine des troubles de Saint-Domingue*, by Raymond. (G) Julien Raymond. Paris 1792. (E)

29. *Fables de Loqman*, 8vo. (Cairo, 1799). (G)

30. Cf the editor's preface, 10 and 11. (G)

31. *Salutaris lux Evangelii*, by Fabricius, 176ff. *Histoire du christianisme des Indes*, by la Croze, 8vo. (The Hague, 1739), 73. Jobi Ludolfi, *Historia aethiopica*, folio (Frankfurt am Main, 1681). (G)

32. J. Ludolfi, *ad suam Historiam commentarius*, folio, (Frankfurt am Main, 1691), proemium 13. (G)

33. (Norimbergae, 1683), chap. 15, p. 34. (G)

34. Ibid., 180. (G)

35. 3 vols., folio (Norimbergae). Cf. the second part which, in the copy of the Imperial Library in Paris is bound as part one. Cf. also the new edition, published also in Nuremberg in 1774, 6:53 and 7:194. (G)

36. Pliny, book 35, chap. 8, para. 34. (G)

37. Letter from Mr. von Murr, Nuremberg, June 2, 1808. (G)

38. *Poems on various Subjects*, by Phyllis Wheatley, 120. (Walpole, 1803), 73ff. (G)

39. Pliny, book 35, chap. 17. Cf. also *Mémoires de l'Académie des Inscriptions*, 35:345. (G)

Chapter 8

1. Great-grandfather of the Russian poet Pushkin. (E)

2. This is the same prince who published the reasons that impelled him to convert to Catholicism, in a brief but excellent work, *Fifty Reasons or Motives why the Roman Catholic Apostolic religion ought to be preferred to all the sects, etc.* in 12-mo. (London, 1798). (G)

3. *Beschreibung des Saal-Creises*, in-fol. (Halle, 1749), 2:28. I am indebted to Blumenbach for this reference and most of the others concerning Amo. (G)

4. In Warden this paragraph reads as follows: "Antony William Amo, born in Guinea, was brought to Europe when very young, and the princess of Brunswick, Wolfenbuttle, took charge of his education. He embraced the Lutheran religion, pursued his studies at Halle, in Saxony, and at Wittemberg." (E)

5. Excussis tam veterum quam novorum placitis, optima quaeque selegit, selecta enucleate ac dilucide interpretatus est. (G) "The Ancients" are the Greek and Latin classics, while "the Moderns" refers to the knowledge and literature created in the period from the Renaissance to the eighteenth century. (E)

6. *Dissertatio inauguralis philosophica de humanae mentis* ΑΠΑΘΕΙΆ. *seu sensionis ac facultates sentiendi in mente humana absentia, et earum in corpore nostro organico ac vivo praesentia, quam praeside, &c, publice defendit autor, Ant. Guil. Amo, Guinea-afer philosophiae, etc. L. C. magister, etc.* 4to. (Wittenberg, 1734). At the end are subjoined several pieces: Among others the congratulatory letters by the Rector, &c. (G)

7. *Disputatio philosophica continens ideam distinctam earum quae competunt vel menti vel corpori nostro vivo et organico, quam consentiente amplissimorum philosophorum ordine,* praeside M. Ant. Guil. Amo, Guinea-afer, defendit Joa. Theod. Mainer, philos. et J. V. Cultor, 4to, (Wittenberg, 1734). (G)

8. *The Monthly Magazine*, 8vo. (New York, 1800), 1:453ff. (G)

9. *Verhandelingen uitgegeven door het zeeuwsch genootshap der wetenschappen te Vlis-singen,* 8vo. (te Middelburg, 1782), 9:19ff. (G)

10. *Voyage autour du monde* by Gemelli Carreri, trans. from the Italian, 12mo. (Paris, 1719), 5:64ff. and 135ff. See also the article "Philippines," *Encyclopédie méthodique.* (G)

11. *Voyage autour du monde,* 142, 143. (G)

12. *Über die Taglische Sprache,* by Franz Carl Alters, 8vo. (Vienna, 1803). (G)

13. *Carta hydrographica y chorographica de las islas Filipinas, hecha por el P. Murillo Velarde, en Manilla ano de 1734, esculpio Nicolas de la Cruz-Bagay, Indio tagalo.* (G)

14. Renamed Mauritius by the British when they took it from the French during the Napoleonic Wars. Grégoire actually describes Lislet as a *mulâtre au premier degré;* that is, someone who was not the child of mulattoes but the offspring of a white and a black parent. A curious instance where even Grégoire was influenced by the very detailed designation of individuals in the French colonies according to their racial origins. (E)

15. This is an allusion to the change from a prerevolutionary institution (i.e., the Academy) to an institution created by the Revolution (i.e., the National Institute). (E)

16. In William Dickson, *Letters on Slavery* (1789), 184 (G). "The Pennsylvania society established in favor of the Negroes" refers to the Pennsylvania Society for Promoting the Abolition of Slavery, founded in 1775 and formally incorporated in 1789, with Benjamin Franklin as its president, by the Pennsylvania Legislature. Cf. Edward Needles, *The Pennsylvania Society for Promoting the Abolition of Slavery* (1848; repr. New York: Arno, 1969). We have not been able to identify the publication of the Society referred to by Grégoire. (E)

17. Buchan, *Médecine domestique* (Paris, 1783), 3:518. (G)

18. Duplanil, *Médecine du voyageur,* 3 vols., 8vo. (Paris, 1801), 3:272. (G)

19. *Narrative of a five years expedition against the revolted Negroes of Surinam,* by Capt. J. G. Stedman, 2 vols., 4to. (London, 1796), 2:xxvi. The French translation of this work, 3:61ff., omitted the word *seconds* in the question addressed to Fuller, which renders it absurd. (G)

20. *American Museum,* 5:2. (G)

21. Brissot, *Voyages,* 2:2. (G) See Chapter 7, note 2. (E)

22. Clarkson, 125. (G) See Chapter 6, note 1. (E)

23. Benjamin Banneker's *Almanack for 1794, containing the Motions of the Sun and Moon, the true Places and Aspects of the Planets, the Rising and Setting of the Sun and the Moon, the E23.clipses, etc.,* 8vo. (Philadelphia).
Benjamin Banneker's *Pennsylvania, Delaware, Maryland and Virginia, Almanack for 1795,* 8vo. (G)

24. This is made public by Fessenden, in a two-volume pamphlet entitled *Democracy unveiled or Tyranny stripped of the garb of Patriotism, by Christopher Caustic,* 2 vols. 8vo., 3d ed. (New York, 1806), 2:52. The author accuses Jefferson of a crime for a deed that is worthy of high praise. (G)

25. *A Topographical Description,* 212 and 213. (G) See Chapter 1, note 36. (E)

26. *The American Museum,* (Philadelphia, 1788), 4:414–17 and 509–12. Grégoire mistakenly wrote that the essay was published in Baltimore, the city where Othello lived. It was written and published at a moment when Northern states, such as Pennsylvania, were debating the abolition of slavery. Othello's main point, argued with considerable eloquence, is that slavery is incompatible with the Bill of Rights and should therefore be prohibited throughout the United States.
The paragraphs that follow, although placed in quotation marks by Grégoire, are not

quotations from the essay itself but a summary of some of the main points made by Othello. (E)

27. *Réflexions sur la traite et l'esclavage des Nègres, traduites de l'anglais,* 120. (Paris, 1788), 10. (G) The page numbers in the section on Cugoano refer to this French translation of Cugoano's *Thoughts and sentiments on the evil and wicked traffic of the slavery and commerce of the human species, humbly submitted to the inhabitants of Great Britain* (London, 1787). (E)

28. Ibid., 184. (G)

29. Ibid., 134ff. (G)

30. The passage that follows, placed in quotation marks by Grégoire, is again not a direct quotation but a summary of the book's argument. (E)

31. Deut. 23:15. (G)

32. English is perhaps the only language that has a special word, *kidnap*—both the verb and its derivations—to designate the act of stealing children. (G)

33. Saint Ambrose (340–397), bishop of Milan, prevented the emperor Theodosius from entering the city and only admitted him to communion after the emperor had expiated at length a massacre he carried out in Thessalonica. Saint Basil (329–379), bishop of Cesarea, defended the right of the church to grant asylum against the prefect Modestus, governor of Cesarea. (E)

34. Cf. the newspaper *The Merchant,* no. 31 (August 14, 1802). (G)

35. Letter of Mr. de Vos to Mr. Grégoire, 27, 1801. (W)

36. In Grégoire's text the Latin original appears as a footnote and only begins with ELEGIA. Warden added the first section to the Latin text, but it is not clear whether this additional material was given him by Grégoire, or whether he had a copy of Capitein's poem in his possession.

Warden's book does not contain any translation into English of the poem. Our translation is based on Grégoire's French text, not on the Latin original, and does not include the section added by Warden. (E)

> Hac autem in Batavorum gratissima sede
> Non primum tantum elementa linguæ Belgicœ
> Addidici, sed arti etiam pictorica, in quam
> Eram pro pensissimus, dedi operam Virum
> Interea tempore labente, institutioni sua
> Domestica catechesios mihi interesse permisit
> Vir humanissimus, Joannes Phillipus Manger,
> Cujus in obitum (cum tanti viri, tum
> Solidor eruditionis, tum erga deum singularis
> Pictatis, admirator semper extitissem) flebilibus
> Fatis. Cum Ecclesior Hagienis protento anno
> Esset ademptus, lugubrem hanc compersui
> Elegiam!

Elegia.

> Invida mors totum vibrat sua tela per orbem:
> Et gestit quemvis succubuisse sibi.
> Illa, metùs expers, penetrat conclavia regum:

Imperiique manu ponere sceptra jubet.
Non sinit illa diù partos spectare triumphos:
Linquere sed cogit, clara tropœa duces.
Divitis et gazas, aliis ut dividat, omnes,
Mendicique casam vindicat illa sibi.
Falce senes, juvenes, nullo discrimine, dura,
Instar aristarum, demittit illa simul.
Hic fuit illa audax, nigro velamine tecta,
Limiua mangeri sollicitare domus.
Hujus ut ante domum steterat funesta cypressus,
Luctisonos gemitus nobilis Haga dedit.
Hunc lacrymis tinxit gravibus carissima conjux,
Dum sua tundebat pectora sæpe manu.
Non aliter Naomi, cum te viduata marito,
Profudit la crymas, Elimeleche, tua.
Sæpe sui manes civit gemebunda mariti,
Edidt et tales ore tremente sonos;
Condit ut obscuro vultum velamine Phœbus,
Tractibus ut terræ lumina grata neget;
O decus immortale meum, mea sola voluptas!
Sic fugis ex oculis in mea damna meis.
Non equidem invideo, consors, quod te ocyor aura
Transtulit ad lœtas æthereas que domos.
Sed quoties mando placidæ mea membra quieti,
Sive dies veniat, sum memor usque tui.
Te thalamus noster raptum mihi funere poscit.
Quis renovet nobis fœdera rupta dies?
En tua sacra deo sedes studiisque dicata,
Te propter, mæsti signa doloris habet.
Quod magis, effusas, veluti de flumine pleno,
Dant lacrymas nostri pignora cara tori.
Dentibus ut misere fido pastore lupinis
Conscisso tenerae disjiciuntur oves,
Aeraque horrendis, feriunt balatibus altum,
Dum scissum adspiciunt voce cientque ducem:
Sic querulis nostras implent ululatibus ædes
Dum jacet in lecto corpus inane tuum.
Succinit huic vatum viduæ pia turba querenti,
Funera quæ celebrat conveniente modo
Grande sacerdotum decus, et mea gloria cessat,
Delicium domini, gentis amorque piae!
Clauditir os blandum sacro de fonte rigatum;
Fonte meam possum quo relevare sitim!
Hei mihi quam subito fugit facundia linguæ,
Cælesti dederat quæ mihi melle frui.
Nestoris eloquium veteres jactate pœtæ,
Ipso Mangerius Nestore major erat, etc.

37. *De vocatione Ethnicorum.* (G)

38. *Slavery inconsistent with the spirit of Christianity, a sermon preached at Cambridge,* by Robert Robinson, 8vo. (1788). He affirms on page 14 that the Africans were the first to baptize their children in order to save them from slavery. (G)

39. *Dissertatio politico-theologica de servitute libertati christianae non contraria, quam sub praeside J. Van den Honert, publicae disquisitioni subjicit J. T. J. Capitein, afer,* 4to. (Lugduni Batavorum, 1742). (G)

40. *The doctrine of perpetual bondage reconcilable with the infinite justice of God; a truth plainly asserted in the Jewish and Christian scripture,* by John Beck. (G)

41. *A valedictory discourse delivered before the Cincinnati of Connecticut, in Hartford, July 4, 1804, at the dissolution of the society,* by D. Humphrey, 8vo. (Boston, 1804). (G)

42. 1 Cor. 7:23. *Pretio empti estis, nolite fieri servi hominum.* (G)

43. P. 27. (G) Capitein, *Dissertatio* (see note 39). (E)

44. Seventh-century French monk whose compilation on ecclesiastical law was frequently republished up to the nineteenth century. (E)

45. *Epistola turcica* (Lugduni Batavorum, 1633), 160, 161. (G)

46. *Staatkundig-godgeleerd onderzoeksschrift over de slaverny, als niet strydig tegen de christelike vriheid, &c. uit het latyn vertaalt door heer de Wilhelm,* 4to. (Leiden, 1742). (G)

47. *Noodige onderrichtingen voor de slaafhandelaaren* (te Middelburg: Verhandelingen uitgegeven door het zeeuwsch genootshap, 1769), 425. (G)

48. *Uit gewrogte predicatien zynde de trowherrige vermaaninge van den apostel der heydenen Paulus, aan zynen zoon Timotheus vit. II. Timotheus, II, v.8 te Muiderberger, den 20 mai 1742, alsmede de voornaamste goederen van de opperste wysheit spit sprenken VIII, v. 18, in twee predicatien in s'Gravenhage, den 27 mai 1742. en t'ouderkerk aan den Amstel, den 6 juny 1742, gedaan door J. E. J. Capitein, africaansche Moor, beroepen predikant op* d'Elmina, aan het kasteel S. George, 4to. (te Amsterdam). (G)

49. Edward Long, *The History of Jamaica, or General Survey of the Antient and Modern State of that island,* 3 vols. (London, 1774; repr. London: Frank Cass, 1970). Chapter 4 of book 3 (2:475–85) is devoted to Francis Williams. Long was an outspoken supporter of slavery, and the following extracts from the chapter on Williams give a sample of the mentality against which Grégoire's book was directed (E):

> With the impartiality that becomes me, I shall . . . leave it to the reader's opinion, whether what they [*sic*] shall discover of his genius and intellect will be sufficient to overthrow the arguments, I have before alledged, to prove an inferiority of the Negroes to the race of white men . . .
>
> Being a boy of unusual lively parts, (Williams) was pitched upon to be the subject of an experiment, which, it is said, the Duke of Montagu was curious to make, in order to discover, whether, by proper cultivation, and a regular course of tuition at school and the university, a Negroe might not be found as capable of literature as a white person. In short, he was sent to England, where he underwent a regular discipline of classic instruction at a grammar school, after which he was fixed at the university of Cambridge, where he studied under the ablest preceptors, and made some progress in mathematics. . . . Upon his return to Jamaica, the duke would fain have tried his genius likewise in politics, and intended obtaining for him a privy seal, or appointment to be one of the governor's council, but this scheme was dropped, upon the objections offered by Mr. Trelawney, the governor at that time . . .

Considering the difference which climate may occasion, and which Montesquieu has learnedly examined, the duke would have the experiment more fairly on a native African; perhaps too the Northern air imparted a tone and vigour to his organs, of which they never could have been susceptible in a hot climate . . .

The climate of Jamaica is temperate and even cool, compared with many parts of Guiney; and the Creole Blacks have undeniably more acuteness and better understandings than the natives of Guiney. Mr. Hume. who had heard of Williams, says of him: "In Jamaica indeed they talk of one Negroe as a man of parts and learning; but 'tis likely he is admired for very slender accomplishments, like a parrot who speaks a few words plainly. (E)

50. The words in italics are not by Grégoire. They were taken by Warden from Long. (E)

51. Probably an allusion to the seventeenth-century English poet Edmund Waller, who honored Oliver Cromwell with a poem in 1651, and published a poem in honor of King Charles II when he ascended to the throne in 1660. (E)

52. *Letter to the treasurer of the society instituted for the purpose of effecting the abolition of the slave trade*, from the Rev. Robert Boucher Nickolls, dean of Middleham, 8vo. (London, 1788), 46. (G)

53. In Grégoire's text this is followed by a prose translation into French, while the original Latin is relegated to a footnote. Warden used Long's translation and included in the Latin text the footnotes in which Long points out what he considered borrowings from the Roman poets as well as other weaknesses. We decided to reprint Long's translation and to place the Latin text in this endnote, but without Long's notes. (E)

> Integerrimo et fortissimo viro
> Georgio Haldano, armigero,
> Insulae Jamaicensis gubernatori;
> Cui, omnes, morum, virtutumque dotes bellicarum,
>   In cumulum accesserunt.

> ### Carmen
>
> Denique venturum fatis volventibus annum,
> Cuncta per extensum laeta videnda diem,
> Excussis adsunt curis, sub imagine clara
> Felices populi, terraque lege virens.
> Te duce, quae fuerant malesuada mente peracta
> Irrita conspectu non reditura tuo.
> Ergo omnis populus, nec non plebecula cernet
> Haesurum collo te relegasse jugum,
> Et mala, quae diris quondam cruciatibus, insons
> Insula passa fuit; condoluisset onus,
> Ni vixtrix tua Marte manua prius inclyta, nostris
> Sponte ruinosis rebus adesse velit.
> Optimus es servus regi servire Britanno,
> Dum gaudet genio scotica terra tuo:
> Optimus heroum populi fulcire ruinam;

Insula dum superest ipse superstes eris.
Victorem agnoscet te Guadaloupa, suorum
Despiciet merito diruta castra ducum.
Aurea vexillis flebit jactantibus Iris,
Cumque suis populis, oppida victa gemet.
Crede, meum non est, vir Marti chare, Minerva
Denegat Aethiopi bella sonare ducum.
Concilio, caneret te Buchananus et armis,
Carmine Peleidoe, scriberet ille parem.
Ille poeta, decus patriae, tua facta, referre
Dignior, altisoni vixque Marone minor.
Flammiferos agitante suos sub sole jugales
Vivimus; eloquium deficit omne focis.
Hoc demum accipias multa fuligine fusum
Ore sonaturo; non cute, corde valet,
Pollenti stabilita manu, Deus almus, oandem
Omnigenis animam, nil prohibente dedit.
Ipsa coloiris egens virtus, prudentia; honesto
Nullus inest animo, nullus in arte color.
Cur timeas, quamvis, dubitesve, nigerrima celsam
Caesaris occidui, saendere Musa domum?
Vade salutatum, nec sit tibi causa pudoris,
Candida quod nigra corpora pelle geris!
Intergitas morum maurum magis ornat, et ardor
Ingenii et docto dulcis in ore decor:
Hunc, mage cor sapiens, patriae virtutis amorque
Eximit e sociis, conspicuumque facit,
Insula me genuit, celebres aleure Britanne
Insula, te salvo non dolitura patre!
Hoc precor o nullo videant te fine regentem
  Florentes populos, terra, deique locus.

    FRANCISCUS WILLIAMS

54. *Lawn* is here used in the sense given it by Johnson; namely, an open space between woods; which has a particular propriety applied to the cornfields of Jamaica (note by Long).

55. *The interesting Narrative of the life of Olaudah Equiano, or Gustavus Vassa, the African, written by himself,* 9th ed., 8vo. (London, 1794), with the portrait of the Author. (G)

56. The two volumes that have been published constitute the smaller and less interesting part of his writings. (G)

57. *Letters of the late Ignatius Sancho, an African, to which are prefixed memoirs of his life,* 2 vols. in 8vo. (London, 1782). (G)

58. Imlay, 215. (G) See Chapter 1, note 36. (E)

59. *Letters of the late Rev. Laurence Sterne, to his intimate friends,* 3 vols., 8vo. (London, 1775). (G)

60. Although Grégoire put this paragraph in quotation marks, he wrote a summary

and not a translation of the following lines by Sancho: "Commerce was meant by the goodness of the Deity to diffuse the various goods of the earth into every part, to unite mankind in the blessed chains of brotherly love. society and mutual dependence; the enlightened Christian should diffuse the riches of the Gospel of peace with the commodities of his respective land. Commerce attended with strict honesty, and with Religion for its companion, would be a blessing to every shore it touched at. In Africa, the poor wretched natives, blessed with the most fertile and luxurious soil, are rendered so much the more miserable for what Providence meant as a blessing: the Christians' abominable traffic for slaves, and the horrid cruelty and slavery of the petty Kings encouraged by their Christian customers, who carry them strong liquor to enflame the national madness, and powder and bad fire-arms to furnish them with the hellish means of killing and kidnapping." *Letters of the late Ignatius Sancho* (London, 1782), 2:4–5. (E)

61. Vol. 1, letter 7, passim. (G) Grégoire actually cites sentences from various letters. Only the first three lines of the quotation refer to letter 7. (E)

62. Letter from M. Giraud, French consul in Boston, dated October 8, 1805. He knew Dr. Peter personally. (G)

63. *Notes on Virginia.* (G)

64. *Poems on various subjects, religious and moral, by Phillis Wheatley, Negro servant*, 8vo. (London, 1773); and 12mo. (Walpole, 1802). (G)

65. These lines were added by Warden. Grégoire included his translations of Phillis Wheatley's poems in the text, and added the original English version as a footnote. (E)

Chapter 9

1. Louis Dominique Cartouche (1693–1721), a notorious French bandit. (E)

2. Samuel Pufendorf (1632–94) was a famous German jurist. (E)

3. *The American Museum*, 8vo. (Philadelphia, 1788), 4:161; and (1791), 9:192ff. (G)

4. *Lettre aux citoyens de couleur et Nègres libres*, 8vo. (Paris, 1791), 12. (G)

5. Dallas, 1:4. See Chapter 2, note 30. (E) Barré-Saint-Venant also proposes that the plough should be introduced into our colonies. (G) See Chapter 2, note 43 for Barré-Saint-Venant. (E)

6. Genty. (G) *De l'influence de la découverte de l'Amérique sur le bonheur du genre humain*, 8vo. (Paris, 1788). (E)

7. The first part of this sentence paraphrases the following statement by Richard Price, English Unitarian minister, friend of Franklin and defender of the American Revolution: "it is self-evident that if there are any men whom they have a right to hold in slavery, there may be *others* who have a right to hold *them* in slavery" (from the chapter "Of the Negro Trade and Slavery" in *Observations on the Importance of the American Revolution, and the Means of Making it a Benefit to the World*, reprinted in *Richard Price and the Ethical Foundations of the American Revolution* by Bernard Peach [Duke University Press, 1979]).

The second part of the sentence is footnoted in both the Warden and the Usteri translation as a reference to the *Essay on the Treatment and Conversion of Slaves* by the abolitionist James Ramsay. Grégoire probably added this footnote in the manuscript copies he sent to the two translators after the French text had already gone into print. (E)

8. Grégoire refers here to Usteri and to Warden. (E)